RACE ON TRIAL

Black Defendants in Ontario's Criminal Courts, 1858–1958

PATRONS OF THE SOCIETY

Blake, Cassels & Graydon LLP

Gowlings

McCarthy Tétrault LLP

Osler, Hoskin & Harcourt LLP

Paliare Roland Rosenberg Rothstein LLP

Torys LLP

WeirFoulds LLP

The Osgoode Society is supported by a grant from
The Law Foundation of Ontario.

The Law Foundation of Ontario
Building a better foundation for justice in Ontario

The Society also thanks The Law Society of Upper Canada
for its continuing support.

RACE ON TRIAL

Black Defendants in Ontario's Criminal Courts, 1858–1958

BARRINGTON WALKER

Published for The Osgoode Society for Canadian Legal History by
University of Toronto Press
Toronto Buffalo London

Toronto Buffalo London
www.utppublishing.com
www.osgoodesociety.ca
Printed in Canada

ISBN 978-0-8020-9909-9

Printed on acid-free, 100% post-consumer recycled paper
with vegetable-based inks.

Library and Archives Canada Cataloguing in Publication

Walker, Barrington, 1970–
Race on trial : black defendants in Ontario's criminal courts, 1858–1958 /
Barrington Walker.

(Osgoode Society for Canadian Legal History) (Canadian social history series)
Includes bibliographical references and index.
ISBN 978-0-8020-9909-9

1. Blacks – Legal status, laws, etc. – Ontario – History. 2. Discrimination in criminal justice administration – Ontario – History. 3. Blacks – Ontario – Social conditions. 4. Race discrimination – Ontario – History. I. Title.
II. Series: Osgoode Society for Canadian Legal History series
III. Series: Canadian social history series

HV9960.C22056 2010 345.713'0508996071 C2010-905025-8

This book has been published with the help of a grant from the Canadian Federation for the Humanities and Social Sciences, through the Aid to Scholarly Publications Program, using funds provided by the Social Sciences and Humanities Research Council of Canada.

University of Toronto Press acknowledges the financial assistance to its publishing program of the Canada Council for the Arts and the Ontario Arts Council.

Canada Council for the Arts | Conseil des Arts du Canada
ONTARIO ARTS COUNCIL
CONSEIL DES ARTS DE L'ONTARIO

University of Toronto Press acknowledges the financial support of the Government of Canada through the Canada Book Fund for its publishing activities.

For Georgina

Contents

Foreword

THE OSGOODE SOCIETY FOR CANADIAN LEGAL HISTORY

In recent years legal historians have been increasingly interested in the social history of the law and in the law's impact on, among many other social phenomena, race relations. This ground-breaking study investigates the relationship between Ontario's Black community and the criminal courts from the mid-nineteenth to the mid-twentieth centuries. Using a sample comprised of capital-case files and the assize records for Kent and Essex counties, counties with relatively large Black populations because they were termini of the Underground Railroad, Barrington Walker investigates the 'limits of freedom' for Ontario's African Canadians. He contrasts formal legal equality with pervasive patterns of social, economic, and attitudinal inequality. The records allow him not only to analyse attitudes of the dominant community but also to provide rare but important glimpses into Black life in Canadian history.

The purpose of the Osgoode Society for Canadian Legal History is to encourage research and writing in the history of Canadian law. The Society, which was incorporated in 1979 and is registered as a charity, was founded at the initiative of the Honourable R. Roy McMurtry, formerly attorney general for Ontario and chief justice of the province, and officials of the Law Society of Upper Canada. The Society seeks to stimulate the study of legal history in Canada by supporting researchers, collecting oral histories, and publishing volumes that contribute to legal-historical scholarship in Canada. It has published eighty-two books on the courts, the judiciary, and the legal profession, as well as on the history of crime and punishment, women and law, law and economy, the legal treatment of ethnic minorities, and famous cases and significant trials in all areas of the law.

Current directors of the Osgoode Society for Canadian Legal History are Robert Armstrong, Christopher Bentley, Kenneth Binks, Patrick Brode, Brian Bucknall, David Chernos, Kirby Chown, J. Douglas Ewart, Martin Friedland, John Honsberger, Horace Krever, C. Ian Kyer, Virginia MacLean, Patricia McMahon, R. Roy McMurtry, Laurie Pawlitza, Jim Phillips, Paul Reinhardt, Joel Richler, William Ross, Paul Schabas, Robert Sharpe, James Spence, Richard Tinsley, and Michael Tulloch.

The annual report and information about membership may be obtained by writing to the Osgoode Society for Canadian Legal History, Osgoode Hall, 130 Queen Street West, Toronto, Ontario, M5H 2N6. Telephone: 416-947-3321. E-mail: mmacfarl@lsuc.on.ca. Website: www.osgoodesociety.ca.

R. Roy McMurtry
President

Jim Phillips
Editor-in-Chief

Acknowledgments

This book has taken a very long time to complete. It began as a doctoral thesis at the University of Toronto under the supervision of Franca Iacovetta. Though it has gone through many changes since its original incarnation, many of the core ideas in the book were developed during the years I worked under Franca's supervision and for that I will always be grateful to her. I would like to thank the Department of History, University of Toronto, for its generous financial support and the Ontario Graduate Scholarship Program for research funds. Thanks also to the many archivists at the Archives of Ontario and Library and Archives Canada who helped me track down sources. David Goutor, Ugo Nwokeji, Mona Pon, Catherine Carstairs, Carolyn Prodruchny, Lisa Mar, and Carole Gillis provided much support and friendship during the early years of my doctoral study.

I would also like to thank my colleagues at the Centre of Criminology at the University of Toronto for providing a space to work (which became all the more crucial once baby Miles arrived on the scene) and a sense of community during my time there as junior fellow in the latter stages of my graduate work. This was a pivotal period in my intellectual growth. Terry Roswell, Andrea McCalla, Dena Demos, Dawn Moore, Renisa Mawani, Charles Ladi Fiki, and Carla Cesaroni became good friends during some of the most productive and happy years of my career. Carolyn Strange and Mariana Valverde were mentors and important influences on my work during this time. In particular, I owe a great debt to the late David Sealy, whom I met at the Centre in the fall of 2001 and with whom I developed the closest friendship of my life. I was never the same after I met him and I will never be the same after his death. David left us far too early and suddenly, in December 2009, but his spirit will stay with me as I continue to write about the things he held dear. His ideas, distilled through our many hours of long-distance conversations between Toronto and Kingston, have profoundly affected my work and my life. Words cannot express the depths of my loss. I will always miss him tremendously.

Thanks to my colleagues in the Department of History at Queen's University for voting to grant me the tremendous privilege of regular and permanent academic employment and a place to reflect, write, and teach among so many talented and accomplished scholars. This book has been published with the help of a grant from the Canadian Federation for the Humanities and Social Sciences, through the Aid to Scholarly Publications Program, using funds provided by the Social Sciences and Humanities Research Council of Canada.

Thanks also to Len Husband at the University of Toronto Press and to Jim Phillips of the University of Toronto Faculty of Law and the Osgoode Society for Canadian Legal History for supporting this project through various ups and downs. Jim's editorial talents and his assistance in sharpening the legal dimensions of my arguments have been invaluable. He helped to make this book much stronger than it would have been. Curtis Fahey and Gillian Watts also provided invaluable editorial support. Wayne Herrington expertly and patiently guided the book to its final stages. It has been an honour to work with him on this project. Any weaknesses or shortcomings are my own. I also wish to thank the various readers who reviewed the manuscript.

Above all, I would like to thank my family. Norma Walker, Barrington Walker, Sr, and Heather Walker have been incredibly supportive over the years, as have been my in-laws, Philip Riel and Agnes Agawa. My sons, Miles and Ellis, have provided many (mostly) welcomed distractions over the years and they are far bigger than I thought they would be upon publication of my first book. I especially want to thank my wife, Georgina Riel (Waabishki Maqwa Kwe), who has been with me through all the travails and neuroses of graduate school and 'junior' professordom and without whom none of this would have been possible. It's finally finished, Georgina. This book is dedicated to you.

Barrington Walker
Kingston, Ontario
February 2010

RACE ON TRIAL

Black Defendants in Ontario's Criminal Courts, 1858–1958

Introduction

From the early nineteenth century until the post-Second World War era, Blacks in Canada lived in a state of paradox, caught between formal legal equality and deeply entrenched societal and economic inequality. Their experiences were shaped by the expression of 'race' in a racial liberal order which granted them full legal equality and the rights of citizenship but nonetheless legally supported racial discriminatory behaviour against them. Over this long period of time, Blacks faced a daunting number of barriers to full inclusion in Canadian society. They were effectively (while not legally) restricted to the lowest forms of menial wage labour, and faced restrictions upon where they could live and where they could travel through 'sundown laws' (curfews or by-laws that mandated that Blacks had to be out of town or indoors by a specific time in the evening). Blacks also had to contend with barriers that determined where they could be educated and worship. In the early twentieth century, potential Black immigrants who longed for another Canaan where they might be protected from the harsh realities of Jim Crow America also faced barriers to entering Canada, which was firmly committed to a 'Whites only' policy.[1]

In 1929, during a period which Robin Winks has labelled the 'nadir' of the Black experience in Canada, Stephen Leacock inquired of Edward Bayly, Ontario's deputy attorney general, regarding the 'rights of the Negro in Canada.' He was writing on behalf of one of his post-graduate students, who, following a recent Ku Klux Klan attack on an interracial couple in Oakville, had been inspired to embark on an ambitious undertaking: a book documenting the history of the Blacks in Canada. Bayly responded: 'The law on the subject has been properly indicated in American Courts, but so far as I know, no major case has ever been before the Courts of Ontario. If so I have never heard of it. The rights in this country of negroes are exactly the same as those of white people.'[2]

The obligation of a theatre owner to sell tickets does not ordinarily exist, Bayly continued; 'he can, if he chooses, refuse to sell seats to statesmen, judges, University Professors etc, and if the refusal is not accompanied by an assault or insult, he can refuse to sell seats in a theatre or even food in a restaurant should he care to do so.' Finally, he noted that 'the reason the question has seldom arisen is because there are very few negroes in Ontario, except in the counties of Essex and Kent, and apparently they are not litigious; at any rate one never hears of them in court, except for petty offences.'[3] Bayly's conclusion was seemingly contradictory: despite pervasive 'Jim Crowism' (presumably societal discrimination and anti-Black social attitudes), the rights (that is, legal rights) of Blacks enjoyed equal status under the law.[4]

Bayly's words reflected the dominant attitudes towards race and rights in Canada in the early twentieth century, and, no doubt, this clearly settled the question of Blacks' equality before the law for others like him: White male middle- and upper-class legal officers who embodied legal authority and power in Ontario. This is a study of one small group of those elusive, non-litigious Blacks who warranted only a derisive passing mention in Bayly's letter, people brought before the criminal courts between 1858 and 1958.

Blacks in Canada

Bayly's blindness to the challenges that Blacks faced in late 1920s Canada was part and parcel of a long tradition of unfamiliarity with the experiences of Blacks in colonial and post-Confederation Canada, a country that has historically prided itself on its supposed racial equality. The history of Blacks in Canada begins as early as the seventeenth century. The first Blacks to arrive in Canada in large numbers were slaves. Canada had its own version of the phenomenon that U.S. slaveholders famously termed the 'peculiar institution.'[5] First in seventeenth-century New France and later with renewed vigour after the British conquest in 1763, Blacks, as elsewhere in the sprawling Atlantic world, were bought, sold, and compelled to submit to a lifetime of coerced labour. Slavery everywhere was a system of racially based economic coercion that was legally codified, and Canada was the first place where the law (of property ownership) was integral to producing blackness. Through legally supported, racially based slavery, blackness was quite literally a product of the law, the dark side of modernity.[6]

After the British conquest of New France, the institution of slavery was strengthened by the colonial government's decision in 1763 to ensure that slavery endured during the transition from French rule.[7] Yet, while Britain created the conditions for slavery to flourish north of its New England colonies, after the conquest it also created the conditions for its demise; Blacks' agency and resistance during this era sowed the seeds of freedom, particularly between 1783 and 1867.[8] In the midst of its bitter conflict with American colonists during the American Revolution, Britain offered freedom to Blacks who were willing to flee from their masters to British military lines. Approximately 3,500 Blacks – mostly former slaves who are now canonized in the literature as 'Black Loyalists' – took up this offer. Most settled in the Maritime provinces of New Brunswick and Nova Scotia. Once these Black Loyalists arrived at their new destination, they found that the British failed to live up to their promise of freedom and equality in exchange for their loyalty to the crown. Many chose to strike out for West Africa – Sierra Leone – to secure their full freedom.[9] In the aftermath of the War of 1812, an eerily similar situation played itself out again. Black slaves were given the opportunity to abscond from their masters and join the British for the promise of freedom in British North America. Many Blacks followed the lead of their predecessors of a generation before and set out for freedom, only to find that once again the British rhetoric of full equality was not justified. These Blacks, dubbed the Refugees, were not even afforded the dignified title of Loyalists (or late Loyalists) and found themselves condemned to the lowest echelons of the society and economy of the Maritime colonies.[10]

Between the 1820s and the 1860s, this symbiotic relationship between Black slavery and freedom in Canada, the latter being born of the bitter fruit of the former, would emerge once again. By the 1820s, slavery was virtually dead as an institution in Canada owing to various legislative and judicial measures taken against it.[11] In 1833 the British formally abolished the institution throughout the empire. Canada thereafter became the terminus of the Underground Railroad in the United States. The numbers of Black fugitives grew dramatically with the passage in 1850 of the American Fugitive Slave Act, which created one of the largest influxes of Blacks in Canadian history.[12] Most settled in Canada West. Similar to the experiences of earlier Black settlers, Black life in Canada West was marked by legal freedom and social and economic inequity and marginalization. Blacks were free but they had not arrived at the Canaan they had imagined.

This history of deferred dreams at the end of the Underground Railroad would endure until the end of the Second World War and the emergence of a modern civil rights movement in Canada. The period between the mid-nineteenth century and the post-Second World War era was a time of social inequality, immigration restrictions, ugly discourses of scientific racism, legally supported segregation, as well as other forms of 'Jim Crowism' and resistance to full civil equality (military service in both wars was the quintessential example). Black Canadians would have to wait until the 1960s and 1970s – the era of civil rights, changes in immigration policy, and official multiculturalism – before they approached anything resembling true equality. And, of course, this is still very much an unfinished revolution.

Black Canadian history has been shaped by a number of important approaches or 'orientations' – to use a term coined by James W. St G. Walker – over time. These orientations are classified according to 'the role assigned to Black people in the making of history.' Walker suggests that the development of the field has been characterized by a move from a scholarship that focuses mainly on White attitudes towards Blacks (both negative and beneficent) to one that focuses mainly on Blacks themselves.[13]

Much of the earliest scholarship on the mid-nineteenth-century African Canadian experience was produced in the early twentieth century and dwelt on the themes of White justice and sympathy and, ultimately, the freedom granted to Blacks. Alongside studies of American fugitive slaves given sanctuary from the harshness of the American South's chattel-slave system, these works stand out as examples of early scholarship shaped by the central motif of Canada as a 'haven' for people of African descent.[14] Decades later, scholars did move away from a crude and uncritical treatment of Canada as a haven for Blacks; the theme of discrimination occupied a central place in their work. These later studies went to great lengths to shatter the myth of Canada West as a safe harbour from racial hostilities. It is also unfortunately true that much of this work focused on the Black experience in Canada as a tragic story of temporary migrants and émigrés; this is typified in the bulk of the scholarship on the eighteenth-century Black Nova Scotian 'Refugees' or the 'fugitive slaves' of nineteenth-century Ontario. Here the Black experience in Canada was posited as essentially an extension of the African American experience, a chapter in the African American's fight against or flight from racial discrimination.[15]

Works that emphasize Black achievement and the role of community are also well represented in African Canadian historiography. This literature focuses on charismatic figures who made important contributions in the face of overwhelming odds, and it ignores, for the most part, the struggles of everyday Black men, women, workers, and families. Examples are biographies featuring prominent abolitionist leaders like Samuel Ringgold Ward or Mary Ann Shadd Cary, the first woman to run a newspaper in Canada.[16] Community studies also figure prominently in African Canadian historiography. Despite their failure to problematize the idea of 'community,' these studies do convey something of the everyday lives of Black men and women; they also acknowledge the importance of Black agency. Among the most sophisticated Black community histories are works on the earlier migration and settlement of Black Maritimers, including studies of the Black Loyalists of Nova Scotia and Sierra Leone and, at a micro level, the Africville settlement in Halifax.[17]

Recent work by Black feminist historians is concerned with the omission of Black women's history from Canadian social history, including Black Canadian historiography. These scholars argue that Blacks' historical invisibility is 'part and parcel of the endemic racism which fuels the Canadian intellectual tradition.'[18] While they have made an invaluable contribution to social and cultural history, their work, nonetheless, is often overtly philiopietistic, focusing on women of 'exceptional merit.' What is problematic about much of this literature is not only its 'Black survivors' orientation but its tendency to over-emphasize positive historical figures and images and romantic stories of triumph in the face of overwhelming odds.

With the notable exception of some of the literature on slavery in Canada, far too much Black Canadian historiography deals with elites while ignoring those who lived at the bottom or on the margins of the social order. The law has also not been fully explored by historians of Black Canada, a surprising omission given its important role in shaping the Black experience in Canada from the days of slavery to life after it. This study is a challenge to conventional and often celebratory Black Canadian historiography and maintains that Black Canadians who were guilty of the most serious criminal offences are worthy of serious attention, for they too are part of the history of Black Canada and remain especially so today given the spectre of the Black criminal that drives so much of the discourse on race and immigration in Canada.[19]

Where History Meets the Law

Historians have long mined legal sources to write social and cultural histories from below. Labour historians have accepted that the law played a pivotal role in buttressing the capitalist order and in shaping the experiences of workers. Their work has explored the 'regulatory order' in which workers were enmeshed, such as the law of master and servant in the mid-nineteenth century, legal regulation of trade unionism, moral/legal regulation of working-class families, culture and behaviour, and the rise of the penitentiary. Studies of the role of the state and its responses to crime among the working class address both adults and juveniles.[20]

Just as the law shored up the capitalist order, so too did it both profoundly shape and reflect normative ideals of sexuality and gender. Women and men encountered the law in a number of different contexts: as the victims of violent crime and as perpetrators, as transgressors of the law, and as targets of social control and moral regulation.[21] Regional studies of rape and other forms of heterosexual conflict in the late nineteenth and early twentieth centuries, for example, are an important lens through which scholars have developed our understanding of how gender and sexuality were articulated in Canadian law. These works pay particular attention to sexual conflict in the realms of individual experience and community and social regulation as well as its regional, spatial, and geographical dimensions and how it served as a site of debate over regional development and nation building. This body of scholarship has also alerted us to the importance of looking at the legal prosecution of rape in the context of 'a matrix of changing social and political relations and shifting cultural dispositions towards alleged perpetrators and victims.'[22] Women were doubly victimized in the prosecution of rape because trials often were a test of their character, their 'rapeability.' Men's characters were also often on trial when they appeared in court prosecuted for rape, and legal authorities frequently deemed men on the margins of respectable society particularly dangerous.[23]

Gender and class analyses have thus taken firm root in legal histories and socio-legal studies; the literature on 'race' and the law in Canada is embryonic by comparison. To date, much of this literature is in the field of Aboriginal history and explores the role of the law in the colonization, racialization, and subordination of Canada's Aboriginal peoples. For Aboriginal peoples, the law operated as part and parcel of a larger matrix of economic and social relations which included the establishment of White settler colonies, the appropriation of the land and resources of indigenous peoples, and the imposition of the 'queen's law' upon peoples who had long had their own complex mores with which to remedy 'crime.' The best work in this genre also shows how Native people negotiated their experiences with the law and demonstrates that legal and government authorities' ideas about Indian character and culture were influential in shaping the post-trial reports which helped determine sentencing.[24] In various locales, particularly in remote regions where the reach of the law was quite limited, maintenance of White legal order would have been difficult without the complicity and even active participation of indigenous peoples. Alongside White lawmakers and enforcers, Natives served 'as scouts, guides, trackers, constables' and, in the courtroom, crown witnesses.[25] Aboriginal issues are often considered apart from those involving other racialized groups in Canada. Yet many scholars now recognize the importance of putting the experiences of various racialized groups side by side to allow for a more comprehensive analysis of how processes of racialization and the law work. Such an approach is – at least in part – taken up in this book.

Much recent scholarship deals with the stories of various racialized groups in Canada's legal system. Two approaches dominate this literature. The first is historical sociology, which draws on statistical data and illustrative examples to examine systemic discrimination in the criminal justice system. Central to this work is its exploration of the historical antecedents of discrimination, in its various guises, in today's criminal justice system.[26] The second approach employs a 'singled out case method,'[27] allowing for rigorous analyses of the cultural and ideological dimensions of how racial categories were created in and through the law. An example of this approach is James Walker's analysis of race and rights in cases brought before the Supreme Court of Canada. Walker analyses four cases involving the struggles of African Canadian, Indo-Caribbean, Chinese, and Jewish litigants. These cases are assessed against the background of 'Jim Crowism' in private establishments, racially biased practices in immigration policy, discriminatory legislation preventing Chinese men from employing or 'managing' White women, and restrictive covenants upon the sale of private property. In each instance, Walker provides a sophisticated treatment of Canadians' racial attitudes and finds compelling evidence of systemic discrimination in Canadian jurisprudence. Similarly, Constance Backhouse's work on race and the law also sheds light on the racially coded nature of Canadian justice, the architects of which have always vehemently insisted upon its neutrality and colour-blindness. By focusing on cases involving Aboriginals, the Inuit, Blacks, and Chinese, Backhouse is able to demonstrate 'the central role of the Canadian legal system in the establishment and enforcement of racial hierarchy.' She also points to the systemic nature of racial oppression. Rather than 'isolated, idiosyncratic and haphazard acts,' Backhouse argues that the law was located in 'systems and structures that girded the legal system of Canada's racist past.'[28]

Using the methodology of the case study, Backhouse and Walker show us how 'common sense' knowledge about race was a product more of social attitudes than of biological reality. Each author pays close attention to how discussions about 'race' played out in legal records and in the context of individual trials at different historical conjunctures and various local contexts. Both are also attuned to the broader culturally created (pseudo) scientific knowledge about race, and how these meanings shifted over time. James Walker argues for the importance of recognizing how global manifestations of race relations and 'race,' given shape by European colonialism and the traffic in slaves across the Atlantic, were 'articulated in Canadian terms': 'Canadian events ... [were] participants in a widespread cultural system.'[29] Backhouse similarly notes that the concept of race is 'built upon shifting sands.' Her work also rightly insists that any study of the history of race in Canada must be attuned to the importance of 'whiteness' – its simultaneous position of privilege and transparency – an approach that Canadian historians, with a few notable exceptions, have been too slow to develop.[30] Neither Backhouse nor Walker, however, recognizes that racist discourse is not solely embedded within matrixes of overtly discriminatory discourse and practice. As Ann Laura Stoler has cautioned, racial formations often lurk within ostensibly 'progressive' political agendas as well.[31]

This book is a history of legally supported and expressed racial discrimination in Ontario, but it also attempts to go beyond the discrimination paradigm that characterizes much of the historical scholarship on race and the law. Blacks certainly did confront legally supported discrimination; however, focusing on the discriminatory aspects of the law provides only a partial picture of how the law shaped the Black experience in Canada. Aboriginals and Blacks, for example, were over-represented among those sentenced to hang. Yet a closer examination of legal sources often shows that the outcomes of such cases were by no means preordained.[32] Selective mercy, for example, was meted out to some Aboriginal murderers, often because legal elites believed that the actions of these murderers were a function of their innate racial and cultural proclivities. Many elites therefore began to see these murders as culturally specific. This is a pattern that was reflected in the law's treatment of many other marginal populations including Blacks.[33]

Critical perspectives on law and the (post-)colonial condition provide analytical tools to sift this pattern out of the historical evidence. Critical theory is anathema to many historians; many of us will uneasily recall the acrimonious debates surrounding theory and historical practice in the last decade of the twentieth century. Nonetheless, the central questions posed by this book are in part framed by theory. This book is indebted to critical perspectives on the law that have emerged out of the legal profession over the past thirty years and that provide students of history with a powerful critique of 'Legal Liberalism': the dominant set of beliefs among many legal practitioners and scholars that the law operates as a transparent and neutral arbiter of social conflict.[34] Post-colonial Studies, a set of theoretical insights about power relations under colonialism, the material, psychic, and bodily forms of domination and resistance that have grown out of the historical materiality of colonial struggles in a variety of contexts over space and time, is critical for understanding the relationship between race and the law because the law has played a pivotal role in maintaining colonial relations of power.[35] Black Canadians' experiences in the criminal courts resonated with the unequal power relations that emerged within colonial practices throughout the world.

Post-colonial Studies also helps us to understand the experiences of Blacks in Canada in the context of the symbiotic – rather than merely antagonistic – relationship between the colonizer and the colonized. Similar to other works on the histories of race, this book points to Frantz Fanon's famous chapter 'The Fact of Blackness' as a signifying moment.[36] Fanon's stunning analysis of blackness as a form of 'crushing objecthood' in his recounting of his encounter with a White child on a train in which his distorted body was 'thrown back' at him through the eyes of the terrified child is a powerful parable of how blackness is constituted under White looks.[37] This book is, in essence, a study of blackness through the eyes – the legal artifacts – of the dominant culture.

Where Fanon's work shows how Blacks were turned into objects under the gazes of Whites, Edward Said's seminal *Orientalism* situates this process of objectification in the very creation of the West itself. The West's creation of 'the Orient' and, more broadly, 'the Other,' says Said, was the product of 'a battery of desires, repressions, investments, and projections.' Thus, Said insists that Orientalism is in large part a 'flexible *positional* superiority which puts the Westerner in a whole series of possible relationships with the Orient without ever losing him the relative upper hand' owing to 'extraordinary European ascendancy from the late Renaissance to the present ... the scientist, the scholar, the missionary, the trader, or the soldier was in, or thought about, the Orient because he *could be there*, or could think about it with very little resistance on the Orient's part.'[38] Homi Bhabha, who is both one of Said's intellectual heirs and one of his critics, has refined Said's thesis with two key ideas: the malleability of racial stereotypes in particular and, second, the 'unidirectional' conceptions of colonial power found in Said's work. That is, under colonialism both the colonizer and the colonized were dramatically affected by this relationship. Their very identities became enmeshed; neither could exist without the other.

Racial stereotypes of Black Canadians were (and are) intricately linked to their creation as colonial subjects. White elites in this book were also shaped by colonial power as well, for, through their contempt, loathing, pity, and even paternalism, they inextricably bound themselves in a relationship with the 'Other' and defined themselves in relation to the very people they despised and pitied. The stereotypes that fuelled this dynamic were also often ambivalent. White Canadians projected wildly contradictory stereotypes onto Black Canadians (childlike and cunning, savage and infantile) and exhibited a strange mixture of both longing and loathing for them.[39]

Race on Trial: Case Files and the Courts

Writing a history of Black Canadians based on criminal case files presents many methodological challenges common to all historians who use them. These challenges stem from the well-known concerns about the fragmentary nature of case files and the difficulty of recovering muted voices of marginalized populations through documents created by elites. In the introduction to a pioneering collection of essays titled

On the Case: Explorations in Social History, the editors note that despite their limitations, case files show how complex power relations played out in local contexts. They also claim that case files help us explore important issues, such as how some groups were affected by the institutional power of medicine or law, or how dominant gender and racial ideologies shaped the discourse and actions of elites and relationships between experts and clients.[40] This work has evoked pointed criticism and even hostility from some quarters. Nonetheless, the collection and the roundtable discussion that followed in the *Canadian Historical Review* still stands as an important mapping of the sorts of methodological interventions that are shaping historical inquiry.[41]

The major challenge when one is confronted with researching the history of race on trial in a racial liberal order where colour-blindness is an integral part of legal formalism is the initial step of finding cases involving Black defendants. In this study, when the race of the defendant was not readily apparent from reading the case files, jail records were consulted. These records are exhaustive, listing the name, religion, age, 'race,' and disposition of all the defendants who passed through the province's gaols, as well as the charges against them, the sentences imposed, and the courts (whether Police Court/Magistrate's Court, County Judge's Criminal Court, or the Assize Court) in which they were tried. In some instances, either to supplement depositions or in lieu of them, this study also makes use of judges' bench books, which contain the notes that various judges scribbled as they presided over trials. It also draws on newspaper reportage of various trials in order to get a sense of how their proceedings extended beyond the courtroom into the realm of popular discourse.

The cases upon which this study is based are drawn from three sets of court and extrajudicial records: the criminal assizes, the county judges' criminal courts, and death-penalty cases. The first two records are limited to the counties of Essex and Kent (see chapter 1). While the amount of documentation found in the Criminal Assize files greatly varies from file to file, they typically contain a complaint, an indictment, a recognizance to prosecute, a recognizance for the granting of bail, and, most important for this study, sworn depositions. The assizes involved serious cases heard before the Supreme Court on an itinerant basis. Supreme Court judges travelled on circuit to local towns on commissions of assize. The history of Ontario's criminal assizes dates back to the early days of settlement in Upper Canada. This extensive history can be touched upon only briefly here, but essentially the criminal court evolved in relation to the demographic and political evolution of Upper Canada following the Constitutional Act of 1791 and the creation of a legal system patterned on British legal traditions but forged in light of colonial and post-colonial political, social, and geographical developments. The Judicature Act (1794) created the province's civil and criminal courts with the establishment of the Court of King's Bench, the highest criminal (and civil) court in the province.[42] The Upper Canadian courts created by these acts, including those most relevant to this study, the criminal assizes (Oyer and Terminer and General Gaol Delivery), laid the foundation for the post-1850 evolution of the courts. This evolution, in turn, formed the basis of the court system upon Confederation. An 1851 act allowed for appeals in felony cases but stopped short of empowering judges to award new trials; this was addressed by an 1857 act which allowed convicted persons to apply for a new trial at the Court of Queen's Bench or lower courts.[43] In 1890, on the cusp of the creation of a criminal code, there existed only courts of assize, Nisi Prius, Oyer and Terminer, and General Gaol Delivery, the latter with jurisdiction over 'treason, felony punishable by death, homicide, or libel.'[44]

The county judges' Criminal Court records, from which I have compiled the second group of cases drawn upon for this book, are exhaustive, chronicling the cases of every Black criminal defendant to appear before the criminal division of the county court. These minute books detail the 'colour' (race), occupation, education, habits, age, religion, and marital status of all offenders. As well, a history of each trial is sketched out, including the prisoner's date of commitment, the presiding judge, the prisoner's plea, the verdict, and, in the event of a guilty verdict, the sentence. These courts also have a rich history of jurisdictional evolution. In 1849 the district courts were renamed county courts in recognition that population growth had dramatically increased the province's original four districts to twenty. The evolution of these districts largely coincided with the geographical boundaries of Upper Canada's counties.[45] In 1869 the county courts, by virtue of a federal act, were granted criminal jurisdiction. The act 'provided for the trial with the consent of the accused, out of session and without a jury, of persons committed to jail for offences triable at quarter sessions'[46] who waived their right to a jury trial. This history of waiving jury trials began with the Speedy Trials Act in 1869 and continued with Oliver Mowat's 1873 act to improve (and reduce the costs of) criminal procedure. According to Nancy Parker, by the turn of the twentieth century, 20 per cent of all indictable offences in Canada were tried under its provisions. This 1873 act also conveyed a formal title to the criminal business of the county court, which had been conferred upon it since 1869 (see above): the County Judge's Criminal Court.[47] An act passed in 1934 enabled these courts to hear appeals that the Criminal Code or the Summary Convictions Act assigned to the county courts.[48]

Death-penalty cases involving Black defendants from throughout the province are the third group of cases explored in the book. The cases here are drawn from the post-1867 era, but such cases in Canada have a trajectory that predates Confederation. In British North America, each colony was responsible for its own death-penalty cases, and the evolution of criminal law and administration of criminal justice was different in each colony though the overall patterns were roughly congruent.

In the 1750s, the New England planters and merchants who governed the affairs of Nova Scotia primarily inherited English criminal law while looking to the colony of Massachusetts for a concise 'code like' way of organizing and identifying offences. In contrast to England's vast number of criminal and capital offences (numbering in the hundreds), Nova Scotia's Assembly created fourteen offences without benefit of clergy (i.e., capital offences) in 1758, adding a few more in later years. In 1841 a more wholesale reform of the Criminal Code took place, including a drastic reduction of the number of capital offences to two (treason and murder) in 1851.[49]

In Quebec, the criminal law was based upon English law as of 1763. In Upper Canada the evolution of the criminal law closely followed English practices and precedents including English penal codes. In the nineteenth century, a widespread movement lessened the harshness of the codes (a trend that was also evident in Nova Scotia, as mentioned above). An 1833 Upper Canadian act, for example, listed eleven felonies for which a sentence of death could be meted out.[50] By the 1850s, all property offences were removed from the list of capital crimes, excluding robberies and burglary.[51]

Confederation made the criminal law Ottawa's responsibility, although its administration was left to the provinces. The Criminal Procedure Act of 1869 made the penalty of death the sentence for five crimes: treason, murder, rape, attempted murder, and carnal knowledge of a girl less than ten years of age. From 1873 a convicted rapist faced the prospect of a death sentence or a prison term ranging from life to not less than seven years. By 1877, those most likely to hang were those convicted of murder.[52] In 1892, as a result of legislation introduced by the Conservative government, Canada's criminal law was codified and incorporated many elements of the common law, leaving most capital offences unchanged. The Canadian Criminal Code of 1892 carefully laid out provisions for criminal culpability (the legal term for responsibility), appeals, and the executive review of cases.

In the pre-Confederation era, the colonial executive had primary responsibility for the review of cases.[53] In the post-Confederation era, the power to determine the prerogative of mercy shifted from local executives to Ottawa and the governor general in council.[54] This process was first set out in the rules of procedure laid out in 1869 and had achieved the status of legal codification by 1893. The procedure was the same in all cases from the era shortly after Confederation until the abolition of the death penalty in 1976. The governor general in council decided whether to commute death sentences automatically or according to the particulars of individual cases.[55]

Whether or not persons found guilty and sentenced to death applied for executive clemency, these processes were implemented. In all cases, judges were asked to send reports and most expressed their opinions both 'on the nature of the trial and the decision of the jury' as well as the 'impact of the crime on the community and the suitability of the condemned person for a reprieve.'[56] Above and beyond documents related to trial and appeals, the Remission Branch of the Department of Justice had a long history of seeking out 'information and evidence concerning the condemned person's background character, personality, conduct in prison, and other relevant matters from police, custodial officers, and other responsible sources.' In addition to these formal assessments of criminal defendants, other materials of a more informal nature often found their way into the case files of the condemned, including petitions and letters. Moreover, beginning in the 1880s, the opinions of psychiatric experts – 'alienists' in the late nineteenth century and psychiatrists by the 1920s – began to emerge as evidence. Juries, however, did not readily accept insanity defences because the legal definition of insanity was quite narrow.[57]

Empiricizing Race on Trial

Collectively, the county judges' Criminal Court records, the Criminal Assize indictment case files, and the capital case files reveal much about the types of crime, conviction rates, and the commutations granted in death-penalty cases.

Table 1: Types of offences

Court	Offence	Number	% of Total Sample
CJCC*	Murder	0	
	Property Crime	32	24
	Rape/Seduction	8	6
	Other	12	9
	Total	52	39
Criminal Assizes	Murder	7	6
	Property Crime	24	18
	Rape	6	5.2
	Other	22	16
	Total	59	44
Capital-Case Files	Murder	21	15
	Rape	1	0.75

*County Judge's Criminal Court

As Table 1 reveals, of the fifty-two cases involving Black defendants disposed of between 1907 and 1958 in the Kent County Judge's Criminal Court, thirty-two (or roughly 60 per cent) were property crimes and twenty (or 39 per cent) were violent crimes including sex crimes like rape and seduction or carnal knowledge. Three-fourths of the Black defendants who appeared before the court were found guilty. In a quarter of the cases, violent offenders were found not guilty or had their cases dismissed. Admittedly, the drawback to these data is that they do not indicate the race of the victim, but data exist for the 1907–17 period which allow us to draw some comparisons between cases involving Black and non-Black defendants.

Out of the fifty-two White defendants who appeared in Kent County court for the crime of theft (Table 4), the highest sentence meted out was two years' imprisonment. By contrast, though the sample of Black defendants was only a fraction of this number – 4/56 or roughly 7 per cent – the highest sentence handed down for this charge was four years' imprisonment, or double the highest sentence for White offenders. Regarding the more violent crime of robbery, four Black offenders were charged with robbery during this period; three out of four or 75 per cent were sentenced to three years in prison. By contrast, in a total of 185 cases, only four Whites were charged with robbery. Of these

Table 2: Sentencing

Court	Guilty	Not Guilty	Dismissed	No Bill	Unclear	Total
CJCC* – Murder	0	0	0	0	0	0
CJCC – Rape/Seduction	6	1	1	0	0	8
CJCC – Property	25	7	0	0	0	32
CJCC – Other	8	3	1			12
Assize – Murder	6	1	0	0	0	7
Assize – Rape	6	0	0	0	0	6
Assize – Property	8	6		5	5	24
Assize – Other	11	3		3	5	22

*County Judge's Criminal Court

Table 3: Outcomes in death-penalty cases

Offence	Executions	Commutations	Other/Unknown
Murder	10	6	5
Rape	0	1	0

four cases (two cases of highway robbery), the highest sentence meted out was two years' imprisonment, and applied to only one case. The statistics suggest two things. First, the sentences for Blacks who committed robbery tended to be higher and were imposed with greater frequency. Second, legal officials demonstrated a palpable reluctance to charge Whites with the more serious crime of robbery. Black theft, it seems, was often constituted as a violent crime in the law and in the courts.

The surviving records of criminal cases brought before the assizes of Essex and Kent (Table 2) – a region with a high concentration of Blacks in the nineteenth and early twentieth centuries (see chapter 1) – are the second main data set used in this book. In the overall sample, 18 per cent of the cases were property offences and of these a slight majority resulted in guilty verdicts. Most resulted in either a not-guilty verdict or a grand jury finding of 'No Bill.' In contrast, of the twelve rape and murder cases tried in the Criminal Assize, all but one resulted in a guilty verdict, and, as we shall see, Black men who were charged with sexually assaulting white women were dealt with significantly more

Table 4: Theft and robbery in Kent County, CJCC,* 1907–17

Offence/Group	Total	Guilty	Not Guilty	Unclear	Highest Sentence	Lowest Sentence
Robbery – Black	4	4	0		3 yrs	1 yr
Theft – Black	4	1	3		4 yrs	1 mo
Hwy Robbery – White	4	3		1	2 yrs	15 mos
Theft – White	52	31	15	6	2 yrs	suspended

*County Judge's Criminal Court

harshly by the courts than those charged with similar offences against Black women or compared to White rapists of White women.

The third group of cases examined in this book – twenty-two to be exact – are province-wide death-penalty cases (Tables 2 and 3). All of those on trial were men and with two exceptions all were murder cases. (The case of the African American Arthur Lucas, one of the two last men executed in Canada, falls outside the time period of this book.) Nearly half of these men, 45 per cent of the total, were hanged. Those who managed to escape the gallows did so in a number of different ways. Most (27 per cent) were granted commutations by the Upper Canada and Canada West legislature in the pre-Confederation period and by the federal government in Ottawa after 1867. Other means of escaping the rope, as evidenced in the remaining 18 per cent of these cases, included deportation, acquittal upon an appeal, and death while awaiting the execution date. (The outcome of one of the earliest cases is uncertain.)[58]

We also cannot lose sight of the broader national picture with respect to how Blacks have fared historically in death-penalty cases. As a percentage of the total number of persons executed in Canada, Blacks were over-represented. David B. Chandler's work finds that, in the final disposition of murder cases stemming from robbery in Canada in 1946–7, 57 per cent of Blacks were executed (only Ukrainians fared worse at 66 per cent, but the total number of Ukrainian cases was half that of the number for Blacks).[59] Still, an overview of death-penalty cases involving Blacks in nineteenth- and twentieth-century Ontario shows a considerable amount of variability in outcomes. The meaning and significance of this variability, its implications for how 'race' and blackness in particular was constructed in and through the law, is what this book addresses.

Race on Trial: Opening Arguments

This book argues that, when Blacks appeared before the criminal courts, 'race,' whether tacitly or overtly, procedurally or rhetorically, was on trial. The criminal law was an integral part of how race was produced, managed, and expressed in the racial liberal order that framed the Black experience in Canada. Black life under this order had a dual legacy: the rule of law and the myriad ways in which, under its veneer and through the exercise of discretionary power, biological racism pushed against it, often rupturing a rhetoric of 'British justice' and 'fair play' which barely concealed it, or bended to its desires under a cloak of legal neutrality.

Two main thematic threads run through this book. First, the imperatives of social history make it necessary for us explore what criminal court records can tell us about the social history of African Canadians 'from below.' How did the criminal courts deal with Black lawbreakers? How did African Canadians view their relationship with the criminal courts? Secondly, what do these legal cases tell us about how Blacks were constituted as racialized subjects? And what do these processes of racialization tell us about race in a liberal order and, at times, its role in shaping a White Canadian national identity?

Ontario's courts cast Blacks in the roles of both 'dangerous Others' and as pitiable colonized subjects in need of salvation. This was a conversation that took place largely among White elites. And yet Black subjects did at times talk back when they had the opportunity to do so. Those who were brought before the courts to stand trial and, in a few instances, Black lawyers were active agents who used the law in various ways to pursue their own ends. This book also suggests that trials of Black criminals often served as a venue for a larger and important discussion of the very nature of Canadian 'nationhood.' The term nationhood, of course, is not being used here in terms of a strict physical or political geography that encompassed all of Canada, but in the imagined sense.[60] But, while the courts placed these criminals at the centre of the conversations that linked them with ideas of the nation, the criminals themselves were taken up as part of this discussion in ways that can only be described as uneven and ambivalent. White supremacist ideas about blackness were manifested in harsh penalties and widespread anxieties that were perhaps best typified by the alleged dangers – especially sexual – that Black men posed to White women. This discourse positioned Blacks outside the borders of the nation. Yet

Blacks were also imagined in ways that made them central to ideals of British Canadian nationhood. When commentators spoke of Black infantilism and thus the necessity of showing mercy towards a member of a 'childlike race,' or when mob justice and lynching were deemed 'unBritish,' blackness was clearly helping to shape a White Canadian identity through the use of racialized discourse. When White defence lawyers used 'common sense' – but racialized – arguments, they were drawing on many of the narrative conventions of what Natalie Zemon Davis in her work on the courts in sixteenth-century France has called the 'pardon tale,' and, as Carolyn Strange has noted, racial stereotypes had the power not only to inculpate but also to exculpate.[61] The almost missionary zeal with which many of these White lawyers defended the most marginal of Black Canadians, without any hope of remuneration, and their (probably sincere) insistence on the importance of 'colour-blind British justice' all show how whiteness was often forged in the crucible of the trials of Black criminals.

Chapter 1 argues that blackness was very much a product of the law – the law of racial slavery – which set the parameters of Blacks' encounter with the legal system in the nineteenth and twentieth centuries. The law continued to shape the lives of Blacks after the legal abolition of slavery in the British empire in 1833 and the emergence of the Underground Railroad. While most Blacks had a vague notion of a Canaan they would find when they arrived, they were met with the reality of a new country and a new province that often was less welcoming than they had imagined, but nonetheless, as legal persons, the law and its courts gave them an opportunity to redress community grievances and establish social bonds; these cases are an important window on Black nineteenth-century community life.

Chapter 2 examines several death-penalty cases involving Black men charged with murder in Ontario. The evidence presented here confirms the findings of existing work on race and the law in death-penalty cases. Racial reasoning could work either to spare the lives or to seal the fates of those who faced the gallows. This chapter is concerned mostly with how the various conversations about mercy were related to ideas about White Canadian identity and nationhood. The evidence shows not just straightforward racist oppression but the complex legal and cultural articulations of race in a racial liberal order. Depending upon the immediate context, certain codes, tropes, and images that were arrayed to portray Black felons could work either 'for' or 'against' these men in determining what kind of verdict they received. In this way,

Blacks' experiences were quite similar to those of Aboriginal peoples. Also evident in the arguments made by lawyers and in the post-trial comments of various observers is their ambivalence about blackness. This is especially true of cases involving what is now commonly, and unfortunately, referred to as 'Black on Black murder' as well as murders across the colour line. This ambivalence helps us to explain the flexible and contradictory position that Blacks occupied in the imaginations of many Whites. In conjunction with (and, at times, clearly subordinate to) class and gender, blackness was sometimes considered a part of Canada and at other times something foreign to it.

Chapter 3 deals with the theme of Black patriarchy, an issue given short shrift in African Canadian historiography. This chapter examines evidence from the Assize Court and capital cases and explores cases of Black men charged with committing crimes against Black women. These stories are in the legal realm of property crime, rape, murder, and spousal murder. In the majority of the cases explored in this chapter, there is compelling evidence for what I call the 'residual patriarchy' enjoyed by these Black men, bestowed upon them by a White patriarchal legal system. Three particularly rich death-penalty cases are featured in this chapter. The peculiar alchemy of Black patriarchal power and stereotypical ideas about Black masculinity in these cases created scenarios where the exercise of Black patriarchal privilege was not clear-cut.

Chapters 4 and 5 examine the contentious issues of race, sex, and the law. Chapter 4 explores cases that exemplified the 'archetype of sexual danger,' that is, Black men who were charged with raping White women. Each of these spectacular rape trials gives us a glimpse of the rape myth in practice. Not even these most dreaded occurrences of sexual violence, however, precluded the possibility of White elites using them as an opportunity to celebrate British justice and British fair play. The discourses surrounding these trials portrayed the Black defendants as representative of a general threat to White womanhood. But, under the right circumstances, the criminal justice system's dispensation of selective mercy or leniency meant that even a Black felon found guilty of assaulting a White woman provided an opportunity for elites to reinforce or celebrate White Canadian nationhood and identity.

Chapter 5 argues that, while many cases involving race and sex did not fit archetypal rape scripts, nonetheless, the dominant culture's view of the many dangers posed by Black male sexuality profoundly shaped and indeed over-determined these cases.[62] This was evident even in cases where White men assaulted Black women. Once again, British justice, fair play, and Canadian national identity were central themes in these stories. Bayly's claim in 1929 that 'one never hears of Blacks in court' could also serve more generally as an apt description of Blacks in Canadian history. The one hundred years and 133 troubling cases of Black criminals covered in these pages are my attempt to provide a counter-narrative.

1

Blackness and the Law in Slavery and Freedom

For Sale, for three years from the 29th of this present month of July A Negro Wench, Named Chloe, 23 years old, understands washing Cooking &c. Any gentleman willing to purchase, or employ her by the year or month, is requested to apply to ROBERT FRANKLIN, at the receiver general's.

– *Upper Canada Gazette*, July 1795[1]

Canadian Negro Hate is incomparably MEANER than the Yankee article. The parties who exhibit most of this feeling, are as poor, as ignorant, as immoral, as low, in every respect as the most degraded class of Negroes. Our recently arrived slaves, are, in all respects, quite equal to our newly arrived immigrants from Europe ... The blacks [are] as free as the whites, and in law and in fact quite equal to them. Hence the greater meanness of Canadian than American Negro Hate.

– Samuel Ringgold Ward, *Voice of the Fugitive*, 1852[2]

These quotations, each from a formative period in Black history in Canada – the era of slavery and the Underground Railroad – tell two distinct, yet intertwined, stories of Blacks' relationship with the law and how it changed over time. The first encapsulates the period prior to 1833 when Blacks in Canada were the legal property of Whites who could buy and sell them as they wished. During this period Black slaves were the property of their White owners whose rights were sanctioned (though not unequivocally) by the colonial state. The second quotation is emblematic of the challenges Blacks faced in the post-emancipation era, a time when they were granted formal equality under the law and desired full citizenship. Sadly, their desires were only partially realized in the era after slavery.

Blacks in Ontario often turned to the law to protect and affirm their status as free persons when it was threatened by U.S. slaveholders and to seek justice and reaffirm community bonds. Formal equality under the law, while significant, did not mean that the law was neutral; in fact, more often than not it lent its support to racial segregation. The cultural weight of slavery in the Americas tainted Blacks as a distinct and inferior group. As James Walker has pointed out, during the colonial period 'black enslavement [made] a powerful impression upon whites ... it was possible to witness the transfer of status from a legal condition to a biological characteristic, from "slave" to "black."'[3]

This chapter argues that the relationship between slavery and freedom – the ways in which the legacy of the former limited the possibilities of the latter – was also a central theme in Blacks' experiences in nineteenth-century Ontario. It begins with a discussion of slavery and moves to the role of the law in the post-emancipation era through the lens of civil and criminal cases. The latter are drawn from the book's sample of cases from the Essex and Kent assizes and illuminate the severity of the racial climate for Blacks and their resistance to legal authority; they also provide a window on Black community life.

Slavery

One writer has described slavery as Canada's 'best kept secret, locked within the national closet. And because it is a secret it is written out of official history. But slavery was an institutional practice for over two hundred years. Canada also engaged in the nefarious business of slavery.'[4]

The author makes a crucial point; there has indeed been a tradition of Canadian historians ignoring the institution of slavery or giving it only passing reference. But the historiography on slavery in Canada is a growing field. In a literature marked by increasing sophistication, many authors have noted that the institution of slavery did exist in early 'Canada' and was deeply rooted in the colonial empires of France and Britain.

France's vast seventeenth- and eighteenth-century empire included slaveholdings in New France, specifically in 'Canada' – the territory of the Saint Lawrence valley – and on Île Royale (Cape Breton Island) in Acadia. Blacks were present in modern-day Canada as early as 1606; one of the first records of a Black person in Canada was a young (and possibly enslaved) boy by the name of Mathieu da Costa, a Micmac interpreter who worked for French explorer Samuel de Champlain.[5] Oliver Le Jeune, the property of a Jesuit priest, is another of the earliest known Black residents of French Canada.[6]

Slavery in French Canada, though it was racially based, was not confined to Blacks. Aboriginal peoples, members of various First Nations the French called *Panis* (a derivation of Pawnee), were also enslaved. Indeed, most of French Canada's slaves were First Nations peoples rather than people of African descent. On the eve of the British conquest of New France in 1759, there were 1,132 Black slaves out of a total slave population of 3,604 in Canada.[7] As a consequence of Blacks' lower numbers and the higher price that resulted from their relative scarcity, enslaved Blacks were the preserve of the elite while Panis slaves were often found in the homes of the bourgeois middle class.[8] These slaves did not toil on the large plantations that were characteristic of other parts of the empire. Slaves in French Canada, both Panis and Black, performed a variety of tasks, working in fishing, mining, agriculture, and domestic service.[9]

The demography of slavery on Île Royale was different from that of its counterpart in the Saint Lawrence valley. While in the latter the majority of slaves were Panis, on Île Royale, with a slave population of 216, 90 per cent were Black, a result of links with traders in the French West Indies.[10] Nonetheless, the slaves' occupations in both places were similar. Slaves performed the tough domestic tasks that helped to feather the nests of White colonialists: providing childcare, gathering firewood, and hauling water. Outside the domestic sphere, Blacks also served as 'gardeners, bakers, tavern keepers, stone masons, musicians, laundry workers, soldiers, sailors, fishermen, hospital workers, ferrymen, executioners and nursemaids.'[11]

Slavery in New France received royal sanction from Louis XIV between 1689 and 1709, years after the first slaves had arrived in the region.[12] In 1709 the intendant of New France, Jacques Radout, issued an ordinance reaffirming the property status of Black and Panis slaves who had been purchased by Whites. In 1736 colonial officials crafted another ordinance which sought to regularize the process of manumission, which had become increasingly ad hoc and chaotic.[13]

The law of slavery in New France was influenced by the *Code Noir*, a legal document the French designed in 1685 – and refined in 1724 – to govern its slave colonies in places such as Saint-Dominique, Martinique, and Guadeloupe. The code, some sixty articles in length, offered protection to slaves and laid out the master's obligation to his chattel. It allowed for slave baptisms, the recognition of the Black family, the extension of Christian instruction to slaves, and, significantly, the launching of petitions by slaves against non-slaves.[14] Conversely, the code also included provisions for the punishment of slaves who committed crimes against Whites. It gravely 'called for the death of slaves who struck their master or their master's children.'[15] The code was never given formal legal status in New France, but many scholars agree that it did shape the mores and customs of slavery in the region.[16]

Slavery endured as a legal institution in New France until the British conquest of 1760, though in the Saint Lawrence valley it had began to decline by the first two decades of the eighteenth century.[17] Slavery in the pre- and post-Loyalist eras of British rule was characterized by both continuity and change. Between 1760 and 1763 – the years of immediate transition from French to British rule in Canada – slavery was legally strengthened in Canada with the British takeover of the region.[18] During this crucial time, the British assured French slaveowners that they would be permitted to keep their slaves.[19] In 1763 James Murray, the governor of Quebec, as the colony was now known, voiced his support for the continued practice of slavery by inquiring about the possibility of importing slaves from New York.[20] Murray's attitude was a product of a time where 'the entire weight of law and custom in the British colonies tended to support the legality of the institution overseas.'[21]

Legal support for slavery in British North America endured even after the landmark Somerset case of 1772, which many at that time (erroneously) believed made slavery illegal in England.[22] In 1790 an imperial act provided 'the most important legal protection given to slavery by Britain for the northern provinces,'[23] allowing emigrants to bring clothing, utensils, furniture, and slaves into British North America.[24] The legal protections the British provided for slaveowners coupled with the Loyalist influx of the post-revolutionary era caused a rapid expansion in the number of slaves in Canada and, as a consequence, a move away from Panis to Black slaves.[25]

Slavery was thus a fact of life in British North America. Most of the Blacks in Quebec were the property of white Loyalist slaveowners. The

1784 census was the first to count the slaves and it found 304 in the part of the province that would become Upper Canada after 1791.[26] They were ubiquitous in the Loyalist settlements, owned by many members of Upper Canada's political elite.[27]

White Loyalists gave the institution of slavery renewed vigour when they imported their slaves into British North America, but, oddly enough, slavery also reached its nadir during this era. Such was the paradox of slavery during the Loyalist period.[28] Slavery was strongly challenged during the Loyalist era right up until its eventual demise across the British empire in 1833. These challenges to slavery took place in both legislatures and the courts.

One of the first legal attempts to reach a compromise between those for and against the institution of slavery took place in Upper Canada. In 1793 John Graves Simcoe, the first lieutenant governor, led the attack from the colony's highest office. At the first meeting of the Executive Council, Peter Martin, a Black servant in the employ of John Butler, Upper Canada's superintendent of Indian affairs, spoke to an audience of the province's most powerful White men, including Chief Justice William Osgoode and slaveowner Peter Russell. Martin told them the tragic story of Chloe Cooley, a young Black female slave and the property of a Queenston resident, who had been spirited across the Niagara River in a legal sale that she violently resisted. This story inspired Simcoe to act, either because of the injustice of what happened to Cooley, the unseemliness of this public spectacle, or both. Simcoe attacked the institution of slavery by tabling a gradual emancipation bill. This was less than the 'frontal assault' on the institution that many scholars have claimed it was, but it was an important legislative blow to an institution that had powerful supporters in the colony. Simcoe's bill became an act within two weeks of its introduction and was only weakly opposed by a handful of slaveholders. The new act called for the gradual demise of slavery. Those who were enslaved in 1793 would retain this status until death. Those born after the passage of the act would be freed at the age of twenty-five, and any Blacks who were born to a slave younger than the age of twenty-five would be freeborn.[29]

No other part of British North America legislated abolition – even gradually – but elsewhere the courts played an important role in shortening the life of the institution. In Lower Canada, following the Upper Canadian example, anti-slavery advocates brought a gradual emancipation bill before the House of Assembly. Although it was defeated, many jurists, most notably Justice James Monk, were sympathetic to abolitionism and chipped away at slavery's legal foundations. In particular, Lower Canada's courts, in a series of rulings that were disadvantageous to slaveholders, placed the burden of proof of ownership on the slaveholding class rather than the enslaved.[30]

Slaveowners in Nova Scotia were challenged by two forces: the economic and social difficulties of perpetuating the institution in the colony and the campaign of anti-slavery activists. Slaves were present in Nova Scotia before the American Revolution; some ninety-five 'Negroes' were recorded in a 1767 census of the province.[31] These slaves were joined by many others after 1783 but most Blacks in post-revolutionary Nova Scotia were free. In 1775, in the heat of the American Revolution, Lord Dunmore, governor of Virginia, had decided to offer freedom to those who were willing to join British forces. This offer – Dunmore's Proclamation – was followed by the Phillipsburg Proclamation four years later which granted freedom to any slave who absconded and crossed into British lines. Lured by the promise of freedom and a chance to start their lives anew in British North America, some 3,500 Black Loyalists departed New York's harbour and headed north, part of one of the greatest Black freedom movements in the modern era.[32]

In Nova Scotia after 1783 it was often difficult to determine who was a slave and who was free, since the link between slavery and blackness was attenuated. This created a problem for many members of the slaveholding class. Birchtown, a Black settlement on the outskirts of the Loyalist settlement of Shelburne, 'became a haven to which slaves from all over the province could flee, and once safely hidden there it was extremely unlikely that a master could retrieve them.'[33] Other slaveowners had no interest in economically supporting their slaves upon their arrival in Nova Scotia, casting them out to support themselves. Many Blacks occupied a liminal position, caught between slavery and freedom. In a new economic twist on long-standing social arrangements, many former bondsmen had to suffer the indignity of hiring themselves out to their former masters to scrape out a meagre living.[34]

The legality of slavery was also challenged in Nova Scotia and New Brunswick prior to the American Revolution; slavery in Nova Scotia was presumed to be legal and was indirectly reinforced by the courts.[35] In the post-revolutionary era and in the period after the exodus of many free Blacks from Nova Scotia to Sierra Leone in 1792, the legality of slavery was challenged by Blacks and their White supporters. During the same years, two failed attempts to pass bills regulating the practice of slavery failed in the provincial legislature.[36]

The judges who presided over legal challenges to slavery in Loyalist Nova Scotia undermined the legality of slavery through their rulings but stopped short of abolition. This pattern was followed by a number of legislators – many of them lawyers by training – who undermined slavery by refusing to enact bills to codify and regulate the institution. At the same time, like the province's judges, many legislators refused to support abolition even though by 1808, Barry Cahill argues, many slave masters, realizing that the writing was on the wall, petitioned for just such a measure.[37] This was, after all, the year that the transatlantic slave trade was abolished in the British empire.

The reluctance of Nova Scotia's legal officers to abolish slavery in law reflected their view that 'slavery, though arguably a violation of human rights, was both customarily legal and seen to be so, and that prudent judges had therefore to proceed with extreme caution lest they find themselves in the invidious position of determining what the law should be rather than deciding what it was and thus provoke the legislature into overruling their decisions.'[38] The province's judicial elite staked out a position between the legal support of slavery and its legal abolition; this was a gradualist approach to undermining slavery. It made the practice of slaveholding a little more difficult than in other parts of the Anglo-American world and in Spanish and French slave colonies, but it was far from the unequivocal emancipation sought by slaves and their allies.

In New Brunswick, slavery was also challenged in the courts but anti-slavery advocates found the judicial climate there much chillier than Nova Scotia's and certainly Lower Canada's. In a province where slavery endured well into the new century, judges resisted the spirit of the abolitionist ethos that was sweeping much of the Atlantic world at the turn of the nineteenth century. Slavery was not legally recognized in New Brunswick. Nonetheless, in two high-profile cases dealing with the issue of slaveowners' property rights (*R. v. Jones* and *R. v. Agnes*), the courts ruled to protect the property rights of slaveholders. This victory for pro-slavery advocates was significant but ultimately short lived. By the second decade of the nineteenth century, slavery was in its last days in all of British North America.

Freedom

Britain abolished slavery in the empire in 1833, but throughout British North America the institution cast a long shadow over Blacks' lives for years after abolition. 'From slavery grew many of the stereotypical characteristics applied to blacks, particularly notions of dependence, lack of initiative and suitability only for service and unskilled employment.'[39] In Nova Scotia and New Brunswick, for example, the status of post-emancipation Black communities in the nineteenth century was precarious. These communities took root in the era after the mass exodus of free Blacks to Sierra Leone and the migration of the Refugee Blacks after the War of 1812. The British had promised the Refugees complete freedom and had originally welcomed their arrival. But over time it became clear the 'place into which they were welcomed ... was narrowly defined. Carrying the negative status of former slaves and sharing the colour characteristic of the region's service caste, the new blacks were expected to perform manual labour at low rates of pay.'[40] Blacks in the Maritimes, those of both Loyalist and Refugee stock, lived in highly segregated communities. They worshipped in separate churches, sent their children to separate schools, and struggled to earn their livelihood on tiny farms. Theirs was a life on the margin.[41]

The large-scale settlement of Blacks in Ontario took root later in the nineteenth century, the age of the Underground Railroad, which began as a trickle during the War of 1812 and steadily grew as the Fugitive Slave Law of 1850 gave American slaveowners the right to recapture absconded slaves who had escaped to the northern states. This pushed the frontier of legal freedom farther north, into British North America. The exact number of Blacks who lived in Ontario in the mid-nineteenth century has been the subject of some contentious debate. Beginning in the late 1820s, American fugitive slaves made their way to Upper Canada/Canada West. Between 1851 and 1861, the population increased dramatically. According to the official data, the numbers of Blacks in Canada West at the time of the 1851 census was approximately 4,669. According to published census data from 1861, ten years later the figure jumped to 13,566 though some contemporary accounts of the fugitive slave population place the number at upwards of 40,000.[42] Michael Wayne's study of the official census disputes the claims of both contemporary observers and the official census. A careful reassessment of the original manuscript records leads Wayne to argue that popular contemporary (and often cited) accounts of the fugitive slave population were greatly exaggerated, while the official census record suffered from errors which left out about 4,000 or so Blacks. Wayne suggests that a more accurate count is in the neighbourhood of 17,000. The tendency for contemporary observers to assess the numbers of fugitives at

40,000 or so, coupled with an overestimation of the number of Blacks residing in Canada West in the 1850s who were native-born Canadians as opposed to fugitives, gave rise to the specious argument that the vast majority of fugitives – approximately two-thirds – returned 'home' to the United States.[43] By 1871, Wayne claims, the Black population of Canada West stood at about 13,500, roughly a 20 per cent decrease from the prior decade, an indication that about 20 per cent of the Black population made its way south, a significant number but not the 'mass exodus' often reported in accounts of the era.[44]

By 1881, the census recorded yet another decline in Ontario's Black population, down a little over a thousand to 12,097.[45] This downward trend continued over the next thirty years; by 1911, 6,747 Blacks appeared in the official record, increasing slightly to 7,220 by 1921.[46] The figures published in the 1930 and 1940 censuses show that the numbers fell again; there were reportedly 3,319 Blacks in 1931 and 3,632 in 1941. However, an almost 50 per cent decline from 1921 leads one to suspect that the Black population was considerably under-represented in both counts.[47] Winks, for one, cites (and perhaps laments?) the fact that the Black population was under-reported in various census years between 1911 and 1951, as a result of the fact that 'a considerable number of Negroes "passed over" each decade into "white" classifications – not through intermarriage since the intermarriage rate was low, but presumably through electing to consider themselves white.'[48] Winks provides no empirical data to substantiate his argument, though at a theoretical level it points to the malleability of racial categories, as well as the need to pursue more actively the process of how constructions of whiteness affected the Black Canadian experience. But, given the severe discriminatory climate for people of African descent in Ontario and elsewhere in North America, Winks's explanation certainly seems plausible. It is clear that Blacks were the victims of under-enumeration; this well may account for the oddities in the reported figures for the 1951 census, which tabulated the number of Blacks residing in the province of Ontario at 6,926.

Most Blacks in Ontario settled in the counties of Essex and Kent. The history of both counties, located in the southwestern part of the province, also known as the Thames valley, began in 1792 when Upper Canada was divided into nineteen districts, including Essex and Kent. In 1841 Kent County was joined with Essex County and Lambton County to form an administrative unit called the Western District. In 1847 Kent became a separate district and in 1850 Canada West implemented a county system, terminating the system of districts.[49] Kent County consists of nineteen towns, townships, and villages, the largest among them Chatham. From humble beginnings as one of the earliest settlements in western Ontario, Chatham grew into an important urban centre by the turn of the century. Essex County, bounded by lakes and rivers on three sides, was comprised of seventeen towns and smaller townships; Windsor emerged as the county's urban centre.

Blacks comprised a small percentage of the total Canadian population, but in certain areas their numbers were quite significant. In Ontario, Blacks made up nearly 20 per cent of the total population of Chatham (Kent County), 25 per cent of Amherstburg (Essex County), and 33 per cent of Colchester (Kent County) in the 1850s.[50] Indeed, between 1861 and 1941, roughly half of Ontario's Black population lived in the two counties, a trend that continued well into the twentieth century.[51]

Black Freedom and the Law

During this time the law continued to play as important a role in the lives of Blacks in Upper Canada as it had in the era of slavery. The abolition of slavery in the British empire coupled with the colonial government's determination to protect fugitive slaves from U.S. extradition created a frontier of legal equality for Blacks, a significant development given the history of slavery in British North America and the continued existence of slavery throughout most regions of the Americas. On the heels of the abolition of slavery in the empire, the legislature of Upper Canada gave the lieutenant governor in council the power to capture and extradite 'Fugitive Offenders from Foreign Countries' but authorized him to refuse if he deemed it necessary.[52] According to Winks, the discretionary power this act placed in the hands of the lieutenant governor was crucial, since 'he could be counted on to exercise compassion towards a fugitive slave whose only crime was self-theft, a patent impossibility where slavery did not exist.'[53]

The lieutenant governor's discretionary power remained a central feature of the adjudication of fugitive slave cases in Canada. In 1833, a year already heavily significant in the lives of Blacks in Canada, the courts proved to be a source of shelter for fugitive slaves. Lucie and Thornton Blackburn had escaped slavery in Kentucky only to be recaptured in Detroit; they were then rescued by an organized group of determined Blacks who spirited them away to freedom. This couple, who would later go on to own Toronto's first cab company, were shielded from extradition to the United States by the lieutenant governor.[54] Subsequently, two other fugitive slaves, Solomon Moseby and Jessie Happy, both escaped slavery in the United States by stealing horses from their masters and riding across the border to freedom. Neither was extradited to the United States to stand trial. In the case of Moseby, the government had decided – contrary to established practice – to extradite him but was met with stern opposition by the Black community of Niagara, which freed him from custody and helped him to relocate to Britain.[55] By the 1840s, pressure was mounting on both sides of the border for an extradition treaty to address the problem of criminals from both countries crossing the border to escape prosecution, resulting in the Webster-Ashburton extradition treaty of 1843. This in theory should have had an effect on fugitive slaves, all of whom violated U.S. laws by escaping slavery. Yet no slave was ever returned to the United States under its terms.[56] This was true in the case of John Anderson, a Missouri fugitive slave who, after murdering his master's neighbour during his escape, was not extradited to the United States after an appeal.[57]

These extradition cases are persuasive evidence of the legal haven that emerged for African-descended people in British North America after 1833. Indeed, the historical record provides clues that some Blacks experienced satisfaction bordering on euphoria after initially arriving under the 'Lions Paw.' Upon his arrival, one ex-slave declared: 'The colored people in London are ... getting along as well as they can expect ... I do not know of one who suffered so much here as he would in slavery.' Another, in St Catharines, said simply: 'I reached Canada about a year ago. Liberty I find to be sweet indeed.'[58] It is also true, however, that social and economic barriers to full inclusion in British North America severely impinged upon Blacks' new legal freedoms. Even while many Blacks found some comfort under the British flag and a refuge from chattel slavery in the United States, they were not regarded as equals. Many Whites continued to hold ideas about Blacks' cultural and social inferiority which existed on a spectrum from paternalism to overt racism.

Over time, Blacks began to realize that they were in the midst of a White settler colony and an outpost of the British empire which grew increasingly hostile to them. As more Blacks arrived in Ontario, the attitude of the host society began to sour. Much to the chagrin of White Ontarians, however, many of these 'unwelcome guests' became permanent settlers.[59] As a consequence, residential segregation became a fact of Black life in Ontario. On the voluntary side of the ledger, White elites, with the complicity of a handful of Black leaders, settled upon Black settlements – in essence self-segregation – as an answer to the dilemma posed by the pressing need for Blacks to make the difficult transition from slavery to freedom. Between 1829 and the outbreak of the American Civil War, a number of these schemes – the Wilberforce, Dawn, and Buxton settlements and the Refugee Home Society – were initiated in Upper Canada/Canada West.[60]

Discrimination flowed readily out of this context and it was a pervasive feature of life for Blacks in nineteenth-century Ontario. Blacks in 1850s Canada West encountered 'substantial prejudice.' They suffered indignities such as widespread unemployment (though its severity varied across the province), White opposition to interracial social gatherings and marriage, and the erroneous but 'widely held view that there was a disproportionate number of Negroes in prisons, jails or the insane asylum.'[61] These aspects of Black life were both cause and effect of a social environment where it was not uncommon for Blacks in 1850s southwestern Ontario to have to endure epithets like 'nigger' in their day-to-day interactions with Whites.[62]

Blacks' struggle for equality through formal education is one of the most important themes in the history of post-emancipation Black Canada. Because so many Blacks had been denied an education as slaves, they were driven to obtain a formal education and to serve as an example, a model of success, to other Blacks. In addition, Donald Simpson argues, 'most black immigrants were anxious to be treated as complete persons. As slaves they had no personal rights' and getting an education was seen as means to acquire them as well as economic well-being, citizenship, and the opportunity for full civic participation.[63]

For interested social observers of the day, the issue of race in the public schools was an important barometer of popular racial sentiment and feeling. Benjamin Drew, a Boston abolitionist who compiled narratives of ex-slaves in Canada West in the mid-nineteenth century, reported that in London, like many other communities, the 'common schools are open to all without distinction to color.'[64] Yet, despite the lack of a legal colour bar to integrated education, when Drew visited two schools in June 1855 he found that one had 13 Black students in attendance out of a total of 174, and the other had 4 Black students present out of a total of 190. Why were the attendance figures so dismally low if the law allowed equal access to the schools? Drew had an answer: 'The principal reason for this neglect of common school advantages by the colored people is the prejudice of whites. Many of the whites object to having their children in schools where the blacks are admitted. Under these circumstances, it is unpleasant to the colored children to attend the public schools – especially if any of the teachers happen to be victims of the very prejudice which they should induce others to overcome.'[65]

Similarly, in Amherstburg the opposition to Black children in the common schools was so entrenched that the school trustees declared that it was preferable to 'cut their children's heads off and throw them into the road side ditch' than to send them 'to school with niggers.'[66] In Hamilton, White opposition to integrated schools was also so pronounced as to compel Blacks to petition the governor general for the right of admission to the common schools.[67]

The law had an important – albeit shifting – role to play in this unfortunate state of affairs. Prior to 1850 the law prohibited segregated schools. The 1843 School Act made it unlawful for school officials to exclude 'any class or description of persons resident within the School district to which some common school belong.'[68] The School Act allowed the creation of separate – principally Roman Catholic – schools, but Whites' attempts to block Black children from the common schools in locales such as Sandwich and London were clearly illegal.[69] In 1850 the provincial government amended the School Act in part by adding a provision that legally supported race-based schools, allowing 'any group of five Negro families to ask local public school trustees to establish such a school for them.'[70] In 1859 a new act again recognized separate schools 'at the behest of the heads of 12 or more families. It authorized the establishment of one, or more, separate schools for Protestants, Roman Catholics, or Coloured people.'[71] Although the law did not prevent Black children from accessing the public schools, for many Whites who were eager to maintain the colour-line in the province's classroom, the act created an opportunity to force Black parents to place their children in separate schools. For, while the act theoretically called for these schools to be set up by request, in reality many school boards were in a position to compel Blacks to resort to segregated education.[72]

The vast majority of Blacks resisted the idea of separate schools and in a handful of instances well-heeled members of the community took the fight to the civil courts. In one case, *Washington v. Trustees of Charlotteville*, a Black farmer launched a lawsuit against the trustees of the Simcoe County school board. The school board had gerrymandered the school district in an attempt to exclude Black children from the schools.

The plaintiff won the case after three trials but 'it was a Pyrrhic victory; he had to sell his farm to cover the court costs.'[73] A similar decision was reached in 1861 in the case of *Simmons v. Chatham*, where, once again, Chatham's school board gerrymandered the school district to create separate schools for Black children. Legal decisions such as these had limited effectiveness, however, since the courts, unfortunately for Blacks, 'could not rule where separate schools were not formally involved.'[74] As Benjamin Drew had observed, informal patterns of discrimination in the school system endured.

Thus, the law of freedom in Ontario created a complicated reality for Blacks. It passively supported and reflected rampant anti-Black racism in and through the exercise of its power while at the same time it secured Blacks' formal citizenship rights. Blacks' experiences in Ontario's criminal courts mirrored both of these tendencies. In the mid-nineteenth century and beyond, many ex-slaves and freemen in Canada courted the possibilities born out of a life after slavery. Yet many found that life at the end of the railroad could lead them before the criminal courts. Along with fugitive slave narratives and the published travelogues and personal essays of elite Black anti-slavery leaders, court proceedings provide one of the few records of Black life during this period.

The Criminal Courts

One sensational case shows the dramatic possibilities of the law of freedom in the era of the Underground Railroad. In 1858 news of an event known as the 'Slave Case' rocked the city of Chatham. On 5 October 1858 a group of U.S. Southerners were on a Great Western Railroad train in the vicinity of the city. Among the passengers was a ten-year-old slave child named Sylvanus Damarest. During a brief stopover, a crowd of 100 to 150 Black men and women – along with a sprinkling of White abolitionists – forcibly wrenched the boy from the train and out of the possession of his White master. Six members of a group known as the Chatham Vigilance Committee were charged and appeared at the Kent County fall assizes. Vigilance committees were an important feature of community activism among Blacks (and a few sympathetic Whites) and quite common in Ontario where Black communities sought to resist U.S. slave catchers.[75]

When the story appeared in the press, on both sides of the border it was characterized by pro-slavery versus anti-slavery rhetoric. For example, the Detroit *Free Press* ran a story which also appeared in the

Brantford *Expositor*. The story emphasized the violent nature of the vigilance committee, referring to its members as 'rioters' who wielded knives, revolvers, and clubs. The committee's successful rescue of the young slave was also denounced as a 'kidnapping.' Invoking colonial images, the *Free Press* quoted an eyewitness who claimed that the train was beset by 'stout burly Negroes' who reminded him of the 'Sepoys of India' while the young slave wailed in anguish during his separation from his master.[76]

In contrast to the Detroit paper's coverage, one outraged *Expositor* reader wrote a letter to the editor celebrating the abduction and invoking a rhetoric of British justice and White Canadian nationhood. In highly dramatic prose, the writer lauded the freedom that the young slave attained in Canada: 'Of course the boy was free in Canada. They touch our country and their shackles will fall. One hundred and eighty-three miles from Niagara Falls.' He continued: 'May I be the next to see and [hear] the "burly Negroes" in their shout of triumph.' This case marked an instance when Black male violence – directed at White men – was celebrated, held up to inscribe the essence of White Canadian nationhood. Whites' involvement in the melee also helps to explain this response. The Chatham *Planet*, which, like other newspapers in Upper Canada, frequently ran sensational stories involving Black criminality, was in agreement. It chastised the Detroit *Free Press* for its propensity for sensationalism and for catering to Southern slaveowners.

The presiding judge at the assize trial found six of the 'rioters' guilty and sentenced them to monetary fines rather than jail time. The lowest fine imposed was ten dollars, the highest was thirty. While passing sentence, the judge dutifully noted that in his official capacity he 'knew of no higher law than the law upon the Statute Books,' but he nevertheless 'acknowledged the force of a higher law.' A Chatham *Planet* editorial echoed these sentiments: 'If in releasing this boy the laws of our country were slightly overstepped, we feel that Canadians of every class, creed, and colour are not altogether dead to recognition of a higher law than all human laws.'[77]

This dramatic event deeply resonated with the fugitive slave cases of the era. It also provided an opportunity to showcase the superiority of British justice over its U.S. counterpart, a common theme in Canadian national discourse throughout the nineteenth and twentieth centuries.

For most Blacks, the law of freedom was better than U.S. slavery (or the Canadian version of the institution) but did not quite fit the celebratory script of the 1858 'Slave Case.' The 1850s were an era of heightened racial (and class) tensions brought about in large part by Blacks migrating across the border into Canada West. Cases of Blacks charged with theft are an indication of the economic hardships many faced. One Black man who had the misfortune of facing charges of larceny at the Kent County fall assizes was accused of stealing a gold coin valued at three dollars from a (presumably White) merchant. Though he pleaded that he found the coin in the doorway of the shop while performing his cleaning duties, eyewitnesses testified that they saw him wearing a new hat shortly after the crime was reported. This alone was enough to convict him.[78] In another theft case, a Black defendant was convicted after he was charged with stealing corn from a White man who employed servants. At the Sandwich (Essex County) fall assizes in 1859, one of these servants brought a complaint to the magistrate on behalf of his master, saying that he noticed footprints in his employer's corn field and a quantity of missing corn. Although he was far from certain of the identity of the culprit, he later said that he had heard from another party that a 'colr'd man come out of the field with a bag of corn. When he was later presented with a bag of corn the police found on the prisoner's farm, this same witness admitted he could not positively identify it.' Again, despite such circumstantial and contradictory evidence, the accused was found guilty.[79] In yet another case, a yeoman farmer brought charges against 'a colloured [*sic*] man in the Defendants Barn in the Township of Howard in the act of Stealing Wheat.' The defendant pleaded that he was hungry and intended to take only a handful of peas; he was found guilty since he had admitted to committing theft.[80]

Interracial encounters, festering in the same climate of intolerance that shaped the schools question, could lead to violence. In 1858 three members of a Black family, Acelous Hurst and his two sons, William and Solomon, stood charged with 'murder or manslaughter' and malicious assault for their attack upon a White man named William Ford. The Hurst Family and William Ford had engaged in a heated argument while 'culling staves' on the banks of a river near the village of Thamesville, Camden Township, a largely agricultural settlement located just outside Chatham. The argument became particularly heated when Ford began throwing staves down the banks of the river over the objections of the eldest Hurst, who demanded that he stop. When Ford replied there were 'plenty of little niggers about to pick them up,' this disagreement became violent; Hurst's two sons jumped into the melee. When Ford called for someone to 'take the Black devils off,' he was subjected to a rain of blows, each of the Hurst boys striking him in succession. The Hursts were found guilty of manslaughter after two doctors and a coroner's jury found that Ford came to his death by 'a blow given by a Negro named Hurst.'[81] In this case, the jury showed some leniency; a murder conviction would have meant a trip to the gallows for the Hursts.

These sorts of racial tensions were also evident in a perjury case which came before the Kent fall assizes in 1883. While Blacks were not actually tried in this case, blackness was. This case is illustrative of the commonness of White men's demeaning attitudes towards Black women. In May 1883 Dr John Pomeroy filed a complaint against Nathaniel Farris, charging that Farris had perjured himself when Noah Waffle laid a complaint of being drunk and disorderly against Pomeroy. Pomeroy's complaint alleged that, during the trial, Farris gave a false statement. Farris allegedly testified that one evening, at approximately midnight or 1:00 a.m., he 'heard a lot of swearing' among a group of men at a thoroughfare the locals called Tippin's corner. Farris stopped to listen to their conversation and heard another man at the gathering say that Pomeroy 'had been trying to run a nigger whore.' At the previous trial (the one that so irked Pomeroy), Farris positively swore that he saw Pomeroy on the street that night, a claim that Pomeroy vehemently denied at the trial and in his subsequent complaint.

What was at stake for Pomeroy was not a substantive legal matter. Indeed, in his earlier trial before the 1883 spring assizes on drunk and disorderly charges, the court dismissed the charge, ruling that there was too little evidence to convict. It seemed, though, that what was at issue here was Pomeroy's reputation, status, and respectability, all of which were placed in jeopardy by a public spectacle that linked him not only with unruly behaviour and bad language but, just as important, with dissolute Black womanhood. A number of prosecution witnesses came forward to rebut Farris's testimony in the first trial. All denied that Pomeroy used words such as 'nigger whore' (though one defence witness waffled under intense cross-examination). One witness questioned the validity of the charge against Pomeroy on the basis that 'this conversation about the nigger whore did not take place at the corner but near the main block.' Pomeroy himself testified that he went to his office well before the incident had allegedly occurred, and remained there until about three in the morning, well after the time of the alleged 'crime.' In the end, Pomeroy would have to find satisfaction in the fact that he managed to orchestrate another trial. There, however, he was only partially vindicated since the case against Farris was dismissed.[82]

These examples illuminate the harshness of the racial climate Blacks had to face in Ontario. But it is also true that breaking the law provided Ontario's Blacks, like other members of the labouring and marginal classes, an opportunity to assert their agency by resisting authority figures. Similar conflicts emerged when the law attempted to regulate the bodies and lives of the White working class and agricultural labourers in nineteenth-century Ontario. Many of the themes in these cases resonate and intersect with the history of the larger population of the labouring classes.[83]

A rare documented example of defiant resistance in the face of the law involving Blacks is a court case in 1859 in which the well-known Black abolitionist Josiah Henson was charged with assault.[84] When a Black named William Stewart died suddenly on his Camden farm, the Kent County coroner decided to hold an inquest on the body.[85] After the inquest the coroner took it upon himself to sort out some of the deceased's personal effects, which brought him into direct conflict with two members of Camden's Black community, Josiah Henson and another man named Cyrus Mitchell. After a skirmish erupted between the coroner and Henson and Mitchell, the coroner brought a complaint before a magistrate alleging that the two men had wrestled a key from him during a struggle in which they had kicked him in the leg and injured one of his hands; in addition, the coroner alleged that he was the victim of abusive language.[86] The coroner maintained that Cyrus Mitchell surrendered the key voluntarily and that it was not until the appearance of Josiah Henson that a confrontation had occurred. According to his testimony, when Henson arrived, he ordered Mitchell to take the key from the coroner. The readiness with which Mitchell complied with the order is a powerful testament to Josiah Henson's status among Camden's Blacks. By openly flouting the coroner's authority, Henson asserted himself as a Black leader and patriarch. There is no record of the exact nature of the 'abusive language' Henson was said to have levelled at the coroner, but one eyewitness testified that Henson was overheard telling Mitchell that if the coroner or 'any other white man' came to take the key he would 'take a club and knock their brains out.' Henson and Mitchell were found guilty and they received sizable fines – $20 apiece – but no jail time. Perhaps Henson's fame allowed him to challenge White male authority figures in ways that were simply not available to other Black men and to Black women, while also escaping a jail sentence.

Such open defiance of the law among Blacks is seldom documented in the historiography, even though, as Susan Lewthwaite and other social historians have noted, violent resistance against the authority of constables, bailiffs, and other judicial officers was quite common, particularly in rural areas or frontiers far removed from the formal reach of the law.[87] There are two additional cases involving Blacks in similar confrontations. The 1892 Essex Assize Court dealt with the case of an African Canadian man who, with the aid of several other Blacks, resisted a constable's attempts to arrest him. The constable went before a magistrate to lay a complaint alleging that the accused 'maliciously discharche[d] laud firearms ... [to] prevent his lawful apprehension for the crime of Larceny with intent to do bodily harm.' The police constable later told the court that the accused had managed to 'pull out a revolver when presented with papers for his arrest' and made his escape with the help of 'about half a dozen colored men.'[88] A similar case where the authority of the law was openly flouted – albeit with far less violent overtones – took place in the 1890s in Raleigh Township where F.A. Shreeve was charged with the crime of 'Larceny from Bailiff.' On 5 September 1892 a bailiff of the First Division Court in Kent County laid a complaint with a magistrate alleging that two days prior he had attempted to proceed with an execution against Shreeve for the value of $53.23. The bailiff went out to Shreeve's home to seize 'one horse the property of F.A. Shreeve.' Incensed by the seizure of his horse, Shreeve went to retrieve it from the Raleigh town stable. One of the stable keepers testified that Shreeve had claimed that he did not know why *'his* property had been seized' and took his horse from the stable. When the bailiff returned to Shreeve's place, Shreeve denied knowing anything about the whereabouts of the mare (he also later pleaded not guilty during the trial). Additionally, Shreeve claimed that the mare, in any case, belonged to his father. Soon afterwards, charges were laid against him. It is not clear from the fragmentary nature of the case file whether Shreeve was found guilty.[89]

These cases are examples of the ways in which Blacks, like other working-class and plebeian populations, openly and defiantly opposed officers of the court and the law. But a more common way Blacks asserted themselves was by using the law to address grievances between and among individuals of local communities. A number of cases that came before the courts involved petty quarrels among men which often escalated into serious instances of violence. In 1883 an African American man was shot in the thigh by a White man – described in the court record as a 'Dutchman with Black whiskers' – when, clearly drunk, he wandered across the U.S. border and was discovered sleeping in a shanty owned by the accused. After enlisting the help of a police officer who procured medical attention for him, the victim of the shooting filed a complaint before a magistrate, charging the White man with 'unlawfully wounding him with intent to commit murder.' The defendant maintained that the shooting was born out of his right to protect his property. This is a position that must have carried some weight considering that the complainant was not only Black but also a 'foreigner' and a 'stranger.' Unfortunately, the outcome is unknown.[90]

Black men were tried before the criminal assizes in cases involving various degrees of bodily violence. In the late 1850s and early 1860s, two such cases involving disagreements among Black men went before the Essex assizes. In 1859 one man was charged with 'stabbing with intent' when a stone-throwing incident escalated into a charge of 'stabbing in the Arm and Thigh with a knife or Dirk without just cause or legal provocation.'[91] A year and half later, one man was charged with shooting another whom he suspected of trying to steal something from his place; he discovered the would-be thief only because he went outside to examine his chimney, which was on fire. Despite the defendant's plea that he was merely protecting his property and his person from an intruder, he received a sentence of one year at hard labour in the gaol.[92] Black men also brought complaints against other men for charges like malicious wounding and doing actual bodily harm with a variety of weapons like slingshots, knives, and, of course, fists. These cases show that there was no reluctance to turn to the criminal court to settle quarrels and seek justice in a very public manner.[93]

Blacks also used the criminal courts to resolve disputes that emerged around issues of gender, family, and sexuality. Ontario's Blacks often resorted to the courts to resolve domestic matters – a subject that has been largely, though not entirely, absent from analyses of Ontario's legal records as well as African Canadian historiography. One particular episode, tried before the Kent spring assizes in 1883, involved the trial of a man for maliciously shooting another when a family gathering turned violent. The shooting, which local newspapers named the 'Chatham Shooting Affair,' led to a complaint by one family member alleging that 'Robert Boswell unlawfully and maliciously did shoot Simon Peters in the leg with a gun with intent to cause grievous bodily harm.' Frances Anne Boswell, Robert Boswell's wife, gave sworn testimony in support of her nephew, the victim of the shooting. She told the court that, on the night of the shooting, she was home with her husband

and 'just after dark Simon Peters came to our house and soon after my husband came in [and] he commenced calling me a damned Bitch and slapped me.' Anne Boswell further testified that her husband, angered by Simon's interference in his domestic matters, struck Simon with his fists and beat him very badly. 'I begged him to stop,' she continued, 'but he did not.' Rushing to the aid of her nephew, Anne Boswell took a whip and struck her husband. Robert Boswell then told Peters to leave his home or he would shoot him. As Peters started to leave, Anne Boswell heard the sound of a gun and discovered that Peters was shot in the leg. Later a doctor treated the wound. By the next day, the injury had so worsened that the leg had to be amputated. During the trial, Boswell's counsel mounted an ineffective defence, namely that, as the Chatham *Planet* reported, 'the gun had gone off accidentally, by catching the fence or by some other means.'[94] Boswell received one year's imprisonment in a case that offered up a rare glimpse of Black family life. It also demonstrated the permeability of the boundaries separating the private sphere of domestic violence among Black men and women from conflicts within larger kin networks.

Conclusion

The law was integral in shaping the experiences of Blacks in Canada in the eras of both slavery and freedom. Slavery was legally supported in New France and British North America. Unlike other parts of the Atlantic world where slave insurrections had a central role to play in hastening slavery's demise, in Canada the law was the primary venue through which the institution was challenged and eventually abolished. In the era of Black freedom, the courts and the law supported anti-Black racism in myriad forms, yet again they served as vehicles through which Blacks asserted their rights to equal citizenship, cemented community bonds, and settled disputes. This was evident on both the civil and the criminal side of the law. Subsequent chapters in this book narrate and analyse more stories of Blacks' legal encounters in Ontario and the role of the courts as a site where the Black community both shaped and was shaped by Canada's liberal racial order.

2

Nationhood, Mercy, and the Gallows

Death-penalty cases in Canada were stories not merely about punishment but also about selective mercy and discretionary justice: the power of the state was realized both through its ability to sanction violence and in its authority to spare life through mercy. This tension between mercy and punishment was heightened even more for dangerous outsiders, such as foreigners, Aboriginals, and Blacks. This chapter examines death-penalty cases involving Black defendants. The worrisome body of the Black male criminal was a site where the power of the Canadian state and where powerful aspects of Canadian identity itself could be realized. Black defendants simultaneously represented an opportunity to showcase the considerable power of the state through harsh punishments and a racialized brand of paternalistic mercy.

This chapter makes two substantive and interrelated arguments. First, it argues that lawyers' use of racial stereotypes and imagery could work either for or against Blacks in informing and shaping both the rhetorical strategies in the courtroom and verdicts. When Aboriginal defendants appeared before the courts, legal officials, government officials, and other experts drew upon pervasive notions of their 'savagery' to create 'exculpatory narratives' to mitigate the criminal responsibility of First Peoples. These kinds of legal defences were based on the widespread notion that Aboriginals could not be held to the same standards as more 'civilized' Whites.[1] As another racialized group, Blacks faced similar experiences in the courts.

Second, this chapter shows that, when legal officials debated whether to grant mercy to Black defendants, these discussions were intimately related to a Canadian nation-building project. This project was the product of a constellation of ideas linking race and nation in racial liberal order: the United States was a violent nation compared to Canada with its celerity of justice; (elite White) Canadians could control their passions and maintain their compassion towards (Black) lawbreakers whereas south of the border they would be subject to lynch law; and hanging such lawbreakers was the provenance of the Canadian state, not a mob.[2]

The chapter is divided into two parts. The first examines cases that did not extend across the colour line, that is, 'Black on Black' murder. The second part deals with murder across the colour line. These cases were determined by the interplay of legal factors and social attitudes, the tension between the veneer of the rule of law and biologically rooted racism that characterized the articulation of 'race' in a racial liberal order. In short, Canadian nationhood was forged in the prism of a racial liberal order when race was put on trial.

Good and Sufficient Grounds for Commutation?

There were five cases of Blacks convicted of murdering Blacks between 1868 and 1930. The evidence suggests that, while White elites were less likely to impose the most severe penalty upon such defendants, they were by no means completely averse to it. Further, the trials in these cases were often marked by an absence of conversations about race. Yet race mattered, nonetheless, precisely because the courts were less inclined to mete out the death penalty for Blacks accused of murdering other Blacks.

A rare case of a juvenile offender, seventeen-year-old George Johnston, was tried before the courts in Chatham in 1867. Johnston, described as a 'mulatto,' was sentenced to hang for the axe murder of another man of roughly the same age. Shortly after the close of the trial, the presiding judge, Joseph C. Morrison, wrote a letter to the secretary of state summarizing the details of the crime and the trial, and expressing both his and the jury's reluctance to see the death penalty carried through for this 'particular sort of crime.'[3] Morrison's allusion to a 'particular sort of crime' is frustratingly ambiguous. While ostensibly it appears to refer to the age of the parties involved, it is also quite possible that race was on his mind as well.

Acting on his recommendation, and that of the jury, and on a petition signed by more than one hundred of Chatham's citizens (including a police magistrate, an MP, and a handful of barristers), the federal cabinet commuted Johnston's sentence. This decision was made on the basis that the 'conviction of the boy George Johnston for Murder at the present Kent assizes appears to be founded upon a too stringent interpretation by the Jury of the Criminal Law.'[4] The evidence strongly suggested that 'the melancholy affair was the result of accident in boyish play.' Nine years later, in June and again in November 1877, petitions were sent to Ottawa pressing for Johnston's release from the penitentiary. Each petition noted the 'non-malicious' nature of the murder, emphasizing that the prisoner and the deceased were playmates.[5] Drawing on testimony submitted at trial, these petitions stressed that Johnston and the victim had been 'like brothers,' accustomed to striking each other roughly, and that the murder had been the unfortunate result of two wild boys engaged in rough play. By reinterpreting violence as 'play,' the petitions sought to erase the lines separating play, bodily violence, and murder. This was a common strategy used in clemency campaigns featuring juvenile offenders.

Once under the auspices of White male institutional authority, Johnston showed all the signs of respectability. His 'good character,' it was now argued, was evidenced in the warden's reports, which described his 'conduct and industry in the Penitentiary [as] ... invariably excellent.' He had been 'employed in the stone shed' and, moreover, had 'applied himself to his trade and is now a good workman.'[6] Johnston was released in 1878.

There are limited conclusions one can draw from a single case but it is clear that what distinguishes this case from the majority of others involving juveniles is race. As Carolyn Strange suggests for the period between 1920 and 1950, 'most cabinets were relatively intolerant toward juvenile offenders.'[7] The outcome of the Johnston case suggests that race played a key role, for the defence implicitly added a racial dimension to a pattern of rhetoric that was commonly crafted by petitioners in cases involving juvenile murderers. Clemency campaigns for youths 'were composites of cultural constructs' that frequently cited biological and psychological explanations for their crimes.[8] The added dimension of the unruly blackness of the two boys engaged in rough play may well have added an extra dimension to a common exculpatory script.

The case of James Smith was similarly suggestive of the leniency granted to Blacks convicted of murdering other Blacks. On the evening of 1 July 1874, a party of Black residents in the township of Harwich sat on the docks in Rondeau watching sailboats drift upon the waves into the wharf. One of the men, William Custard, assaulted James Smith's sister, Mary Smith. Placing his hands on her bosom, Custard broke the buttons off Mary Smith's dress and pushed her against a pile of logs. When he was told what had happened, Joseph Smith promised his sister that Custard would be prosecuted.[9] The evening soon turned violent as Custard, 'cursing and swearing,' struck Joseph Smith.[10] Smith returned home, where he witnessed his brother James retrieve a gun from his father's bedroom. When Joseph returned to the scene of the party, he noticed his brother standing with the gun across the road from Custard. Shortly after, Custard was shot dead.[11]

Two surgeons performed the post-mortem examination on Custard's body. Dr Daniel Samuelson testified that his 'head was almost shot away – all that above the ears – all the brain was out on the ground – it was done evidently by a shotgun.' The second examiner, James Sampson, surmised that 'the gun ... was not at the shoulder of the person who discharged it.'[12] This was an important point for the defence strategy and the post-trial discourse surrounding the case. While it was accepted that James Smith had fired the gun and killed Custard, the defence argued that the victim had a bad character and that Custard was the victim of an accidental shooting. It called character witnesses to attest to James Smith's 'good character' and his family's 'good nature' and respectability.[13] One witness declared that the Smiths' 'conduct has always been such that it is almost impossible for me to believe that one of them would intentionally shoot a man in the manner described.'[14] Others concurred and this undoubtedly influenced the jury's decision to add a recommendation of mercy to its guilty verdict. In his trial summary, Justice John W. Gwynne noted James Smith's excellent character and that he had discharged the gun merely to scare the party. In Gwynne's mind, these were compelling reasons to support a commutation of the sentence.[15] A petition submitted to the cabinet mirrored Justice Gwynne's reservations and asked for a commuted sentence.[16] These collective efforts worked. James Smith was spared the death penalty and his sentence was reduced to imprisonment at the Kingston Penitentiary for ten years.[17]

Yet another similar outcome occurred in the 1914 case of *R. v. Frank Smith*. Smith, a Black American from Cleveland, Ohio, was charged with the murder of James Conyers, who was also Black. Following a fight characterized as a 'drunken brawl,'[18] Smith was tried, found guilty, and sentenced to death. Again, however, the jury coupled its guilty verdict with a recommendation for mercy. Almost immediately after the trial, there was a groundswell of public opinion opposing Frank Smith's death sentence.

A key part of this opposition to Smith's death sentence – and a key theme of this book – is how both legal and non-legal actors weighed in on the importance of such sensational cases as a chance to showcase the superiority of the rule of law under British justice, a lynchpin of Canadian national identity. The press played a significant role in articulating this view. The Chatham *Daily Planet*, for example, found the sentence 'neither in accordance with the British fair-play nor yet with the Statement of the authors of the Declaration of American Independence that all men are born with certain inalienable rights, among which are life, liberty, and the pursuit of happiness ... [and] an equal chance for life.'[19] Similarly, the *Planet*'s headline declared: 'THERE IS A GROWING PUBLIC SENTIMENT THAT THE YOUNG MAN DID NOT INTEND TO COMMIT MURDER AND HE DOES NOT DESERVE TO GO TO THE GALLOWS FOR THE CRIME HE COMMITTED.' A month earlier, this newspaper had printed a story about race and sex in Los Angeles, in which a Black man was sentenced to thirty years in prison for 'stealing a kiss' from a White girl.[20] Readers who kept this story in mind while pondering Smith's plight could scarcely have missed the message of the superiority of British fair play.

Legal officials and medical experts drew upon racial stereotypes in their discussions of Smith's guilt. When Dr George T. McKeough described Frank Smith as a 'poor unfortunate,' and a 'child of nature,' this was an expression of his condescending view of a group of people he thought to be racially inferior: 'Seldom have I seen a more pitiable condition of affairs than the following out of the routine of the law in this case. He is a poor child of nature, no parents, without a day of schooling, without the world showing the least bit of interest in him to save him from the cruel and hard meshes of life.'[21] This 'pitiable condition of affairs,' a result of an unfortunate nature and a harsh environment, lay at the root of the crime. McKeough continued: 'I will admit that under high passion he would show little of his characteristics but we have to acknowledge that most of the fatalities of all races are committed under passion. Here is a boy obedient, willing, sympathetic, docile, except in enraged moments, possessing a number of the characteristics that have made his race faithful under oppressive circumstances, parentless, homeless, completely illiterate and wandering upon the world.'[22] McKeough thought that these 'enraged moments' were not typical of

Blacks, a group of people generally 'sympathetic' and 'docile.' Murder in this case was the result, in fact, of a Black's weak mental faculties, rather than criminal intent. As McKeough declared: 'The crime which he has been charged and convicted could not be a crime, for the boy's mental condition and general characteristics *could not involve premeditation*.'[23] Blacks, in effect, lacked the cognitive abilities necessary to commit an act of premeditated murder.

One Black Chatham resident also wanted the state to commute the sentence. A 'respectable' and likely middle-class spokesman, J.C. Richards declared that a petition 'was being drafted up and every effort would be made to present the defence that should have been presented had the young fellow been here long enough to be well known and had money.' While eschewing the White paternalistic rhetoric espoused by Dr McKeough, Richards nonetheless made a similar plea: 'We do not wish to offer any encouragement to the killing of men, but hanging will not be a remedial measure for life taking in such instances as this. He seems to be a harmless, unschooled sort of boy, and had it not been for the row and the drink arousing his temper, the deed never would have been done. The petition will be signed by all classes I am sure when the public understands better all the circumstances.'[24]

Two observers espoused the sensibilities of the temperance movement, pointing to the role that liquor played in this tragedy. One argued that the Canadian government was to blame, owing to its lack of prohibitions against the sale of liquor. The state, he argued, 'legalizes the liquor traffic' with the consent of the public and is 'therefore responsible for the selling of the liquor ... and responsible along with the other citizens of the province for getting the liquor.' Another observer, a 'prominent citizen of Chatham,' agreed and wrote that 'if it had not been for the liquor, the crime would not have been committed,' and that since the state legalized the sale of liquor it was also morally responsible for the crime. At any rate, he added, 'it does not seem to be a case where the extreme penalty should be imposed.'[25]

Writers also made comparisons between the Frank Smith case and the trial of Andrew David, a Chatham-area Native man tried in the mid-nineteenth century for murder.[26] The story of Andrew David was a remarkable instance where a sensational trial had become part of Chatham's local lore and its legacy bore a heavy imprint upon how observers made sense of Frank Smith's case. David was also drunk when he committed his crime. In the minds of those old enough to remember the David trial, drunkenness linked the stories of David and Smith, and hence Black and Aboriginal crime. One 'old timer' commented: 'The Indian said he did not know that he killed a man ... and I believe he told the truth. He said he was drunk at the time and he told the truth ... I don't know whether there was any recommendation for mercy like there is in the case of Frank Smith now awaiting his doom in the Chatham jail, but I don't think there was. The hanging was quite the talk of the town for a good long time after it occurred. I don't think there was many men in the city who witnessed the hanging who would like to see another.'[27]

This 'old timer,' along with Frank Smith's petitioners, who included a prominent local MPP and the foreman of a railway gang in Kentucky, need not have worried that the spectacle of an execution like Andrew David's would be revisited upon the Chatham gaol. A few weeks prior to his scheduled execution, a jailhouse examination conducted by Dr Bruce Smith determined that Smith's ordeal had created a 'weak mental condition' in his patient. A short time later, Smith's sentence was commuted.[28] A major factor in the decision was that 'Smith's crime was committed in the east end of the city, and was the result of a drunken brawl.' Smith was promptly taken to the Kingston Penitentiary to serve out his sentence.

Levi Steward and Frank Jackson: Familiarity and Novelty

The sorts of cultural and racial scripts that shaped cases of Black-on-Black murder did not necessarily produce lenient outcomes or the extension of mercy. Social factors such as class, the reputation of the accused and victims, and the support that defendants received from local communities were important in explaining why some Black-on-Black murders resulted in executions while others did not. So were legal factors. Judges, juries, and government officials who decided which sentences were commuted tended to treat murderers who committed their crimes in the heat of rough play or drunken brawls with more leniency than those who committed acts of cold-blooded murder or killed their victims as a result of failed robbery attempts.

In 1900 Levi Steward was hanged in the town of Sandwich (just outside Windsor) for the murder of 'a feeble old man,' also Black, named Jim Ross.[29] The murder was the tragic result of a botched robbery attempt. In July of that year a Sandwich hotel hosted a picnic, a 'huge gathering of colored people.' Levi Steward and a woman named Sarah Carter were there, as was the victim, Jim Ross, whom town locals affectionately dubbed 'Old Jim.' Steward had empty pockets and had tried to borrow funds from several people at the picnic. Later in the evening, he spotted Jim Ross in a bar, accosted him, and asked the older man to buy him a drink. Ross eventually agreed to do so after Levi Steward reminded Ross that he had hired him to do farm work in the past. Later that evening, Steward followed Ross home, hoping that 'there would be something in it.' Steward later returned to the picnic, suddenly flush with money which he spent freely. Ross had also had a purse and an expensive watch in his possession.

At some time after 2:00 a.m., Ross was found 'lying upon the road not far from his residence ... moaning, alive but unconscious.' One of his servants, William Taylor, took Ross and laid him upon a sofa.[30] Ross never regained consciousness and died the next day. His keys, watch, and a part of his watch chain were missing. While the evidence against Steward was mainly circumstantial, he foolishly incriminated himself by asking the officer who arrested him: 'If the old [son] of a [bitch] dies what will they do to me?' Moreover, Steward asked his paramour, within earshot of the same officer, 'Sarah, what made you tell those men about me knocking down old Ross?'[31] Steward's stupidity sealed his fate. At his trial the jury took less than two hours to return with a guilty verdict, with no recommendation for mercy.[32]

The public was incensed by this crime. Indeed, much of the conversation that this case generated was characterized by racist discourse more commonly reserved for Blacks who committed murder across the colour line. This can be largely explained by class. Many believed that the cruel and heartless murder of 'Old Jim,' a respected and established Black man of considerable wealth, by the hand of a lower-class Black man was outrageous. Dr James Sampson, who presented evidence at the trial, clearly expressed this sentiment. An angry Sampson deemed Steward 'a stupid ignorant mulatto of a very low mental type, as evidenced by all his conduct before and after and since his trial and during the trial itself. He has no education of any kind and is the son of a father who was once tried for murder. The man is surely a moral pervert and should never again be at liberty.'[33] Sampson's remarks demonstrate how class tensions and biases were expressed through the language of race in this case.

The portrayal of Levi Steward as a 'stupid ignorant mulatto of a very low mental type' was also used by his lawyer, who argued that Steward's statement to Sarah Carter did not constitute a confession. William Hanna argued that Steward was simply enquiring for information as to what position he was in. 'He is not an educated man. He is a poor ignorant darkey who did not know what in the world they were proposing to do to him ... he asked ... supposing the old man dies, I suppose they will hang me ... Now there is no admission in that. He was simply asking for some information – with regard to the crime with which he had been charged.'[34] But Hanna did not want to base his defence entirely on the portrayals of his client as an 'ignorant darky' or 'ignorant mulatto' who failed to grasp the gravity of his crime. He also attacked Sarah Carter's credibility. During the trial, he produced several witnesses who collectively described Carter as a woman with a 'bad' reputation.[35] Hanna later revisited this line of argument in his statement to the jury, stressing the absurdity of passing a death sentence on the evidence of a (lowly Black) woman of disreputable character. Hanna asked the jurors:

> Are we going to believe that the prisoner hit [Jim Ross] on the unsupported evidence of Sarah Carter? ... Gentlemen, you saw Carter in the box here. Did she give her evidence in a manner that would carry conviction to you? She has evidently got an unsavoury reputation. What was the woman doing at the hotel carousing around until 7 o'clock the next morning? ... Are you going to send a man to the gallows on the evidence of Sarah Carter as she shewed herself here yesterday? If we were trying a little Division Court case and you were a jury, would you believe her from the manner in which she gave her evidence? Are you, gentlemen, going to believe her in a case of so much importance as this, where life and death is at stake?[36]

After the trial, facing a death sentence, Steward made a dramatic confession in the press, perhaps because he knew the possibility of commutation was slim (there is no evidence of even an attempt on his part to launch an appeal), and recanted his prior attempt to incriminate Sarah Carter and another man.[37] On 6 February 1900, in the presence of the Essex County sheriff, a justice of the peace, and the gaoler and turnkey of the Essex County gaol, Levi Steward was executed.[38]

The Franklin Jackson murder case in the county of Peterborough in 1933 was a lengthier affair than the Steward case but resulted in a similar outcome. In June 1932 Franklin Jackson and Eugene Lee, both Black retired United States Army soldiers, left Wisconsin and crossed the border at Sault Ste Marie, heading towards Peterborough County, Ontario. Attracted by the promise of lower taxes, they had thought of buying some land and setting up a home.[39] Within a few days of settling in the town of Dummer, the pair purchased land and began building a house. Throughout the summer during the construction, the two men spent their nights in a car. However, as late fall approached, the bonds of friendship between the two men had started to fray. Lee took to the house of the White Saultern family who lived nearby; 'as the October nights were getting cold and as Lee was a southern Negro, he did not like the cold and so sought the shelter of the warm house at nights.' Things came to a head during an afternoon in October when Franklin Jackson, annoyed that the older man, Lee, was doing little to assist him, asked, 'When are you going to get the cement and lime?' Lee responded, 'I do not know whether I am or not.' Raising his automatic pistol, Jackson fired six shots and Lee fell to the ground dead. Jackson was charged with murder, tried, and sentenced to death.

Jackson was tried twice. The crown's star witness in the first trial was Ruby Saultern, the youngest member of the Saultern family. Ruby told the court that she had witnessed the shooting and that it was unprovoked.[40] There was also evidence that, after the crime, Jackson was defiant. Ruby's mother, Sara Jane Saultern, testified that after shooting Lee, Jackson 'said he was ready to hang. He said he had shot him and he was ready to hang if it was the laws of this country to hang a man.'[41]

There was virtually no defence mounted by George Gordon in the first trial. He did not call any witnesses or enter any evidence. Nonetheless, Justice George H. Sedgewick's trial summary argued that Gordon did 'all that was possible for the prisoner,' adding that even 'if the prisoner had gone into the box, and had told the story that he put in his statement, and had been able to make that story stand up, it is quite possible that the verdict might have been reduced to manslaughter, though I do not think that there would be any real ground for such a verdict.' The 'story,' as Sedgewick rather derisively referred to it in his trial summary, was Jackson's version of the events on the day of the shooting as transcribed by one of the constables called to the murder scene. Jackson maintained that the shooting was not a calculated and cold-blooded act but done rather out of self-defence when the older man 'reached for his "Gat."'[42]

Gordon's only semblance of a defence in the first trial was his objection to the judge's charge. Gordon argued that, since Ruby Saultern was 'a child of such tender years, lacking experience and training,' her evidence 'should be scrutinized more than that of a person of experience and intelligence.' It was his position that the crime was manslaughter rather than murder. He maintained that there was 'the question of the heat of passion aroused in a man who was in apprehension of death which might occasion him and would be likely to occasion him to continue the act of shooting till the fear of that apprehension had passed.'[43] Unconvinced, Sedgewick summarily dismissed these arguments in his charge to the jury. After retiring for deliberations for about two and a half hours, the jury returned with a guilty verdict. The death sentence was passed and an execution date of 5 May 1933 was set.

The lack of a spirited (or competent) defence and the guilty verdict mattered little to at least one editorialist. The day after the trial, an article in the Peterborough *Examiner* carried the following headline: 'CANADIAN LAW AT ITS BEST.' Portraying Jackson as a 'negro from the United States, a foreigner with little or none of the world's goods, astray from another land without a friend in this part of the world,' the article went on to celebrate the fact that 'the legal rights and privileges of this wanderer were protected as would have been one of the foremost of our own citizens.' Evocative of the rhetoric of nineteenth-century Canadian abolitionism, Jackson's American blackness served as an opportunity to demonstrate the superior nature of British justice, impartiality, and, tacitly, White Canadian nationhood: 'It was pointed out to the jury that, although a foreigner and a man of colored blood, the prisoner was entitled to all the protection that would be given a Canadian citizen. The whole course of the trial, the dignified atmosphere of the hearing, the insistence upon fair play for the accused, the business-like celerity with which a jury was selected and the hearing of evidence commenced, [served] to illustrate once more that in our system of justice this country need apologise to none other anywhere.'[44]

Despite the 'business-like celerity' with which the *Examiner* claimed this trial had been conducted, Jackson was granted a new trial based on several arguments Gordon advanced in the Court of Appeals that were more convincing than the defence he presented at the Peterborough spring assizes. The Court of Appeal granted a second trial on the grounds that the judge erred in his instruction to the jury about a key piece of evidence, Jackson's sworn police statement. In it Jackson stated that Lee, the victim, had pushed him over the wheel of the car and forced him to reach for his gun. Sedgewick informed the jury that this was not evidence of what had happened; rather, he instructed, it was evidence of what the prisoner said had happened and not direct evidence. 'It is only evidence,' said Sedgewick, 'that the prisoner said that in his statement he made that statement.' The appellate court found that Sedgewick erred in his instruction to the jury. It was the judge's duty, the court ruled, to inform the jury that it had to consider the parts of Jackson's statement that explained why he shot Lee. Sedgewick's failure to do so constituted 'material nondirection tantamount to misdirection.'[45]

A new trial was granted for 19 September 1933 in front of Justice Eric Armour. Virtually the same evidence was submitted, though this time three character witnesses testified for Jackson.[46] But the result was the same: Jackson was once again found guilty and sentenced to die on 29 November 1933. Again, Gordon appealed the decision, but unfortunately for Jackson, this time the appellate court unanimously ruled that it could not disturb a fair verdict which was fully supported by the evidence. The appeal was dismissed.[47]

The day after Jackson's second appeal was dismissed, Gordon wrote a letter to the minister of justice in a last-ditch effort to spare his client from the gallows. Gordon urged the minister to consider that Jackson 'was living with eight or ten white persons in a poor, miserable, house in North Dummer Township. A little girl, Ruby Saultern, a poor anaemic child of twelve years of age ... claims to have seen the shooting.' The press portrayed Jackson as the epitome of Black abjection and the beneficiary of the 'celerity' and solemnity of British justice. Gordon's counter-narrative, however, portrayed Jackson as the victim of the unreliable testimony generated by dissolute and impoverished Whites. He argued: 'I cannot get away from the thought that this girl is not telling the truth and dozens in the Court room had the same impression. There is not a negro in this city or county and I do feel that Jackson, being a stranger without friends, to some degree influenced the minds of the jury and for that reason, I am drawing this matter to your attention, with the request that if you think, under all the circumstances, you have studied the evidence, it is a proper case to remit the penalty to that of life imprisonment, I would appreciate your consideration.'[48]

Clearly Gordon, a White defence lawyer, was cognizant of the importance of race in this case. He was well aware that two Black men in North Dummer were an extraordinary sight for the Whites of the township, where only a small number of Blacks lived. Indeed, Gordon's plea for clemency was based largely on the argument that Jackson was the victim of marginal Whites who were unfamiliar with and probably hostile towards Blacks. He did not sway the cabinet. On 30 November 1933 Jackson was executed in the Peterborough County gaol.[49]

The Franklin Jackson case bears some similarities to the sensational 1903 'negro murder' trial of two circus performers in Picton, Ontario, when Edward Johnson was tried for the murder of Edward Clarke. Both men were Black, and foreigners (Americans), in a town where there was no resident Black population. The major difference between the two cases, however, is that Picton jurists rendered an acquittal. Carolyn Strange and Tina Loo argue that in this particular instance, Pictonians, haunted by an 1884 death-penalty case in their town in which an innocent man may have been hanged, were reluctant to risk a potential miscarriage of justice once again. In addition, many Pictonians believed that, while unfortunate, the murder of one Black circus performer at the hands of another had little to do with *their* town.[50] Moreover, the acquittal provided Pictonians with an opportunity to engage in 'public performances that affirmed equality and proved that justice was blind.'[51]

Clearly, then, cases of intraracial murder reflected a complex alchemy of racial attitudes and the internal logic of the law, illustrated, for example, by the relative merits of the evidence presented against the accused and the effectiveness of clemency campaigns. Similar factors were important in determining the more fraught cases of murder across the colour line.

Killing across the Colour Line

In 1868 a White man named Captain Oliver Minor was murdered. Two Black men, Charles Medley and Curtley Bush, were jointly indicted – the former for the murder, the latter for aiding and abetting – and tried separately at the Sandwich fall assizes in front of Justice Henry Beecher. A third man, George Brown, was indicted, but he had absconded. Medley and Bush were sentenced to death but their sentences were commuted. In light of a crime that epitomized a grave threat to the social order – Blacks murdering Whites – why did these two men not hang? Again, the reasons lay in the interaction of social and legal factors.

Eliza Rose, a key witness for the prosecution, testified that on the fateful night she was present while her husband, Joseph Rose, and Captain Minor engaged in a prolonged evening of drinking. At one point during the night, her husband told Eliza to fetch more liquor. Minor quickly joined her, and, after she had fended off his sexual advances, they returned to her husband without the spirits. While Joseph Rose and Captain Minor were engaging in a conversation (in French) near a woodpile, Eliza saw 'a man [who] put his head out back of the wood pile next to the mill' and warned her husband, 'You better come home.' The captain turned towards the woodpile and asked, 'What are you ...

looking at[,] is it me?' This figure in the woodpile, testified Eliza, 'did not reply but struck the captain about the head.' Eliza shouted 'Murder!' and she and her husband began to run towards the street. According to Eliza, as they headed for the street, two men followed 'us ... one of them said he was an officer and he was going to arrest me ... The man who insisted on taking me as an officer struck me across the face striking fire from my eyes and the other man kicked me as I stooped to pick up my husband, in the back of the head and broke my comb. I then called rape ... The men were colored men.'[52]

Eliza's identification of her attackers constituted an evidentiary basis to arrest them. But the importance of broader social and cultural factors is evident in the way she couched her identification of these men. Eliza's cry of 'rape' unleashed a tried and true talisman. Black male violence against White women was not only synonymous with sexual danger in the White imagination. In court it was meant to appeal to commonly held notions of how easily the physical threat posed by Black men could turn into a sexual threat.[53]

Joseph Rose supported his wife's testimony, as did other prosecution witnesses.[54] But this testimony was vigorously challenged in the trials of both men (the prosecution presented the same evidence against each). The accused men were the beneficiaries of solid legal defences, but their defences were based on legal tactics that were heavily influenced by dominant social attitudes towards Blacks. For example, one defence strategy was to argue that the darkness of the night would have made it difficult for Eliza Rose to identify her attacker. Under cross-examination, Eliza Ross first testified that she could not discern the identity of the figure in the woodpile, that she 'could not tell whether the man was white or Black.' Later she seemed to reverse her position, stating that she could indeed identify her attacker. When asked whether the darkness might not have affected her ability to identify him accurately, she responded: 'You could see the features of a person close to you – I could distinguish the features of a colored man 10 feet away from me if he was not very black.' This seemingly innocuous response reflects a racialized view of Blacks that equated blackness with darkness. In effect, the darkness served to obscure Black faces and features. Conversely, darkness could also engender a corporeal blackening (of White bodies), thereby making racial distinctions impossible. Both strategies were marked by racial reasoning.

Unfortunately for Eliza Rose, because of gendered stereotypes, the talisman of physical/sexual danger did not work its magic as easily and as readily as she had hoped. When she was asked if she had ever before 'been before the law,' she told the court that she 'had some trouble before' when she had 'brought some boys named Brown and another Taylor [and] another Curry [and] another McMillian before him [Judge Beecher].' These men, continued Eliza, 'came in and brought whiskey and said they wanted my husband to go out and they would do as they liked with me ... I charged them with riot in my house and attempt to violate my person.' The charges against the young men, however, had been dismissed and Eliza received no money from any one for refraining from prosecuting them 'or anything of value other than money.'[55] This line of questioning sought to cast doubt upon Eliza Ross's sexual morality.

The defence also tried to use the disappeared third man in the indictment to create reasonable doubt. George Brown was likely the same Brown who was earlier charged for a 'riot' and attempting to 'violate' Eliza Rose. In fact, one defence witness testified that not only did he know George Brown but he also saw Brown on the evening of 'the 13 Oct last,' after the row. Brown told this witness that he had killed Minor in self-defence after he 'caught the captain with a woman and he went to the woman and the captain and the captain struck him with a stick on the side of the head.'[56] Though in each case the judge urged the juries to exercise caution in their deliberations, both found Charles Medley and Curtley Bush guilty of murder.

Almost immediately after the verdict, Justice Beecher expressed his misgivings to the minister of justice about the trials and the death penalties. In a particularly revealing passage, he wrote: 'With regard to the convict Curtley while it was quite open to the jury to find as they did I would have been better satisfied with an acquittal.' Beecher continued, giving his general assessment and evaluation of the testimony submitted to the court: 'The conclusion I have come to from hearing the evidence and seeing the witnesses, is that there was a love affair between deceased and … Eliza Rose – And … the three colored men … suspecting this [Minor was] determined to disturb it – but with what degree of violence, or whether with any violence it is impossible to say.'[57]

It is not clear why Beecher felt the 'three coloured men' had any reason to interfere with the affair he suspected. More important, Beecher believed that there was 'nothing in the case which suggested robbery or an attempt to rob as a motive for the crime.' Bush's plight in particular created 'strong doubt' in the judge's mind and he wondered 'whether he did aid and abet the murder and whether he contemplated any violence when he went there.' For these reasons, concluded Justice Beecher, 'I do not think this is a case for which life can be safely taken by the law.'[58]

Reverend Isaac Rice wrote an impassioned letter to the governor general on behalf of Charles Medley echoing Justice Beecher's concerns. He raised three arguments for commuting Medley's sentence: the murder was not deliberate; it was Brown rather than Charles Medley who was responsible for the murder; and confusing the two men was quite easy since 'the evening was too *dark* to *unmistakenly* identify parties. Brown and Medley are just about of a [similar] height and complexion, admitting of *easy mistake* in an evening of considerable darkness.' Highlighting the racial and sexual features of the incident, Rice also noted that 'general opinion' believed 'the occasion of the collision was a licentious woman,' adding that 'the captain and the B[oy] were after her and there was no other confederacy than at any Brothel.' Then, turning to the issue of the racial attitudes in the town, he wrote: 'There is a great feeling against the Colored here and a jewry [*sic*] would on this account easier condemn. This is evident from condemning Young Bush Curtley who is but a mere Boy and doubtly as innocent of any conspiracy in the case as I am and yet he is unhesitatingly turned over to the gallows, who should by all means be at *once pardoned*.'[59]

Medley (it is not clear from the legal records what happened to Bush) had his sentence commuted to life in prison on the grounds that 'some doubt may exist as to the identity of the party who struck the blow which proved to be fatal to Minor.'[60] Medley was to serve out his days in the Kingston Penitentiary. The commutation process tended to paper over legally suspect convictions and this was especially true in the case of people of colour.[61]

Border Crossings: Race and Nation, Colour and Class

The story of Curtley Bush and Charles Medley illustrates that mercy could indeed be served up when murder was committed across the fault line of race, particularly when convictions rested on a shaky legal footing. There was a symbiotic relationship between *socially suspect* and *legally suspect* convictions. In other words, the legal soundness of convictions was often largely a function of larger social concerns about race which operated in two contradictory ways, making race both absent and present. Cases could be considered suspect if the court had failed to live up to the dominant rhetoric of fairness and racial impartiality. Secondly and contradictorily, a conviction could be deemed suspect if there was a question about whether a *real* racial transgression had even taken place and whether a crime was an affront to entrenched racial hierarchies. These factors were at play in Windsor in 1904 when James Slaughter murdered a White man in Tecumseh House, a local tavern owned by an African Canadian man named Wade Hill. Another similar case, in 1934, was the trial of Frederick Turner in Chatham for the murder of a nebulously White man, who was also an 'Other,' a foreigner. The contested spaces of race, nation, and class, and, of course, the internal logic of the criminal law worked in concert to determine the outcomes of each case.

Slaughter, a resident of Michigan, murdered John Redden, a local farmer, after a brief argument which quickly escalated. The victim, described as 'quite intoxicated,' had 'generally made himself quite offensive applying the epithet "nigger" to Slaughter.' A short time later, Slaughter went to the bar to purchase a drink for himself and a soft drink for a young girl, the daughter of the proprietor of Tecumseh House. Redden again approached Slaughter and told him, 'I am not going to buy any drinks for you.' Slaughter responded (rather insolently, it must have seemed to Redden) that he had not asked him to. Following a brief session of slapping or 'sparring,' Slaughter struck Redden over the head with a pool cue, inflicting a severe wound. The owner of the Tecumseh laid Redden on the floor (rather inhumanely, the judge later remarked), where he stayed without medical attention from 6:00 p.m. on the evening of the incident to 4:00 p.m. the next day. Redden was eventually treated for symptoms similar to typhoid fever but it was too late. He died the following day.[62]

The evidence presented at trial produced a contested verdict. The jury unanimously found Slaughter guilty of murder but its verdict was challenged on a number of fronts. Justice James V. Teetzel, the presiding trial judge, was bound by statute to mete out a penalty of death upon the jury verdict, yet he almost immediately expressed doubt. Indeed, during his charge, Teetzel had tacitly acknowledged that manslaughter may have been the more appropriate verdict, a decision he reached after considering the arguments of defence counsel, prominent African Canadian attorney Delos Rogest Davis, one of the first Black lawyers called to the bar in Ontario.[63] Teetzel conceded that he was 'bound by law' to 'pronounce an execution date,' but he decided to wait while Davis submitted Slaughter's case for executive clemency. Teetzel later recommended mercy based on his own assessment of the evidence.

Teetzel's discomfort with the sentence the law bound him to hand down was one of the key factors that shaped this case. External extra-legal factors also influenced its outcome, namely, the ability of the defence counsel to use the defendant's foreignness to his advantage. With his case attracting attention in Michigan, White elites in Ontario were likely more reluctant to mete out the penalty of death to an American Black than they would have been if the accused were a Canadian-born Black man.[64] One rather striking example of the kind of advocacy Slaughter received from across the border came in the form of a letter from J.W. Reynolds, a manager at the Calvert Lithographing Company in Michigan. Reynolds, a Liberal Party supporter, subtly hinted at his political connections and urged the minister to commute Slaughter's sentence. Another writer, a Detroit doctor, sent a letter to a local MP suggesting that nothing short of the 'honour of the fair name of Canada' and the 'honour of the Dominion' were at stake in efforts to save Slaughter.[65]

Pressure from south of the border did not fully explain the decision to extend mercy in this case. Blackness and Canadian nationhood also worked their peculiar alchemy in a number of ways. A crucial factor was the efforts of the defence counsel, Davis, who skilfully handled the trial and successfully mobilized public sympathy among the citizens of Windsor. In his charge to the jury, Teetzel actually made a point of commenting on the Black attorney's considerable achievements, remarking that it was 'pleasing to know that a gentleman with some of the natural handicaps in some countries, that Mr. Davis possesses ... has brought himself so prominently to the front in his profession in this country, and that he is regarded with such respect in this community.' Davis's achievements, then, were proof of a racially enlightened polity that did not exist in 'some countries' (that is, the United States). The Black defence attorney symbolized Canadian racial justice but so too did the body of the Black felon. Teetzel's charge also emphasized the significant degree to which this case occupied the terrain where race met the nation:

> I desire, just briefly and only in a word, to allude to the reference made by Counsel, both counsel to the fact that the prisoner is a colored man, and a resident of a foreign country. Mr. Davis apologetically referred to this circumstance, more he said to satisfy the misgivings of his client and his friends, who did not fully appreciate that they were being tried in Canada under British Justice and coming from a country where we all regret to know, that prejudice too

often prevails to the injury and carnage of justice ... though this man belongs to a foreign country and is a colored man, he will receive the same justice as if he were a white citizen of this country, and on the other hand, neither will he receive less, because he is unfortunate in his colour.[66]

During the trial, Davis mentioned race in only very cautious and strategic – almost apologetic – ways which were meant both to flatter the court and to subtly challenge it to live up to its rhetoric of racial justice. Once the verdict was in, however, Davis's efforts to secure a commutation of Slaughter's sentence betrayed a markedly different tactic, perhaps because the gentlemanly and restrained approach of the trial had not produced the desired verdict. In the next phase of the case, Davis's appeals to the secretary of state and the minister of justice certainly did not shy away from racial arguments.

The appeal was made upon both medical and statutory grounds. Davis argued that Redden's death was unconnected to the blow he received and that the crime did not fit the legal definition of homicide. Moreover, the decision did not consider the role of provocation: 'that PROVOCATION can be given by blows, words, or gestures ... [which] reasonably deprived the Prisoner at the moment of the power of self control.'[67] Furthermore, Davis's application suggested that there was a considerable amount of bias against his client in the way the trial was conducted. Davis pointed out that one of the witnesses, David Kennedy, was 'an intimate friend and neighbour of the Deceased John Redden [and] attended him during his sickness,' and that he had told the jury he had 'knowledge not given in evidence.' Both things should have served to disqualify him as a witness. Davis also pointed to some of the comments made by Justice Teetzel during sentencing; the judge had spoken in severe language to the jury, saying that 'no such man should keep the hotel, and the likes of him should get out of this Country.' These sentiments, argued Davis, had 'influence on the jury [and] affected the prisoner in his trial to his hurt,'[68] as did the fact that Redden was 'a white man' and the prisoner 'a colored man.'[69] Remarkably, the county crown attorney, A.H. Clarke, similarly argued: 'It was generally expected in the community that the verdict would be manslaughter and I think that under the circumstances justice would be done by commuting the punishment to life imprisonment. It is not long since a white man in this County was tried on the charge of murdering a colored man there being a great deal of ill-will between them. In that case the verdict of the Jury was manslaughter and not murder, and in view of the unequal position of the colored man in society I think it would be in the interests of justice that the Government should intervene.'[70]

Davis reinforced the message that a commutation of the sentence was 'generally expected in the community.' Again, the issue of the appropriateness of a manslaughter verdict in this case was key. A day after submitting his application to the court, Davis sent the minister a petition containing some 834 signatures along with a letter from R.F. Sutherland, an MP for Essex, urging the minister to commute the sentence. As a result of these efforts, Slaughter's sentence was commuted.

In 1914 it was reported that Slaughter had been in the 'Insane Ward' for most of his time in prison. One prison official in 1909 claimed that Slaughter's incarceration in the prison asylum was not due to mental illness, but by 1914 he was deemed medically insane.[71] As was often the case with foreigners who committed crimes in Canada, the news of Slaughter's insanity prompted plans for his remission and deportation.[72] Arrangements were made for Slaughter to be sent 'to his own country on the express understanding that he will be received by his mother in Detroit Mich., she having agreed to arrange for his commitment to an institution for the Insane in the United States.'[73]

Murders across the colour line were not only revealing of the lives of Black transgressors but also show how White racial identities were created through the judicial system and the state more generally. In 1934 Frederick Turner, a trucker for a Chatham tobacco factory, was tried for the murder of John Brescina. Brescina, a man of foreign extraction, a Bohemian, was considered only tenuously White.[74] Turner, described in the case file as a 'Canadian, coloured, 20 years of age,' murdered Brescina in June 1934. In this particular case the 'dangerous foreigners' were White and the Blacks were Canadians. The murder took place during a street fight following a quarrel in Chatham's CPR hotel between a group of Bohemians and a party of three Black men. Curiously, Frederick Turner was not involved in this melee; he learned about it only after he joined his friends shortly after the row. The 'colored men,' having added one more to their party, once again headed in the direction of their foes. A verbal exchange led to blows and, eventually, the death of one of the Bohemians.

According to the evidence presented at the trial, Turner approached Brescina, asking him if he knew what the words 'son of a bitch meant.' Brescina responded: 'Yes, you are a Black son of a bitch.' In response, Turner hit Brescina with his fist and knocked him down. When Brescina got up, he was again struck by Turner, and again he fell down. Brescina then rose up (rather unsteadily) and, allegedly, pulled a knife out in order to 'either defend himself, or stab Turner.' Turner 'struck him with his fist, and this time knocked him flat, and his head probably struck on one of the tracks of the C.P.R. or the pavement,' causing 'a laceration of the victim's brain tissue.'[75]

This encounter did more than expose the 'rough' masculinity and language of plebeian street life. It also created a link between a physical contest between these groups of marginalized men and a discursive contest which sought to configure and reconfigure the borders of race and nation. Frank Turner's query, 'Do you know what a son of a bitch is?' had two meanings. While outwardly a simple insult, Turner tacitly deployed it as a rhetorical strategy to 'Other' Brescina, to use his facility with the English language (for in this instance, even the English of a working-class Black man was decidedly more 'standard' than that of this foreigner) as a point of demarcation, differentiation, and debasement. Brescina's response, 'Yes, and you are a Black one,' also carried multiple meanings. Like Turner's epithets, the remark was clearly meant to hurt and provoke its intended target. It was also clearly a strategy that sought to 'Other' Turner and to claim the mantle of whiteness through degradation of blackness.[76] This street contest set the stage for the larger contest which was to follow in the courtroom and in the post-trial commentary.

Crown counsel H.D. Smith called thirteen witnesses at the trial, held on 20 September 1934 in front of Justice Courtney A. Kingstone. One of these witnesses was a City of Chatham civil engineer, called to map out the spatial dimensions of the crime. Smith also called the physician who conducted the post-mortem examination upon Brescina's body, the physician who attended to Brescina prior to his death, Brescina's employer and landlord, Brescina's three companions on the night of the murder, four eyewitnesses, three of whom were CPR employees, and two police officers. The defence counsel, W.B. Beardall, called only three witnesses, Garfield Freeman and Earl Brown, both of whom were Frederick Turner's companions on the evening in question, and Turner himself.

It is clear that these defence witnesses, who were implicated in the affair, found it difficult to counter the interpretation of the murder put forth by the prosecution. For example, Beardall first called to the stand Garfield Freeman, in order to establish that Turner's blows were done out of self-defence since his opponent was armed with a knife. Thus,

Freeman suggested, it was Brescina, not Turner, who was the aggressor. Under cross-examination, however, the prosecution managed to get Freeman to concede that his testimony was, at best, inaccurate and, at worst, a lie:

Q: When [Brescina] fell down the first time Turner got over him, didn't he?
A: Yes sir.
Q: And he was hitting him?
A: Yes sir.
Q: While he was down?
A: Yes.
Q: And what did [Earl] Brown do?
A: Brown took hold of him to stop him.
Q: Brown hauled him off, didn't he?
A: Yes.
Q: What did Brown say to him?
A: That the man had enough.
Q: Brown said to him that he had enough; and if I understand you, at the time Turner said nothing. You saw no knife?
A: No sir.
Q: Either in Brown's hand or Turner's hand?
A: Neither one.
Q: And you never saw Brescina hit Turner?
A: No sir
Q: So it was a rather one-sided fight, wasn't it?
A: Yes sir.[77]

Beardall soon became exasperated with his own witnesses.[78] His frustration mounted as it became clear that Turner, like Freeman, would have great difficulty convincing the court that he acted out of self-defence. Turner said that the Bohemian struck the first blow to his jaw, but this lacked credibility since Turner was the only one to make such a claim. Moreover, in cross-examination, the prosecution hammered away on two central and damning points. Why, the crown asked, did Turner need to be concerned with this fight at all? Furthermore, the victim did not strike back, and even when one of Turner's companions, Brown, called out, 'He has got enough,' Turner refused to stop, striking Brescina with a fatal blow.[79]

The prosecution's case was strong. But this case was not merely determined by the overwhelming weight of the evidence against the accused. Competing rhetorical strategies of Black dissolution and the abjection of (foreign) whiteness complicated this murder across the colour line. The fragility of the 'whiteness' of the Bohemians in this case is evident in the distinct ways in which whiteness was expressed in much of the trial testimony. The signifier 'Canadian' was exposed as a native-born English-speaking person of British origin. When crown attorney H.D. Smith called on John Kucera to testify, he tacitly equated whiteness with a capacity to speak English. Kucera, Smith, and Judge Kingstone had a revealing conversation:

Mr Smith: Q: Do you think you can talk English to me?
A: I can talk but not everything.
Q: Will you try? I will go slowly. It will be better for the jury.
A: Better that man come here and help me some.
Q: You want an interpreter?
A: Yes
Mr Smith: This man, I am told – I have never examined him myself – can talk English some, and I know your Lordship prefers it.
His Lordship: We will get on as far as we can.[80]

Justice Kingstone decided that the proceedings might 'get on faster' with an interpreter when John Bacik and John Secka took the stand.[81] Subsequent testimony shows the range of signifiers that were invoked to make whiteness. Consider, for example, Beardall's cross-examination of T.E. McIntosh, an employee of the Canadian Pacific Railroad hotel, who had testified about the events that preceded the fight. McIntosh's testimony reveals how the category of Canadian was placed in opposition to the category of foreigner and only Canadians were completely synonymous with whiteness:

Q: You said there were about fifteen people in there?
A: I imagine there would be fifteen people when they came in.
Q: Out of the fifteen there were only three who were colored?
A: Yes
Q: So there would be about twelve who were white?
A: Yes.
Q: And of those twelve who were white people, were most of them foreigners?
A: There was four foreigners.
Q: And the rest of them were most of them foreigners too?
A: No, they were Canadian people.

Q: All the rest?
A: Well, I couldn't swear to all of them.
Q: It is a fact that you get a good deal of patronage from these, shall we say, new Canadians that come into your hotel?
A: We get quite a few of them.
Q: Quite often there is quite a gang of them around here?
A: Sometimes we get a few, and times we don't.

The Bohemians were also constituted as the 'Other' through the court's discussions of local geography. There was a fair amount of commentary on the east end of the city as a 'hot spot,' a site of intraclass interracial conflict, which, of course, implicated the Bohemians involved in this melee as much as it did Turner and the other Black men. In Judge Kingstone's introductory remarks to the jury, he noted that 'the altercation ... shows, if nothing else, that between the colored element of the east end and the foreigners there was not a very good feeling.'[82] Indeed, Kingstone was to later reveal that this tension, in conjunction with the jury's ignorance of certain key points of law regarding the issue of sentencing, had much to do with his strong reservations about the verdict.[83]

The idea of east-end Chatham as a 'dangerous area' had even more salience than dominant notions of the dangers posed by the bodies of Black men. For example, during the trial one of the prosecution's strategies was to suggest that at least two of the three men involved in the melee were professional boxers:

Q: You are rather handy with your fists, aren't you?
A: I wouldn't call myself handy with them.
Q: When you have to take care of yourself, you can?
A: I think so.
HIS LORDSHIP: Q: Are you a prize fighter?
A: No sir.
Q: You do not fight for money?
A: No sir.
Q: And Turner has the reputation of being one of the best among your coloured boxers, hasn't he?
A: I have not heard anything about it.
Q: Didn't you know it?
A: No.

Q: Did you ever see him box?
A: No.

Defence counsel addressed this issue head-on during Frederick Turner's direct examination.[84] Beardall was concerned about the effect that the notion that the men were boxers might have on the jury's impression of Turner's capacity for violence. The prosecution clearly wanted to make a case that the skills of professional boxers included a certain macabre expertise in how to kill; hence, these particular Black male bodies were weapons. Justice Kingstone, by contrast, obviously held professional pugilists in high esteem. He described Brown in particular as 'a rather good-looking coloured man ... looked like a fighter to me – [a] clean cut, good looking fellow.'[85]

Kingstone's charge noted: 'It is quite clear on the evidence that [Turner] struck [Brescina] three times; that it was not necessary on the third occasion, I think you may come to the conclusion, to strike him at all, whatever the attack the dead man made on him, that he was quite incapable of doing Turner any harm at all.' Turning to the issue of provocation, however, Kingstone had a different view. He felt that the jury could reasonably excuse Turner's actions if they felt that 'he was in such a state of passion at the moment,' a passion leading to his 'loss of self control.' In this case, Kingstone instructed, manslaughter would be the proper verdict.[86] Three hours after Kingstone's charge, the jury found Turner guilty of the more serious crime of murder with a recommendation for mercy.

In his report Kingstone wrote: 'Turner [n]ever intended at any time to seriously injure Brescina, and that in all the blows that were struck there is no evidence that he did anything other than use his fists.' He also cited the importance of the dissolute environment of east-end Chatham as a mitigating factor, noting that he was told by the crown attorney at Chatham of the 'bad blood' between the coloured population and the foreigners in the east end of the city. 'I do not think the fight was really premeditated,' concluded Kingstone. 'I am of the opinion that the ends of justice would be well served by commuting the sentence on the accused to that of life imprisonment.'[87]

After the trial, Turner's defence was spearheaded by African Canadian lawyer B.J. Spencer Pitt and E.D. Cross. The evidence is silent about why or how it was that these two lawyers came to Turner's aid. In any event, they took the case to the Ontario Court of Appeal while simultaneously applying for clemency. The minister of justice, in turn, requested that he be given time to see how the Court of Appeal would handle the case.[88] The case was heard on 16 November 1934. Noting the inappropriateness of asking it to deal with an issue of executive clemency, the Court of Appeal dismissed the appeal on two points of law. First, the court argued, 'we cannot say the verdict was unreasonable. There was ample evidence to go to the jury.' Second, the court held that 'the judgment of the Trial Court may be set aside where there has been a wrong decision of any question of law – there has been no wrong decision of any question of law – or where there has been a miscarriage of justice. We are unable to say there is any miscarriage of justice.' However, the court, differentiating between its role and the broader discretionary power exercised by the minister of justice, also noted: 'We are all of the opinion that this is a case where the exercise of clemency would appear perfectly proper and just ... we have not in any way expressed a view that executive clemency would not be appropriate under the circumstances.'[89] Four days later, the cabinet ordered that the sentence be commuted to life in prison.[90]

After the commutation of Turner's sentence in 1934, subsequent efforts were made for 'additional clemency.' In 1935, 1938, and 1940 Turner's requests were denied, each time on the basis that such an appeal was 'too soon.' In 1940 Turner tried to bolster his case by requesting an exercise of clemency in order to allow him to join the army, in effect offering his body in service to the Canadian state. This request, however, was also denied; Turner would simply have to wait for the passage of more time.

That time came in 1945. On the basis of a penitentiary warden's report, which declared that Turner's 'conduct and industry have been very good,' coupled with observations from Kingstone's trial report – namely, the judge's unease with the verdict – Turner's case was now deemed to be 'favourable for clemency.' It was also reported that the Reverend W. Constantine Perry, pastor of the African Methodist Episcopal Church in Toronto, had been working behind the scenes, pressing for Turner's release and offering to 'give every assistance in re-establishing the prisoner and assisting in his rehabilitation should clemency be granted.' These circumstances prompted the director of remission services at the Kingston Penitentiary to advise that Turner be released to the supervision of the Reverend Perry.[91] In short, a penal sentence of roughly ten years, not death by hanging nor life imprisonment, was the price that Turner paid for killing a Bohemian – the embodiment of abject whiteness from the wrong part of town. Over time there was

WINDSOR MAN IS FOUND GUILTY OF CHATHAM MURDER

Death Sentence When Assizes End

LOCAL YOUTH CALM WHEN HE HEARS VERDICT. 3 PALS WHO TESTIFIED AGAINST HIM ADMIT ROBBERY ARMED

CHATHAM, Feb. 28.—Charles "Chuck" Cross today stands in the shadow of the gallows. The 20-year-old Windsor colored youth heard the foreman of the assize court jury at 8.07 o'clock Thursday night pronounce him guilty of the murder of John Labadie, early on the morning of September 22 last.

Before the verdict was given by the jury, Edward "Ted" Powell, 20-year-old colored youth of Windsor, who had been indicted with Cross for the killing of Labadie, and who yesterday took the stand to give evidence against Cross, was arraigned and pleaded guilty to robbery while armed. This morning, John Sanders, 20 and John Evans, 18, also colored and having their homes in Windsor, pleaded guilty to the same charge. Both had given evidence at the trial of Cross.

Victim of Robbery

Gun Owned by Evans

Prompt Data Is Demanded

C. of C. Party Away Today

Prize For Essay Writing

Acting Mayor Sees Eaton's

McLarty, Fraser In New Offices

About Work

Lacasse Raps Blue Ruin Cry

Windsor *Times Star*, 28 February 1930: Charles Cross found guilty of murder in Chatham.

consensus that manslaughter was a more fitting verdict than murder. In addition to these all important legal considerations, it seems likely that the authorities in this case did not fully view the crime as a murder across the colour line.

The pattern in cases of both intraracial and interracial murder is clear: cold-blooded murder rather than killing as a result of a melee or brawl tended to result in death-penalty verdicts. In February 1930 an African Canadian man named Charles Cross was tried for the murder of the White male owner of a Chatham gas station during a robbery. Three of his accomplices also appeared before the court in separate trials. A large headline in the *Border Cities Star* signified the seriousness of the crime: 'TRIAL OF WINDSOR FOUR IN LABADIE KILLING.' It was also reported that this trial had been the one of 'chief interest' among all the other cases tried at that year's spring assizes.[92] The other three men involved in the crime – each of whom testified against Cross – were given lengthy prison sentences, whereas Cross was sentenced to hang on 19 May 1930. However, even a case such as this one yielded unexpected results: at the eleventh hour, swayed by a petition bearing some 1,500 signatures, the minister of justice commuted Cross's sentence to life in prison. Because Cross's accomplices' testimony was used to convict him of a murder in which they had a role, the *Border Cities Star* suggested, many in the city of Chatham felt that the sentence was unduly harsh, a sentiment that was strongly expressed in the petition.[93]

Another sensitive case of murder across the colour line was *R. v. Jerry Simmons and Glen Lotharp*. In 1954 these two Black men, both citizens of the United States, were charged with a murder that was the unfortunate result of a botched robbery at a service station in the Woodson Township, Norfolk County. Both were sentenced to death for the crime but the latter's conviction was eventually overturned.

Many of the township's citizens were outraged. In fact, Harold E. Stafford, one of the defence attorneys in the trial, argued that widespread anti-Black sentiment in the township warranted a change of venue. He conducted an informal poll of twenty townspeople, who, he concluded, 'seemed to think the two Negroes were guilty before they were even tried.' The poll also revealed 'a certain feeling against Negroes and three out of four people said they deserved to hang.' His request was denied.[94]

While a visceral strain of anti-Black sentiment was stirred up in the township, in the courtroom a paternalist strain of liberal racism was evident. At a key juncture during Lotharp's trial, the defence presented *voir dire* (jury absent) arguments that challenged the admissibility of some of the evidence, including Simmons's police statement to an Ontario Provincial Police detective. Simmons's attorney, Harold E. Stafford, maintained that the case of *Regina v. Sankey*, which went to the Supreme Court of Canada, was a relevant precedent. Arguing before Justice Barlow, Stafford maintained: 'In this case the accused man was an Indian, and the court felt that, as such, he was more susceptible to the influence of those in authority.' I suggest, Stafford continued, 'that this argument applies in the case of a Negro.' Stafford held that his clients' natural susceptibility to authority, coupled with the fact that the police put them through a rigorous four-hour examination, meant that their statements possibly had been coerced. In other words, Blacks and Aboriginals shared a childlike nature that limited their criminal responsibility. For his part, the crown attorney argued that *Sankey* was not an applicable precedent since the accused in that case was 'an Indian who could neither read nor write, which was different from Lotharp.' Justice Barlow was not swayed by the paternalistic arguments presented by the defence. Sidestepping the issue of race entirely, he ignored the claims put forth by either side and instead chose to rule carefully on the admissibility of each defendant's police statement.[95]

After his appeal was dismissed and the federal cabinet denied his request for clemency, Simmons was hanged in the Simcoe County jail for his part in the crime. In Lotharp's case, the jury recommended mercy. Upon a successful appeal, Lotharp's conviction was overturned, the court citing the trial judge's failure to instruct the jury adequately on a key part of Lotharp's defence, 'namely – were the acts of Simmons in the struggle with the deceased done in execution of the common purpose to commit robbery, and were those acts known, or should they have been known, to Simmons to be a probable consequence of the prosecution of the aforesaid common purpose?' Because the judge ruled out the consideration of manslaughter, the jury did not deliberate on these key points. Lotharp was granted a new trial – for robbery – at which he was convicted and sentenced to fifteen years in prison.[96]

The Cross case, and to a lesser degree that of Lotharp, suggests that even when death penalties might have been appropriate, according to the conventions of the law at the time, appeals and post-trial deliberations were used to address verdicts that jurists felt were socially suspect or problematic. These two instances, both involving murder across the colour line and resulting in verdicts that may have had the appearance of an unbalanced dispensation of justice because of racial bias, fit this criterion.

Murdering White Males as a Crime against the State

To law-enforcement officials, murders of police officers were the most abhorred crimes. As C.H.S. Jaywardine has shown, in the period between 1948 and 1954 all of the six men convicted of killing an officer were executed.[97] The Canadian Association of Chiefs of Police has always had a very firm position on the effectiveness of capital punishment as a deterrent to violent crime, particularly in the case of crimes against police officers and corrections officers. The association espoused this view from the 1950s until the abolition of the death penalty in 1967 – and still does. In the 1960s, among police officers and police departments, capital punishment constituted an 'umbrella issue' and the 'ultimate expression of the doctrine of crime control.'[98]

During the period under investigation in this book, police officers were overwhelmingly White men. When the murderers of police officers and corrections officers were Black men, these crimes were also murders across the colour line. The interracial nature of these crimes thus added another incendiary element to tense situations. Next to the highly sexualized and racialized murders of White women, this kind of crime perhaps created the most anxiety. In my sample there are two such cases: the trial of 'M' for the murder of a member of the police force of London, Ontario, in the late nineteenth century,[99] and Chester Crosley's trial for the murder of a guard at the Kingston Penitentiary in the 1930s. On 28 June 1898 a poster was issued by the sheriff of the city of London (page 75). Thus began a case that created intense interest in London and beyond: a case involving a 'mulatto,' 'peg-legged' transient charged with the murder of a White police officer.

On 30 September 1898 M, a U.S. citizen, was apprehended in North Yakima, Washington State, and plans were made to begin extradition proceedings. First, however, provision had to be made to send someone to retrieve him along with one of two witnesses.[100] Approximately a month after M was apprehended and brought to Canada, P.M. McPhillips, a prominent lawyer, was retained to serve as defence counsel. McPhillips wired a formal objection to A.S. Hardy, the attorney general of Ontario. He argued that his client was 'an American Citizen and he claims the benefit and protection of the Ashburton treaty existing between the United States and Canada and he claims that he is not properly before the Canadian Courts upon the charge upon which he is about to be tried.'[101] McPhillips most strenuously objected to the fact that, according to M, he had been arrested in Washington State on the charge of 'selling liquor to Indians' and confined to a jail cell there for fifteen days. M also alleged that 'on the pretence of taking him to Seattle' to stand trial for the charge of selling liquor to Aboriginal people, he was instead brought into Canada and 'arrested on the charge of murder at Victoria B.C.' McPhillips claimed that the Ahsburton Treaty between the United States and Canada meant that M should not have been brought to Canada on the charge of murder. Further, he argued that M had been brought here 'by artifice' and in 'violation of the laws existing between these countries.' He thus urged the attorney general to return M to the United States and dismiss the case on the basis that he had not been legally extradicted.[102]

McPhillips also sent additional letters to the attorney general, bemoaning the fact that with a January trial looming, he was not yet ready to mount a proper defence since he was still without a copy of the evidence taken at the coroner's inquest, as well as a list of crown

$500.00 FOR CAPTURE

—OF—

MURDERER!

London, Ont., June 28th, 1898.

Wanted here for the murder of an officer by shooting on the night of June 24th.—A tramp with wooden leg, a peg from knee down, described as follows:—35 to 40 years old, about 5 ft. 8 in. tall, broad chested, walks very erect, very dark complexion, has colored blood or Indian in him, perhaps both; has black hair, short and said to be curly; was on 26th dressed in dark clothes and had dark hat with stiff brim and soft crown; is making for Michigan through the woods and by rail track, was on night of 27th thirty miles this side of St. Clair River, going west.

W. T. T. WILLIAMS,

Chief of Police.

The Trial of 'M.' Police poster, London, 1898, Library and Archives Canada, RG 13, vol. 1438.

witnesses. Neither could McPhillips locate 'four or five' of his 'most important witnesses,' some of whom were a 'thousand miles away.' This also led him to wonder aloud about who would pay to bring his subpoenaed witnesses to the London assizes.

William Lount represented the crown in this case. Like McPhillips, Lount was also a prominent attorney and a member of Ontario's Conservative Party establishment, sitting as a Tory MP in the House of Commons between 1896 and 1897 and doing a stint as a justice in the Court of Common Pleas from 1901 to 1903.[103] Predictably, Lount cynically called McPhillips's requests for postponement 'excuses,' suggesting that the defence counsel was 'only jockeying to escape trial.' He insisted there was no 'sufficient reason to warrant any postponement' and, further, that there were no 'witnesses who can give material evidence on behalf of the prisoner.'[104] His arguments evidently carried the greater weight, for, despite what appear to be valid objections on McPhillips's part, the trial proceeded.

A little over three decades later, the task of bringing Chester Crosley before the courts to stand trial for killing a corrections officer was a relatively simple affair. There was no 'manhunt' or debates about extradition, for Chester Crosley was a prisoner in the Kingston Penitentiary.[105] On 11 July 1936 Crosley had slashed 'White male nurse Toomey' in the prison dispensary and also fatally wounded a White prison guard named John McCormick.[106]

The Trials

M's trial opened at the Middlesex assizes in London on 23 March 1899. The Toronto *Globe* reported that the 'crowd of spectators' included 'a large number of ladies.' The prosecution called numerous witnesses both to identify M as the man who committed the offence and to construct a 'chain of evidence' beginning with an assault on a local resident, a man of sixty named James Ross, and ending with the murder of a police officer. The stark inequities in this case are illustrated by the very uneven quality and quantity of the evidence mustered by each side. Prior to the trial, McPhillips had expressed concern that he had neither the resources to procure defence witnesses for trial nor any idea how he himself would be paid for his services. The crown, by contrast, spared little expense. The first two witnesses were law-enforcement officials brought in all the way from Texas: a former jailer at the Georgetown jail, and a constable from the town of Taylor. The jailer, who had been working at the Georgetown jail in June 1898 when M was doing time there, told the court about M's escape from custody in June 1898, his theft of the jailer's firearm, and his skill as an expert train jumper. The jailer's testimony was also used to provide a physical link that tied M to the crime. The jailer identified an article of M's clothing – a Stetson hat – which was found at the scene of the murder. The second Texas lawman, it seems, was there primarily to dispel commonly held assumptions about Texan 'lawlessness,' mainly the 'mistaken idea' that it was 'a common practice in Texas to carry firearms.'[107]

These opening witnesses provided a compelling narrative of M's 'bad antecedents' (as presiding Justice J. MacMahon later described M's personal history). Enlisting a remarkably large number of witnesses (well over sixty), the prosecution turned its attention to tracing M's movements from the U.S. side of the border into Canada and, eventually, his appearance in the vicinity of London, Ontario. A diverse cross-section of witnesses all claimed to have spotted the 'mulatto peg leg' at appropriate times and places. Their statements also reveal their unequivocal derision of and even fascination with M. On the third day of trial, for example, no fewer than twenty-four witnesses went into the box for the purpose of 'tracing [M] from Strathroy to London and then from point to point in [London] to the corner of Ontario and Dundas street where the late P.C. Toohey learned that the one legged tramp had gone north and followed him.'[108] Indeed, a troop of railway engineers, stationmasters, 'Roadmasters,' 'watchmen,' and conductors collectively traced M's route on the rails. Two others testified that they gave M some food, another that she gave him water upon his arrival in Strathroy (just outside London). Several railway watchmen testified that they saw M arrive in the city of London. One watchman in particular, the James Ross whom M had allegedly assaulted, gave what was considered a 'key' piece of evidence. He identified the prisoner and claimed that M had delivered a 'violent blow' to his left cheek 'which left him senseless.' M's arrival was verified by still more witnesses, including one who claimed that while reading the newspaper 'a mulatto with a peg leg and a coat on his arm came along and swore at [my] little girl, who was sitting on the sidewalk, for being in his way.'

The courtroom drama gained momentum as the procession of witnesses traced M's movements nearer and nearer the scene of the crime. After the alleged assault of the watchman, a witness contacted the police, starting a chain of events leading to a police officer's murder. Once the police were alerted, they, along with 'some boys,' began to search for M; this development created the ever present threat of mob violence. Indeed, from M's standpoint, the line between the police, vigilantes, and a mob might have seemed inconsequential if not non-existent. One of the 'boys' followed closely behind Police Constable Michael Toohey (who was not wearing a police uniform), as the officer pursued M into a thicket of bushes. The witness testified that he heard two shots and heard someone say 'Hold on there';[109] moments later, two members of the Guelph Battery found the body of Toohey 'kneeling, head, foremost, on the ground, his right hand under his chest, and the left arm out a little from the body. The revolver was picked up from under his open right hand.'[110] A hat, similar to that described by the lawmen earlier in the trial, was found near Toohey.

Finally, the prosecution addressed the 'flight of the prisoner.' More witnesses testified that they saw the prisoner in and around town in the days following the shooting, as well as his getaway. A resident of Hyde Park, an area five miles west of London, recounted a rather odd encounter with M, who showed up at his house asking for something to eat. While M ate his meal, this witness told M that 'it was lucky he was not in London, because it was reported that a colored man with one leg had shot a policeman, and that he might be arrested.' The following day, M made stops at the homes of various other witnesses, each of whom granted his request for food. M's last stop was Mary and Malcolm Campbell's farm. While M was there, two county constables arrived and asked John Campbell 'if he had seen a one legged man.'[111] The chase resumed through the Campbell farm. When one of the constables fired a shot at M, he reportedly 'returned the fire.' The press reported that when the police fired again, 'the tramp,' M, 'merrily waved his hat in the air and walked on.' As M's pursuers drew nearer, he proclaimed that he 'knew what he was wanted for and he would never be taken alive.'[112] M managed a dramatic escape from his pursuers and was not seen again until he was arrested in Washington State.

McPhillips found it difficult to mount an effective defence. Overcoming the sheer number of prosecution witnesses must have seemed like an insurmountable task. Furthermore, McPhillips was unable to procure any witnesses on behalf of M (likely owing to a lack of time and money and the fact that, according to the *Globe,* the spectators had shown 'very little manifestation of sympathy for the prisoner'). McPhillips thus turned to his only viable option. He attacked the veracity of prosecution witnesses – a common tactic that, nonetheless, won him little favour with the presiding judge. While questioning the detective who examined Constable Toohey's body, McPhillips suggested that the officer's hand, not the defendant's, was 'clutching the pistol' (invoking a different picture of the incident than the prosecution, which maintained that at the scene of the murder 'the revolver was picked up from under his open right hand, which was under the body'). When the detective was on the stand, McPhillips claimed that '30 or 40 persons had been arrested on the strength of the descriptions sent out by the police.'[113] Though the judge ruled that this evidence was irrelevant, McPhillips pressed on and 'insinuated that certain witnesses for the defence who came from Texas had been taken into custody by the police.' Moreover, reiterating the substance of his pre-trial efforts, McPhillips also suggested that his client had been arrested on another charge (not murder) and was wrongfully before the court. The judge dismissed both arguments, particularly the latter.[114] Despite the hostility he received from the bench, McPhillips touched upon all of these points once again in a three-and-one-half-hour address to the jury, during which he characterized the prosecution's case as 'a tangled mass of statements unworthy of credence.' McPhillips even 'had the officer's tunic passed around among the jurymen and insinuated that the garment showed evidence of having been tampered with after the tragedy.' He reportedly 'concluded with an impassioned plea for the prisoner, whose aged mother, he said, might at that very moment be shedding tears for her absent son,' while M, looking on, 'wept copiously.'[115]

The court was little moved by this performance. In his charge, the judge all but dismissed a key aspect of McPhillips's defence: 'It is unnecessary that a policeman should be clothed with a warrant in order that he might arrest an offender, for the crime imputed to the prisoner for the assault upon Ross. In the performance of his duty, while he was apprehending the man accused of the crime, if the person knew that he was an officer of the law, it was his duty to submit without a murmur.'[116] As a 'member of the criminal class,' he continued, addressing M, 'your acts upon entering this country showed that you have no respect or feeling for age or youth.'[117] M, predictably, was convicted.

Similar themes emerged in the case of Chester Crosley, who was twice tried for murder. The first trial commenced at the Frontenac County fall assizes in September 1936. This too took place in a highly charged atmosphere, one replete with White supremacist representations of Black masculinity. An article in the Ottawa *Evening Journal* on Crosley's first court appearance painted a vivid picture: 'Crosley's feet were shackled when he was brought into the court room accompanied by armed guards. A penitentiary keeper sat directly behind him and other prison officials were stationed in the court room and outside the doors. The room was jammed with spectators. The giant Negro's appearance came a few minutes after the Fall Assizes grand jury brought in a true bill on three counts, charging him with the murder of John Toomey hospital nurse in penitentiary hospital, and with disabling convict Felix Paquette.'[118]

The image of the 'giant Negro' was a cliché of White supremacist rhetoric. In fact, Crosley was average to slightly below average in height and stature.[119] Nonetheless, as the trial commenced in February 1937, this sort of rhetoric, the exaggerated physical danger that this man posed to his jailers, became a central thread of the prosecution's case.

The timing of Crosley's case was key because it was tried in an era of penal reform. In 1936 the Archambault Commission was entrusted with the task of investigating the country's penal system. The investigation had been prompted by the harsh reality that 'no less than twenty riots and disturbances' had occurred in the previous eleven years.[120] Also, Crosley's high-profile defence lawyer, W.F. Nickle, a sitting member of Parliament at various points in his career, was a major advocate of penal reform.[121] Indeed, Nickle had been a member of a 1921 parliamentary commission (the precursor to the Archambault Commission) charged with investigating the operations and 'the conduct of the officers of the Kingston Penitentiary.'[122] That same year, he also headed a commission of inquiry into the treatment of female prisoners.[123]

Nickle entered a plea of not guilty, contending that his client's mind was altered during the crime. 'If the negro was guilty of murder it was because he was under the influence of drugs at the time.'[124] Crosley's state of mind became a central and contested issue in both trials. In each trial, both sides marshalled several psychiatric 'experts' to make their case. The defence attempted to portray the crime as a result of Crosley's 'drug crazed' state – a state induced by the drug ephedrine. To make the case, Nickle called upon Dr John Wylie, a professor of preventative medicine at Queen's University in Kingston. Dr Wylie had examined Crosley and told the court that he found the prisoner to be a 'physical wreck ... a moron and of a low mental type ... [and] also a drug addict.'[125] Dr Ross, another physician, concurred, maintaining that Crosley 'did not know the nature and quality of his act or know it was wrong.' Ross was of the opinion that 'a long-continued use of drugs, such as barbital, would break down a man's mind; would cause hallucinations and dull his moral sense.' His conclusion was that 'on the morning in question the accused was not responsible and was incapable of forming the intent to kill.' Another doctor was called as an expert witness for the defence. Earlier he had been reluctant to certify Crosley as insane, but during the trial he said he 'now believed, after hearing the evidence and noticed the demeanour of the accused during the trial, that he was insane.' Dr Armour, a 'well known Toronto alienist,' was somewhat more equivocal than the defence's other expert witnesses; he concluded that 'the accused was in the same condition as a man intoxicated with liquor, verging on delirium tremens' and, further, 'that it was perhaps only by chance ... that Crosley attacked McCormick and Toomey.'[126]

Testifying for the prosecution, Dr Julian Loudon, chief physician at St Michael's Hospital in Toronto, definitively stated that Crosley was 'not a mental case.' Moreover, he also refuted defence arguments regarding the addictive nature of ephedrine and the notion that it could drive anyone to commit a violent act. Others corroborated the evidence given by Loudon. Two physicians, one the superintendent of the Ontario Hospital in Whitby and the other a physician at a hospital bearing the same name in Brockville, were of the opinion that Crosley 'knew the quality and nature of the act and knew it was wrong.'

The evidence of these expert prosecution witnesses was not enough to secure a conviction in the first trial. That trial ended amidst much scandal – even outrage – when the jury was unable to come to a verdict after being twice sent back by Justice Keiller Mackay. Of the twelve members of the jury, only one voted for acquittal. An angry Justice Mackay remarked: 'I am very sorry that one of our citizens should assume such an attitude, but I am powerless ... One life has been taken and others may also ... To the 11 jurors who gave honest and careful consideration I express my thanks. To the 12th I have nothing to say and do not care to say anything.'[127] Justice Mackay's anger was reflected in press coverage of the trial. An Ottawa *AM Journal* editorial castigated the one holdout on the jury, sardonically remarking: 'He had made up his mind, was not open to argument – everybody else was out of step.' Even 'more annoying to the people of Kingston and Frontenac,' the piece continued, 'is that the convict in question is not a native son, was not a resident of the county before he was sent to prison. The county has no moral responsibility for the expenses of his trial: this cost falls upon Frontenac because the penitentiary stands within the county borders. It would seem fair that in trials of convicts in penitentiaries the cost should be assumed by the Dominion treasury.'[128]

The second trial, held six months later at the fall assizes, produced a more agreeable verdict for Kingston's citizenry. Once all the evidence was in, the jury took little time in reaching a guilty verdict.[129]

While White elite medical experts and alienists figured prominently in both trials, Crosley did not merely complacently watch as they decided his fate. The press frequently remarked upon his outbursts and utterances. The portrayal of these outbursts was, in some respects at least, ambivalent, reflecting feelings of pathos, contempt, and, ultimately, even awe. The shackled, 'burly,' 'squat,' 'heavy shouldered,' 'thick shouldered,' and 'thick set' 'Negro' often interrupted the court proceedings and in so doing undercut the dominant construction of him as subhuman, a belief that was shared by the prosecution and his own lawyer.

During an examination of one of the guards at his first trial, for example, Crosley jumped to his feet and cried: 'I can't stand any more of this. Let me out of here. I've had 17 years in prison and I know what the guards are. I have too much respect for the judge and jury to interrupt this court but I simply can't stand it any more.'[130] As the trial wore on, Crosley became even more adept at using rhetoric that both embraced and condemned the White male legal apparatus which was to decide his fate. The *AM Journal* carried this report of one episode in the first trial, during the crown's cross-examination of Dr Wylie, a key defence witness: '[Crosley] turned to Justice Keiller Mackay, sobbing and said: "Stop him from introducing racial feelings into this trial ... I was born in this country and nowhere in the world is a colored man treated like he is under the British flag. Make him stop these South American tactics."'[131]

Cloaking himself in the dominant rhetoric of colour-blind British justice and Canadian nationhood through a disavowal of 'South American tactics' (presumably U.S. Jim Crowism) was clearly one of the strategies Crosley used to assert his humanity under circumstances in which such a possibility was highly circumscribed. The judge was compelled to respond: 'You will get a fair trial here Crosley. It makes no difference if a person is Black or white, man or woman, there will be no discrimination by the law.'[132] In 1945 Justice Mackay, while sitting upon the Ontario High Court, acted upon the sentiments he expressed in this trial by writing a decision to strike down restrictive covenants in *Drummond Wren*, a decision that was widely heralded at the time. Nonetheless, three years later the Ontario Court of Appeal overturned his ruling.[133]

Crosley also attempted to undermine the defence crafted by W.F. Nickle which focused on his mental enfeeblement, insanity, and drug addiction. Again, in the first trial, Crosley 'dramatically challenged his defense counsel's claims of insanity' by declaring 'I am not crazy now.' The seemingly nihilistic act of subverting his own defence was, in reality, an act of asserting his agency. His refusal to accept the premise of his own counsel's defence again became evident when, in the second trial, Crosley interrupted his defence attorney's examination of key witnesses. While one medical expert gave testimony in support of the defence's arguments, Crosley, in an act described by the Montreal *Gazette* as a 'wild outcry,' stood up and shouted: 'I want justice in this court. They're telling lies!' As he was removed from the courtroom for his impertinence, his attorney remarked: 'I don't care if you send him back for the balance of the trial ... Certainly I can't keep him quiet.' About a day before Crosley's defiant remarks and his removal from the courtroom,[134] inmates in the Collins Bay Penitentiary, an institution that was then three miles from Kingston,[135] made a show of solidarity with Crosley in the form of a sit-down strike. In response, the guards locked the prisoners in their cells.[136]

During the closing arguments of the second trial, the crown urged the jury not to send this 'dangerous man,' a 'leader among convicts,' back to the penitentiary where he might kill again. Nickle stuck to the strategy he relied upon throughout the case. Addressing the jury, he argued that 'the poor mentality' that Crosley 'had from early life was weakened by overdoses of drugs' and, moreover, '[he] was born a lame duck – he never had a chance. Doctors said right here he is a mental defective. On top of that he is given a dose of drugs.' Claiming that no less than the 'principles of British Justice' were at issue in the case, Nickle insisted: 'I am not asking for sympathy, but if there is any reasonable doubt, *that creature in the box is entitled to it.*'[137] Clearly, Nickle barely, if at all, considered his client a human being. His comment starkly illustrates that the rhetoric British justice was not antithetical to White supremacy and indeed could be an integral part of it.

After the jury rendered its verdict, Justice Nicol Jeffrey 'sentenced him to die on the gallows on December 6.' It was at this point that Crosley's resistance to the scripts enacted in the courtroom received its most poignant expression. With the court's rapt attention, Crosley delivered 'a dramatic one hour speech ... stunn[ing] the crowded courtroom as he addressed the Bench in precise and sometimes solemn words.' Those words constitute a powerful illustration of how subaltern people could speak to power, even under the most constrained circumstances.[138] Crosley stated: 'In the course of these two trials I have paid particular attention to everything that has been said, and as far as my counsels are concerned they have endeavoured to put forth their best. I have no complaint to make against my counsel. They have laboured hard; very few in the court room know how hard they have laboured, outside of the court room, that is to say visited the penitentiary during the day and in the hours of the night. I can even go far as to say that financially they are in debt.'[139] Turning to the evidence submitted by medical experts, Crosley then questioned the validity of the testimony of alienists (who had been procured to 'defend' him): 'Towards the latter part of the week I discovered something of rather scientific and suspicious character as one of those, I do not know how you apprehend me, I would call them sworn doctors. They termed me suspicious. Through their examination they have only touched upon two or three dreadful fits. That is not necessary for me to dwell upon ... I jumped up today because I could not help it. Today I am the same man, and a few weeks ago I was the same man. There were times when my time bother[ed] me, throughout the years I have spent in prison. It would bother anybody.'[140]

In conjunction with his own assessment and critique of the expert-driven discourse that lay at the heart of the case, Crosley also returned to a theme he had invoked earlier, namely, the relationship between blackness and Canadian nationhood.[141] He refused to accept the dominant culture's insistence that the two were mutually exclusive. Referring to one of his earlier 'outbursts,' Crosley declared: 'Even though I am a criminal, my skin may be Black, but I was born in Canada. I think civilization and patriotism and civilization in Canada is as great if not greater than any other country even though it is a smaller country ... It is apparent all the way through, and ever since I have been in this country. Before I was in the geographic part of the continent, the place known as the next door neighbour to the United States and below the Mason Dixon line, [I] would not be allowed to speak the way I am speaking now and there is only one place in the world where a Black man can speak and I realize it now ... as you know all across Mason, Dixie [there is] mob violence and applying the torch.'[142]

While Crosley praised Canadian 'civilization' and 'patriotism' as laudable national characteristics, he was unapologetic in his criticism of Quebec. He recalled his experiences in the St Vincent de Paul penitentiary, the institution where he was incarcerated before being transferred to Kingston, as his justification. Crosley told the court that while at St Vincent he had been 'disciplined many times.' On one such occasion, 'they took me down and placed me on the table which if a man is sentenced as you know for being strapped ... They lashed me until the blood ran from my body. You are not supposed to draw blood according to what I have heard from Ottawa. Immediately after they put a gag in my mouth. The gag consists of something like a halter you put on a horse and around this is gauze. The gauze is to absorb the saliva in your mouth so you can hardly breathe. So I was jacked up until my toes almost touched. There I remained for twenty four hours ... There is one consolation. I am going to be hung, I am not going to be hung by a Frenchman.'[143]

Crosley need not have worried about being 'hung by a Frenchman' at all.[144] He didn't even live to see his execution date for he was discovered dead in his cell at the Frontenac Jail about a little more than a month from his scheduled execution. An inquest revealed little, 'prominent medical authorities' being 'unable to state definitively the cause of death.' In a rather surprising gesture, and an unexpected epilogue to this case, Crosley's lawyers offered to bury him, recognizing his humanity in death in a way that they did not – or, arguably, simply could not – during his life.[145]

Crosley had had few supporters writing to the minister of justice and cabinet on his behalf. He had to speak for himself. He did this powerfully and eloquently in the face of courtroom discussions that had sought to dehumanize him. As for M's case, it produced a range of conflicting public responses. Some observers felt that hanging the 'negro tramp' would constitute a miscarriage of justice. They felt that M's conviction was questionable since it touched on issues of international law; hanging him would thus constitute an international incident. Others pointed to the immediate details of the case. At the close of the trial, McPhillips, M's counsel, presented the minister of justice with a petition signed by individuals whom the Reverend Robert Johnston, a member of St Andrew's Church in London, described as 'thoughtful and wise men.' He also stressed that 'every signature represents a calm and informed judgment as no person was asked or urged to sign except as an expression of his own judgment.'[146] These petitions cited four main reasons for the minister to consider the commutation of M's sentence: M did not receive the consideration from the jury warranted by the evidence; even if M committed the crime, darkness, evidence of a scuffle, and M's ignorance of the fact that he was engaged in a struggle with an officer who had a pistol 'clutched in his right hand' and that he had shot out of self-defence precluded a fair trial; the jury and the general public at the time of the trial were so prejudiced against the prisoner that he did not receive the justice to which he was entitled; and, lastly, 'no miscarriage of Justice would take place if a new trial were granted or that the crime should be reduced to Manslaughter.' Perhaps the most impressive petition was presented by McPhillips. It was 'signed by forty members of the London Bar, setting forth that in their opinion that if [M] is guilty at all, he is guilty of no greater or higher a crime than manslaughter.'[147]

One London attorney also wrote the minister of justice in support of commutation, but his letter suggests that not all members of the bar agreed with McPhillip's strongly worded petition. Arguing that there was 'neither malice nor premeditation before the act, but simply self defense,' the writer also urged the minister to consider that he could 'make [M] atone for his sin by a lifetime of imprisonment [and] profitable labour.' He concluded: 'He is without friends, without money, homeless, wandering from place to place a vagabond among men. Surely he is a fit subject for the exercise of Mercy.'[148] Other letters echoed the same themes, but they also invoked racial tropes to strengthen claims that M was a good candidate for the extension of mercy.

The issue of racial prejudice alluded to in the petitions was not the only way race figured into arguments for commutation of M's sentence. Racial reasoning, at least in part, tacitly informed the letter of a London doctor who wrote that 'if mercy can be extended to him on the ground of his antecedents and the wild sort of life which he has been accustomed, I shall be exceedingly happy.' Yet another letter, written by Archdeacon Evans Davis of the St Jarvis Rectory, more explicitly expressed late-nineteenth-century notions of 'blood admixture.' The archdeacon urged the minister to consider 'the Man's Blood[,] half Indian and half negro. Such a man,' wrote Davis, 'I can understand being impulsive, hasty and being capable of committing any crime if pushed to it.' Besides the question of blood, the archdeacon also stressed the importance of social and political factors, particularly American racism: 'In the south such men seem to be treated worse than dumb brutes. Instance the recent butchering of the coloured people in the South – not merely lynching but the dismemberment of the body to [*sic*]. A coloured man's only chance down there where such brutal treatment is dealt out to him, it seems, is to use [the] same weapon of self-defence. Brought up in ignorance of religion, civilization, and of law, one is forced to the conclusion that he is no worse than his surroundings were calculated to make him.'[149]

The archdeacon's letter went on to deal with the particulars of 'the crime,' which, in his view, 'was certainly not premeditated or planned' but an act of self-defence.[150] Tellingly, the letter constructed a hierarchy in which the question of blood was the most important point of consideration in this case. The invocation of the lynching ritual in the American South signified the context within which such a volatile mixture of blood inevitably led to bad results. Moreover, as in the Crosley case, configuring the trope of the lynching ritual as fundamentally American provided an opportunity to foster Canadian nation building, for extending the prerogative of mercy would reaffirm the superiority of British justice. None of the appeals upon M's behalf, neither those invoking legal arguments nor those focusing on the question of M's 'antecedents,' 'environment,' or 'blood,' ultimately held sway with officials in the Department of Justice or the cabinet. As with all of those, Black or non-Black, who killed police officers, M's conviction stood. On 17 May 1899 a London coroner's jury witnessed M's execution and viewed the body after the sentence was carried out within the walls of the Middlesex gaol.[151]

Conclusion

Death-penalty trials of Black men in nineteenth- and twentieth-century Ontario were more than straightforward stories of racial oppression. On the contrary, these cases are evidence of the complexities of race's expression in the law in a liberal order. Race was expressed in multiple ways and upon multiple registers. First, these cases provided forums where White elite jurists, through the exercise of mercy, in cases involving outsiders, could demonstrate the superiority of British justice. The cases were often suffused with White condescension and paternalism towards Black defendants who were deemed incapable of premeditation, unable to control their passions, and incapable of appreciating the gravity of their crimes. It was a dehumanizing strategy that was quite often rather effective. White jurists also used these cases as a stage to articulate a particular vision of Canadian nationhood, one where the celerity of British justice trumped the social disorder of lynch law in the United States. Cases of murderers such as Frederick Turner and James Slaughter and Franklin Jackson illustrate this tendency most strikingly. Nonetheless, even a story such as that of the insane inmate Chester Crosley, a case that ended in an execution, shows the power of the rhetoric of the superiority of British law, rhetoric so powerful that the presiding judge, Keiller Mackay, had to respond to it when Crosley challenged him to do so.

The second major conclusion to be drawn is that the law, while far from neutral in the sense that legal formalists often imagine it to be, clearly had its own internal logic and that this logic, to a great extent, shaped the outcome of these cases. As this chapter has shown, while murders across the colour line clearly invoked more anxiety among jurists, the press, and various communities, it is also clear that murder cases in the main had to meet the legal criterion for murder set out in the Criminal Code. Murder convictions that were handed down for socially suspect reasons were susceptible to legal challenges in the form of appeals or in other cases were commuted. The exception to this pattern seemed to be murders where Black men killed White males who embodied state authority: police officers and prison guards.

3

Black Patriarchy

Race and racialization remain important themes in this chapter, but the focus shifts slightly to Black social, gender, and familial history. In the process, I also consider the issue of Black patriarchy and how it was expressed in and through the law.

This chapter owes a great debt to a generation of feminist scholars who have turned to legal sources to unpack the history of gender conflict through cases of family violence, spousal murder, and rape. Following in their footsteps, I study cases of family violence and spousal murder both for their value as sources of cultural and social history and for what they reveal about the courts as a site where various struggles about the meaning and nature of family and marriage, and the nature and function of the law itself, took place. Similarly, detailed examinations of rape and other forms of heterosexual conflict have been instrumental in informing my understanding of how the law has historically perpetuated and reproduced male power since (and this is still sometimes the case) all too often it was the character of the victims rather than the deeds of their attackers that was on trial. The perpetuation of male power was even evident, ironically, in statistically rare cases of female murderers of partners and spouses. These defendants were the beneficiaries of dominant ideas of 'womanly virtue' that mitigated their criminal responsibility in the eyes of elite jurists and some non-elite jurors, precisely the persons who had the power to grant life or pronounce death.[1]

Despite their great contributions, feminist legal scholars have had relatively little to say about the experiences of non-White men involved in cases of family violence. While they have rightly identified the male power and privilege that was produced and deployed in the courts, they have not done enough to consider how this male privilege was both implicitly and explicitly White male power. Similarly, few, if any, of the critical insights born out of this body of work on domestic violence and gender conflict have been applied to the gender history of Black Canadians, which has generally eschewed the sort of gruesome stories recounted in this chapter in favour of profiles of middle-class female achievers and relatively pastoral and celebratory renderings of Black community life. The exceptions to this general pattern are accounts of women and slavery in pre-Confederation Canada.

This chapter attempts to answer two central questions. First, how much, if any, of the privileged position enjoyed by White men was conferred onto Black men because of their gender? Secondly, what were the terms of Black men's engagement with legally conferred and articulated White patriarchal power? Stated differently, how much of this privilege was conferred by the law's internal logic and how much was accrued to Black men via the social and cultural attitudes that structured gender relations beyond the court? Finally, what role did Black men's subordinate status play in shaping the contours of their male privilege?

The chapter examines seven cases involving conflict between Black men and women in instances of property crime, rape and murder, and spousal murder. It argues that Black men enjoyed a residual but fragile form of patriarchal power bestowed upon them by the dominant culture.[2] Black men in nineteenth-century Ontario, many of whom had recently escaped from chattel slavery and/or profound legal discrimination in the United States, brought with them certain ideas about proper gender roles. Among these was the notion that a man should be head of a household and exert patriarchal control over his home and his community. However, the grim realities of material deprivation and the seasonal nature of the work available to Black men meant that this patriarchal ideal could not be fully realized.[3] As cultural critic Michael Awkward has argued, one must be cognizant of Black men's 'limited access to the prevailing social fiction of masculinity.'[4] As the trials under scrutiny in this chapter were highly dramatic, even sensational, in character, and as there are relatively few of them, we must be careful not to overreach in our conclusions. Still, all of the trials examined here are powerful moments of Black patriarchy at work in the court. Collectively, they provide a window on gender and domestic conflict within Black families and communities in nineteenth- and twentieth-century Ontario.

Some of the cases provide compelling evidence of Black residual patriarchy, while others are suggestive of its limits. It is clear that, in many cases, Black men were the direct beneficiaries of a system which often showed blatant disregard for Black female victims of crime. However, while some cases provide compelling evidence of the patriarchal privilege and power Black men enjoyed over Black women, other cases provide less direct evidence of Black male privilege. Competing definitions of Black masculinity were played out in these trials. Many legal officers and medical experts believed that Black men were particularly prone to acts of violence and, by extension, domestic violence. This was a recurring theme in these cases, as was the idea that Black men were unable to control their passions or, in some cases, fully appreciate the severity of their crimes. Both were thought to be a function of their inherent racial proclivities, mental defects, or both. Thus, the peculiar alchemy of Black patriarchal power, madness, and White supremacist constructions of Black masculinity suggests that Black patriarchal power was less than absolute.

George and Eliza Ross

On 16 September 1882 George Ross, a fifty-year-old African Canadian labourer, was arrested and charged with breaking into the house of his estranged wife, nineteen-year- old Eliza Ross, and her housemate, Susan Darrey. Ross had violently destroyed the women's possessions. He did not stop there. Curiously, he stole bedding, two dresses, one chemise, one undershirt, and other clothing from the premises.[5] The crime with which George Ross was charged – larceny – does little to convey the issues of patriarchal entitlement, gender, and sexuality that informed this case. At the Police Court hearing in front of Police Magistrate Alex Barttle, Eliza Ross described her relationship with George Ross, her husband of five years, in some detail, noting that 'he used to whip me and [I] used to go home from him previous to our separation.'[6]

From an early age, Eliza Ross's father and her husband were the two predominant patriarchal figures of influence in her life, but she would eventually assert her independence from them. Eliza told the court that on the day of the incident she met her husband in the market where he 'called me names.' Later, a nearby on-duty police constable found George Ross burning assorted goods,[7] which he believed to be stolen. Ross was promptly tied up, arrested, taken to the police station, and charged with larceny.

Eliza's story was one of domestic abuse, belittlement, and patriarchal control but it would be a mistake to see her as merely a victim of George's domination. It was Eliza Ross who filed the complaint against her husband on 18 September 1882 in front of magistrate Barttle. Her autonomy was clearly articulated in her assertion that she had been 'living separately from her husband ... for two years.'[8] Moreover, she further strengthened her claim of autonomy by showing that she was a breadwinner (and, perhaps a matriarch). She testified: '[I] worked and earned the goods ... about three weeks [for] two dollars and a half per week ... I [also] worked at the Montruels a month ... I made about three dollars per week.' In addition to her work as a domestic servant, she 'took in sewing and cooking for a living.' Her financial independence allowed her to confidently depose that the goods that her husband had produced 'were taken from my house ... free from the debts and obligations of her husband and free from his control or disposition.'[9] Eliza made this claim during a time when married women (at least in theory) were being given the right to control and dispose of personal property – including wages – by virtue of the Married Women's Property Act that was passed in 1872. This, along with her related claim of autonomy and independence, is perhaps what Eliza Ross hoped would override the deeply embedded patriarchal mores of a nineteenth-century common law perception of marriage, which, though it held that men had certain legally prescribed duties and obligations to their wives and children, was very slow to recognize the property rights of women in Upper Canada.[10]

Despite Eliza's presentation of a respectable image of Black womanhood, the Windsor jail records indicate that about a month later she was charged with running a 'disorderly house,' or house of prostitution. But, given the limited options open to women without male partners in nineteenth-century Ontario – particularly Black women – it is perhaps not surprising that Eliza Ross may have resorted to brothel keeping in order to survive.

Ultimately, Eliza Ross did not have the satisfaction of seeing the crown secure a conviction against her husband. In examining the reasons behind this, we can see how in this instance the legal system supported Black patriarchy. The defence attorney successfully exploited nineteenth-century common law ideas about the marriage contract that were woven into the fabric of Anglo-Canadian jurisprudence. He objected to the charges brought against his client for two main reasons: first, 'a wife cannot give evidence against her husband,' and second, because a husband and wife were 'one in law,' there could be no charge made against a husband for stealing from his wife.[11] We know for certain that the case against George Ross was dismissed, likely by the grand jury, but how this occurred is not entirely clear from the fragmentary and (contradictory) nature of the jail records and the criminal assize indictment. George may well have been summarily acquitted at the criminal assize, where the rules of evidence trumped the nascent liberal reforms that were remaking the legal landscape of property law and would reach their crescendo in 1884. In any event, the formal charges and the verdict passed down in this case point to the concrete links between marriage and masculine entitlement.

Sexuality, however, was also an important subtext in this case. Consider, for example, the sexual undertones that characterized George Ross's actions on the day he broke into his estranged wife's house. When George Ross entered Eliza Ross's home, he was clearly attempting to extend his abuse of her body and psyche to her possessions. George's destruction of Eliza's property was also highly sexualized. The invasiveness of this action, and its sexual undertones, hints at the possibility of a sexually tempestuous relationship between George and Eliza.[12] Moreover, George Ross's behaviour might have also been a symbolic attempt to exert his sexual dominance over Eliza while also reclaiming her as his wife. His trial, then, reinforced codes of normative and natural heterosexuality.

Black Womanhood, Rape, and Black Patriarchy

If sexual conflict was the subtext of the case of George and Eliza Ross, two rape cases highlight much more overtly the issues of violence and sexual conflict among Black men and Black women. The cases of Jonathan George and Allan Saunders shed light on the interlocking discourses of Black male sexual violence, Black patriarchy, White paternalism/patriarchy, and dominant codes of dissolute Black womanhood through which Black patriarchy was articulated.

On 24 December 1867 Jonathan George stood charged with the rape of Hannah Brown in a Windsor courtroom, while his alleged victim and four other witnesses took the stand on behalf of the prosecution.

Hannah Brown, a resident of Detroit, recounted the particulars of the alleged assault on 12 June of that year. Brown, who at the time was visiting an acquaintance, decided to go for a walk when she 'met the prisoner,' who asked her if she 'would take a walk with him to a Mrs Dennis.'[13] Upon their arrival at Dennis's home, they found the house unoccupied. As she made her way back to the main street, Hannah testified, 'the next thing I knew was he threw me down – he took me in his arms ... and he choked me [and] my clothes were thrown over my head.' When she 'tried to make a noise,' George persisted. 'He made me open my legs,' said Brown, 'he [forced] me to open my legs ... [and] got between my legs, he got his privates into mine [and] he told me that if I did not give way he would keep me there all night.'[14] Having 'accomplished his purpose,' George let her go. Brown made her way to Mrs Keys's house. Fear kept her from telling anyone of the incident for days (she told the court that her attacker told her not to tell her mother about the assault). Only after returning to the safety of her mother's house in Detroit did Hannah Brown muster the courage to tell her mother what happened. Shortly after, Brown returned to the Canadian side of the border to identify the prisoner; he was arrested soon afterwards.[15]

The defence argued that this was a consensual sexual encounter but Hannah Brown courageously stuck to her story and relived the trauma of her rape by recounting its details while the elite White men presiding over the trial scrutinized her moral character. When the prosecution asked about her familiarity with the accused prior to the assault, she told the court she had not 'had connection with him nor made any arrangement with him ... I did not know him prior to the Sunday I came over.' Hannah was emphatic that she went with him only with the intention of taking a walk, that she had 'been with the prisoner before but not alone.'[16]

Other witnesses gave testimony that corroborated Hannah Brown's story and undermined the prisoner's credibility. Hannah's mother testified that, when she heard what had happened, she 'came over to see if I could see [Jonathan George] ... he was pointed out to me and I called out to him. I then charged him with the crime and he denied it.'[17] Another prosecution witness, Emiline Keys (the woman with whom Hannah Brown resided during her stay in Windsor), said that 'the morning after the [alleged] outrage I saw her dress hanging [off] torn [and] muddy.' Yet another witness testified that he 'had a communication with [Jonathan George] in jail about 4 weeks ago ... he wanted me to go see Mrs Thomas... [and] talk with her.'[18] The very same Mrs Thomas, along with another man named Theodore Dunn, presented evidence for the defence, suggesting that the encounter between Hannah and Jonathan was consensual. Thomas stated that 'they were at my house on the evening in question, they came there about the same time; I think [Jonathan George] went out first and she went out afterwards – I think they went away together from my place.'[19] Theodore Dunn, the second defence witness, testified that he saw Brown and George on a date, locked arm in arm as they strolled along the sidewalk at 10 p.m. When he was cross-examined, however, Dunn admitted that he was not sure of the exact date but 'it was the night she said it was committed but I don't know the night myself.'[20] Jonathan George was found guilty and sentenced to hang on 24 December 1867. Rape was a capital felony in 1867.

As observed in the previous chapter, the commutation process was often initiated to address socially suspect legal convictions. In this case, what made the conviction socially suspect was the race of the *victim*. If George's victim had been a White woman, (see chapter 4), it is very unlikely that the commutation process would have been initiated. Over the course of the next several years, the sentence would be dramatically reduced for both legal (changes in the Criminal Code) and political reasons.

Shortly after the sentence was passed, the residents of Windsor mobilized on Jonathan George's behalf. Most notable among them was the warden of Essex County, the county clerk of the peace, and the deputy reeve for the city of Windsor. The petition that George's supporters drew up can be seen as evidence of an oppositional discourse in this case, a discourse that defended George, a Black man, by invoking dominant notions of the sexual depravity inherent in Black womanhood as the antithesis of respectable (White) womanhood.

The petition, signed by over 400 residents of Windsor, argued that 'the circumstances connected with the trial of said Jonathan George, disclosed no special facts of an aggravated character beyond the crime itself.' The consensus among many in Windsor was that Jonathan George 'bore a good character and was not before charged with crime.'[21] This assertion of Jonathan George's allegedly 'good character,' however, was largely linked to (or, at the very least, was in no way threatened by) dominant ideas about dissolute Black womanhood. The petitioners were quite secure in their view that commutation to imprisonment for a certain period '*would be sufficiently adequate to meet the demands of this case*.'[22] Evidently, the cabinet and the minister of justice were moved by the petition and by the sheer numbers who signed it. Shortly thereafter, the sentence was commuted to life in the provincial penitentiary.

Remarkably, in 1871, Windsor's White elites once again mobilized on behalf of Jonathan George. Whereas the first petition argued for the commutation of this sentence, the second asked for a full pardon and an outright release. It made two points: Jonathan George's innocence and the dissolute character of a woman he could not possibly have sexually assaulted.[23] This petition stated that Jonathan George had suffered long enough in prison for a crime he did not commit. Evidence of his innocence was twofold. First, George's exemplary behaviour as a prisoner was a 'manifestation of his innocence' and warranted 'merciful consideration.' Indeed, the warden of the Kingston Penitentiary himself concurred, saying that there was 'not a mark' against Jonathan George since the beginning of his prison term. Secondly, the petitioners claimed that '[Hannah] was the first person to sign George's petition after his conviction[,] stating publicly that she would not have arrested your petitioner had she thought anything serious would have resulted from it.'[24] The petition also described Hannah Brown as a woman of an 'abandoned character,' who had once spent many months in Detroit's House of Correction.

This rhetoric of 'abandoned character' was invoked even more vigorously in yet another petition produced on Jonathan George's behalf about three years later. Indeed, buttressing this renewed effort were key texts which were central to what amounted to a community project of reclaiming respectable Black masculinity at the expense of Hannah Brown. Attached to the petition was a somber-looking letter from the Detroit Metropolitan Police Department which certified that on 25 November 1867 Annie (Hannah) Brown, 'a colored woman 27 years old,' was sentenced to the House of Correction for six months. The story was confirmed by a brief attached note written by a clerk at the Detroit House of Correction. In addition, a handful of affidavits were submitted by residents of Windsor, attesting to Brown's 'low character.' One man testified that he 'was well acquainted with Anna Brown' and 'knew her to be a prostitute pursuing that profession' in Windsor and Chatham. 'I myself,' he added, 'have had carnal knowledge of the said Anna Brown on several occasions both at Windsor and at Chatham.' Equally damning for Brown was a sworn statement from a woman named Elizabeth East, the keeper of a boarding house, who said that she knew Jonathan George well; he had boarded at her house for six years. She also knew Anna Brown, 'who was continually calling and enquiring for George.'

On the basis of rumours and Brown's actions, East declared her *'a bad woman.'*[25]

A month later, the Department of Justice put in a request to the warden for a report on George's conduct. The warden's assessment was a ringing endorsement of George's character and, by extension, the claim of his innocence. Drawing upon powerful biblical imagery, the warden wrote: 'George is trusted and respected by every officer in the Prison, and the general impression here is that like Joseph with Potiphars' wife, he was accused and convicted because he would *not* commit the offence charged.'[26]

In 1874 the minister of justice, Telephore Fournier, released Jonathan George. He believed that, because George had been in prison only for three years at the time of the previous application, releasing him then would have been 'premature.' After reviewing an application signed by 'the Mayor and Sheriff of the County of Essex and by other respectable parties,' the minister reversed the previous decision. The presiding judge also played an important role in this case. His report concluded that 'if the state of the law had been at the trial as it is the present day, in all probability he would not have sentenced the prisoner to a longer period of confinement than seven years.'[27] This was a reference to a change in the Criminal Code's sentencing guidelines for rape in 1873, which allowed judges to impose lighter sentences. The remarkable quest to free Jonathan George now drew to a close.

The early-twentieth-century rape trial of Allan Saunders produced quite a different outcome. On 23 September 1908 Timothy Gray went before Windsor Police Magistrate Barttle and filed a complaint against Allan Saunders of Maidstone Township, Essex County, on the grounds that he 'did unlawfully ravish and Carnally [know] one Mary Gray wife of Complainant.'[28] Timothy Gray told a police magistrate that he had known Allan Saunders for a year. Gray had arrived in Maidstone about a month before the trial and arranged to do some farming with Saunders.[29] On the day of Mary Gray's assault, 22 September, Timothy Gray said that during the course of a conversation between him and Saunders, Saunders asked where he could get a cork for a bottle. In response, Gray told him he could 'get one at the house [as] the little girl Lizzie [Gray] might have one.'[30] When Gray announced that he had to go for a 'harness' of water two miles away, Saunders took advantage of his absence. Mary Gray, who was suffering from severe burns to her face at the time, informed the court that shortly after her husband left to get water for the household 'the prisoner came to the door, spoke as usual [and] asked how my scalded face was.'[31] Under the pretext of getting a bottle cork from Lizzie, Saunders entered the house, closing the front door just as Lizzie attempted to exit, a small baby in tow. 'He asked me if I give him some,' testified Mary Gray, 'and I said no and he said yes and I said I did not do such things.'[32] Mary continued: 'He said it was not wrong for any married woman to do such things ... he [then] dragged me into the bedroom. I told him to turn me loose that I would tell my husband. He closed the middle door as he grabbed me and turned the button on the door. He asked me when I was going to tell Tim and he threw me across the bed and pulled up my clothes and ravished me. I tried to break loose I was sick and weak and my face was very sore I hollered as loud as possible I could [but] I could not speak very loud [as] my mouth and face was very sore.'[33]

According to Mary Gray, after the attack Saunders asked her if she wanted to 'take some tablets he had if he brought them down.' She refused his offer. Mary also said, 'I told my husband what he had done to me as soon as he returned home.'[34] Gray said that he returned to find his wife was 'very much excited and nervous.'[35] Despite Mary's obvious distress, it appears that Allan Saunders's intimidation extended beyond her body and exerted itself on Timothy Gray, causing him to wait a full day before fulfilling his duty as family patriarch by bringing in a complaint to the police magistrate. During the day of the attack, testified Timothy Gray, he said 'nothing to [Allan Saunders] because he had threatened to shoot anyone that interfered with him.'[36] Saunders was sentenced to two years in prison, demonstrating the court's insouciance with regard to the issue of sexual violence against women generally and Black women in particular. The case was also a rather stark reminder of an unpleasant truth about Black men's power: it often rested upon the subjugation of Black womanhood. The exercise of this power was supported by dominant patriarchs.[37]

Once Again before the Bench

Jonathan George had attracted much support from White elites in Windsor who had campaigned to free him from prison in the 1860s and 1870s. He found himself back before the criminal courts again in the early twentieth century. Now in his sixties, he was a rather strange old man with a white beard and white wisps of hair. Once again George stood trial for committing a crime upon a Black woman but this time the charge was murder. Though well publicized, this trial did not garner quite as much attention among the Windsor citizenry as did the first. In May 1904 Eliza Williams's body was discovered in her home; she had been violently murdered. Police sergeant Abraham Nash found her body lying on her dining table with her head facing south in the blood-splattered room.[38] In a case that the *Evening Record* tellingly suggested was based primarily upon 'circumstantial evidence,' several witnesses testified for the prosecution at both an inquiry into Williams's death and, later, at the Essex fall assizes.

The evidence presented at the preliminary hearing and at the assizes was quite compelling. For instance, one witness, a neighbour of Eliza Williams, testified that she spoke to Eliza a week before the discovery of her body. During their conversation, Eliza Williams said that she 'had had some words with the defendant' and asked her neighbour if she had heard their conversation. When she responded no, Eliza commented that 'he thought the whole town would have heard.'[39] A receipt was produced at the trial, written by one of Eliza Williams's former employers, Mary Sprague; she told the court that she 'was in the habit of writing receipts for [Eliza],' who was in all likelihood illiterate.[40] By presenting this as evidence, the prosecution intimated that money was, perhaps, the root of the disagreement between Jonathan George and Eliza. In addition, the prosecution sought to present evidence of a robbery, which, it was argued, had led to murder.

Nash's search of Eliza's house yielded a discovery of blood on the door. He also noticed that six of her preserves had been recently removed from a kitchen shelf.[41] The preserves were later found at George's house. Now under a heavy cloud of suspicion, George was brought into the police station and questioned by the chief of police. When asked where he got the preserves found at his place, George said that he 'got them at different places he had worked for over the river and here,'[42] and when pressed, George replied he 'got them from white ladies he had worked for over the river.' George denied getting any of these preserves from Eliza Williams even though the jars found in his possession were identified as hers. Indeed, at the fall assizes, two witnesses testified that they gave Eliza Williams the preserves found in Jonathan George's house.[43]

Despite the severity of the charge against Jonathan George – murder – there was an undeniable atmosphere of levity in the courtroom. In an exchange documented in the *Evening Record*, defence counsel Hanna asked one of the investigating officers about his handling of the weapon – a hatchet – used to murder Eliza Williams. The officer noted that it 'looked as if the instrument had been recently washed,' and that lint as well as a hair 'about three inches long' was found on the weapon. When asked what he did with the hair, the officer replied. 'It was lost.' To which Hanna reportedly remarked, 'Oh, you let the hair get away from you.' This comment was met with a 'general laugh' in the courtroom. Hanna received a similar response from the court's spectators when he chastised Sergeant Abraham Nash for ransacking a wooden box in Jonathan George's home, a search that produced no results. Mocking the officer's ineptitude, Hanna sardonically remarked, 'I suppose you had your eye out for more preserves.'[44]

The presiding judge dismissed the case on the grounds that the prosecution failed to establish motive 'regarding threats or robbery.' In other words, while the prosecution established that George had burgled Eliza's home, it failed to establish that violence, leading to murder, was implicated in the theft. Had the charge been larceny, the judge noted, he would have 'probably sent the case to the jury.' After the dismissal of the case, Jonathan George 'left the box with ... glee and shook hands with everyone who showed the most [desire] to do so.'[45] While on technical legal grounds the judge's decision may have had some merit, it is evident that, politically and socially, this crime, given the race and gender of the victim, was not regarded as particularly serious nor threatening to the social order.

Black Patriarchy and Spousal Murder

Three late-nineteenth-century cases of spousal murder were the ultimate expression of Black men's violence against women: the 'Peel Murder' of 1875, the Anderson Veney[46] murder trial in Essex County in 1892–3, and the trial of Hiram Richardson a year later in neighbouring Kent County. These cases show the power and the privilege that Black men exercised over their wives, the horror of their violent outrages, and the invisibility of their victims. The limits of Black men's power, however, were revealed when White men invoked 'race' and the racial inferiority of Black murderers to explain their acts of violence or mitigate their criminal responsibility.

The Peel Murder

On 11 August 1875 George Farr, a White farmer in Peel Township (near Guelph), was awakened around midnight to the sound of someone rapping upon his back door. As he opened it, he saw Henry White, his Black employee. Henry White was looking somewhat peculiar but Farr 'could see no excitement about him.' When White told Farr that his wife, Susannah, was 'in a well,' Farr replied, 'Be off and help the woman out of the well!' Farr repeated this three times but White did not leave immediately, which suggested to Farr that White wanted to lead him somewhere. Dressed in only a shirt and a pair of boots, Farr quickly left his house and ran towards the well, passing White as he approached it. Farr testified that he found Susannah White in the well and her 'feet were up' and her 'head was down' in approximately '2½ feet of water.' George Farr tried to pull Susannah out: 'I caught my arms around her feet and drew them to my breast and tried to get her out alone. [Henry White] came up as I was trying to do this and I asked him to take hold of one of her feet and assist in pulling her out [but] he [did] not make any real effort to get her out before we took hold. As I passed the prisoner, when I was running to the well he said "she's dead anyway."'[47]

In Henry White's subsequent confession in the press, the details of the events leading up to his wife's death became public. In the spring of 1875, White noticed that Susannah 'began to take a liking for a man named Peter Wilson.' Henry soon began to suspect that his wife was involved with Wilson. One evening Henry White told Susannah that Wilson was 'going after another woman'; Susannah, who was probably jealous upon hearing this gossip, leapt to Wilson's defence. 'She would take [Wilson's] part,' recalled Henry White, 'and make excuses for him when [I] told her he was going after another woman, and said she did not believe it. She threatened to tell Wilson what he had said about him, and that [I] had called him a whoremaster.'[48]

On the day of the murder, a huge 'flax bee' was being held in the township. Under the pretext of doing something at the Black church,[49] Henry White asked George Farr to let him off work a little early. On the way to the bee, White met his wife, who, incidentally, had been whitewashing Peter Wilson's house. A sense of unease again settled upon White, who had began to notice a disquieting degree of familiarity between his (perceived) rival and Susannah. White's unease soon developed into 'murderous feelings' towards his wife.

After White took a late-night supper at the house of his brother-in-law (Arthur Smith), things came to a head. When he arrived home, White asked Susannah if Wilson had paid her for whitewashing his house, and she said no. When Henry persisted, asking if he was going to pay, she responded, 'Never mind that.' His ego bruised and his masculinity threatened, Henry White later recalled that he was 'vexed at the way she treated me' and said to himself: 'You won't do it no more.' At that moment, White decided to murder his wife. He 'took a stick of Black Ash that I had laid at the fence on the morning before going to the bee ... for the purpose of striking her if I made up my mind to do it.' As he struck Susannah White on the head with the stick, she cried out, 'Oh! Henry you have killed me.' Henry then asked her: 'Will you go then and sauce me as you have done[?]' Pleading for her life, Susannah responded: 'No, Henry I won't.' To this her enraged husband replied: 'Oh, yes you will,' striking her two or three more times. Henry then remarked to himself, 'If she is not dead then she soon will be,' while he heaved her barely breathing body head first into the well.[50]

A coroner's inquest was held not far from Henry White's home. Susannah White's body (which had to be disinterred before the examination could take place) was in a state of rapid decomposition, with 'the outer skin peeling off when touched with the hand.' But there was still ample evidence of the violence to which she had been subjected, a textual anatomy of Black male violence, patriarchal power, and subjugated Black female subjectivity. The examiner noticed that 'the face was much swollen the tongue protruding from the mouth and swollen – the eyes protruding from the sockets – a bloody froth issuing from the mouth.' The examination further revealed 'a small contusion behind the left-eye between the eye and the left ear; also, a small lacerated wound in the same locality.' Dr Varden and his colleagues also discovered that on the left side of Susannah White's head her 'jaw bone was fractured, being broken off at the point where it turns up.' The cause of death, however, was attributed to severe fractures found on the right side of the victim's head (in fact, a sizable portion of her right temporal bone was broken off entirely). Susannah's wounds could not have been caused by a fall into a well, the doctor opined, but 'must have been produced by a blunt instrument like a club, and it would require great force to break it.' When Susannah White died, concluded the doctor, she 'did so in a state of shock, without any reaction ... a shock to the nervous system.' Varden's final assessment was that 'pressure of the fractured bone on the brain, in connection with the other fractures ... produce[d] death, but not, I think, immediately unless in a state of shock.'[51] Two other examiners corroborated Varden's testimony.

The coroner's report was the centrepiece of the evidence at the trial. At the end, after deliberating for approximately half an hour, the jury returned with a guilty verdict. White was scheduled to hang on 23 December 1875. Months later, sitting in his 'condemned cell,' Henry White publicly confessed to the crime.

The defence had offered little to counter the evidence produced by the crown during the trial; rather, defence counsel hoped that White's public confession would convince officials to exercise their discretionary power and reduce the sentence. Henry White also had supporters who wrote cabinet on his behalf, voicing their objection to the sentence. One was journalist Thomas James, the man who took Henry White's confession. He argued that little could be accomplished by sending a man such as Henry White to death for his crime. Robert Lorrance, one of White's spiritual advisers, urged the minister of justice to consider that the 'only thing in [Henry White's] favour is his ignorance.' Lorrance continued: 'My conviction from the intercourse I have had with him as a minister [is] that more importance should be attached to the provocations, to jealousy which were given him by his wife and the neighbour with whom she was once suspected of too great intimacy ... She was going to the States, that she would not be deterred from going even by her love for her children, and the offer of the man to sell his chattels to White, as he was going to the States also.' According to Lorrance, these statements, rumours, and innuendo *'had their influence on a mind naturally weak in awakening to jealousy.'*[52] This allusion to White's 'naturally weak' mind clearly had a racial subtext.

Thomas L. Davidson, pastor of the Baptist church in Guelph, echoed these sentiments and was more direct about the role that race played in the crime. What compelled Davidson also to ask for the reduced sentence was specifically that White 'came from Virginia twenty years ago as a refugee from Slavery' and that he was a 'man of very low intelligence whose moral sense is below the average for his race.'[53] A similar line of reasoning was apparent in a letter penned by Thomas James from the offices of the *Daily Mercury and Advertiser*. 'When forced to face death,' wrote James, '[White] talks about religion as if he knew nothing about it and simply learned a few pious phrases which he does not understand and cannot appreciate.' White, in James's view, was ignorant and had 'a total lack of moral responsibility.' Indeed, after 'long conversations with him,' James concluded that White 'exhibits the strangest mixture of ignorance, superstition and religious credulity that they ever came in contact with.' In short, White was a 'poor, ignorant superstitious wretch' whose 'brute instincts were his only motive [for the] crime.' Evoking a discourse of White normative masculinity against which lesser, residual Black masculinities were to be measured, James opined that if the sentence were commuted to life imprisonment 'White could to some extent [explain?] his crime, and, perhaps, live to learn something about his position as a man and his responsibility to his God.'[54] The minister of justice was, ultimately, unmoved by these racialized and paternalistic pleas for mercy; the 'law took its course' and the execution went ahead as scheduled.[55]

Veney and Richardson

Between 1892 and 1894, residents of southwestern Ontario and beyond were privy to two highly publicized and unsavoury glimpses of Black domestic life. The first case involved Anderson Veney, who, as newspaper headlines as far away as Toronto reported, was charged with killing his wife, Martha. On the morning of 13 September 1892, for example, the Toronto *Daily Mail* boldly trumpeted: 'MURDERED HIS WIFE: THE BRUTAL ACT OF A JEALOUS HUSBAND.'[56] The tale of the Veneys was recounted in grim detail in both the press and the trial transcripts. One of the key witnesses at the trial, Hattie Primeaux, graphically recounted Martha's murder. From across a vacant lot between seventy-five and eighty feet from the Veney family home, Hattie Primeaux saw Martha Veney between five and six in the evening of the Sunday she was murdered.[57] Primeaux crossed the empty lot and approached the Veney's house. Standing on the step of the Veney's side door, she watched as Martha Veney was 'humming a hymn ... [with a] dish cloth in her hand.' This fleeting moment of domestic tranquillity and piety was abruptly interrupted, Primeaux testified, when Anderson Veney came home. When she heard Martha scream, Primeaux ran to the front door. Martha twice called out 'for God's sake Hattie ...'

> Mr. Veney then was holding her with her left side of the face towards me; all the left side from her mouth down her was all blood, and I says 'for God sake, Mr. Veney stop' and I called twice that way and when he heard me I suppose he heard me holloa – he through [*sic*] her down to the ground and on her he fell. By that I ran to the corner of the house, that would be on the street, and as I looked out I saw Mr. [Weadon] Johnson, and I says, for God's sake run, Mr. Johnson and Mr. Veney is killing Mrs. Veney. I grabbed my little boy and ran into the house and ran out again, and as I looked over that way, he was standing looking at his wife and Mr. Johnson was standing just turning to go back again when he killed her.[58]

Other witnesses offered similar testimony. Weadon Johnson, the neighbour mentioned in Hattie Primeaux's testimony, told the court that on the evening of Martha Veney's murder, he was tending to his geese while engaging in a brief conversation with Anderson Veney.[59] Shortly after their conversation ended, he 'heard a scream' and 'supposed it was a fight scream, I supposed it was boys in the street.'[60] When Johnson arrived there, however, he instead found Hattie Primeaux. As he ran to get help, he spotted Mrs Veney leaning over the gate and then headed to the back part of the house. He continued on to the north side of the house where he found her lying down with 'the blood pouring from her neck ... and a great stream of blood coming from her neck. That horrified me, of course,' he said, adding, 'I saw her gape three times.'[61] In a similar vein, the *Telegram* reported that George Street, another neighbour, 'heard screams from Veney's house,' and when he ran to the back door, a 'frightful scene was presented.' Martha Veney 'lay on the kitchen floor, her throat cut from ear to ear,' while '[Anderson] Veney was walking up and down the room covered with blood with an open penknife in his hand.'[62] Veney suffered small cuts to his neck – apparently the results of a failed suicide attempt – which were described as 'severe [though] in no way likely to prove fatal.'[63] Just a few minutes after he committed the murder, Veney was arrested by Amherstburg's chief constable, Lewis Lemay, who arrived at the Veney home to find Anderson Veney 'up on a night stand with a looking glass.' Lemay grabbed Veney and 'took his knife away from him and took him outside.' With a handkerchief the constable 'plugged the hole [in Veney's neck] so that it would not bleed too much and took him to the doctor's.' Sometime afterwards, Lemay picked up Martha Veney's battered body from the doorway and placed it upon a table.[64]

That very evening, a post-mortem examination of Martha Veney was conducted in Amherstburg's town hall.[65] The inquest that followed is again a graphic and unsettling illustration of how Black masculine privilege could literally be inscribed upon the Black female body. Essex County Coroner Forrest T. Bell and two physicians, Dr J. Proudfoot and Dr James T. Park, had examined Martha's body. At the inquest, a twelve-member jury heard evidence from Park and Proudfoot. Dr Park rendered a medical opinion which attributed Martha Veney's death to a 'haemorrhage from [the] carotid artery and jugular vein.' According to Park, 'the [damage to] the deceased['s] organs was not sufficient to cause death; the wound which was made there with the blade of a dull knife [or] blunt instrument,' he explained, would not have so quickly caused death. But the wound in the neck was another matter. 'She could not have resisted or [fought] after such a wound … she would probably [have] taken a step and fall after receiving such a wound ... [in] probably 3 or 4 seconds.'[66] Dr Proudfoot concurred with Dr Park's testimony. The coroner thus concluded that 'there was reason to believe that the deceased died from violence or unfair means, or by culpable negligent misconduct.'[67]

A little over a year later, a similar tale of spousal murder unfolded in Dresden, a small town in neighbouring Kent County. Hannah Richardson suffered a violent death at the hands of her husband, Hiram Richardson, dubbed the 'Dresden Fiend' in nearby Chatham's newspapers.[68] On the morning of 6 November 1894, Hannah Richardson, dissatisfied with her marriage and probably fearing for her life, decided to leave her husband. Hiram Richardson accosted her in the street as she was moving some of her belongings out of her home and into a wagon with the aid of her friend and neighbour Daphne Warren and William H. Harris, a local 'carter' and peddler. This act of resistance enraged her husband. Angered by the spectacle that Hannah created by such a public show of her insubordination, Hiram Richardson reportedly said, 'If [Hannah] went on moving she'd move away a corpse.'[69] As Hannah was 'fetching something up near the wagon,' Hiram Richardson 'punch[ed] her and knocked her down and said ... I don't give a damn I'm going to kill her.'[70] He then boldly proclaimed that he 'didn't care whether they sent him to prison or to hell [for] killing her.' As Hannah tried to run to Daphne Warren's house – she and her daughter had sought and received sanctuary there the night before – her husband 'caught her by the back of her dress and turned her around.' He then 'struck her on the jaw with his fist and she fell on her side by the wagon and he put his foot on her neck.'[71] Daughter Mary Richardson had witnessed her mother's murder. At one point, she told the court, she tried to come to her mother's defence by striking her father with a stick but he 'knocked me down twice and then went back to mother.' He 'kicked [mother] in the side and on the head and then he mashed her forehead with her heel.'[72]

While her daughter ran off to 'fetch uncle Ross,'[73] Hannah Richardson somehow mustered the strength to crawl over to Daphne Warren's house. Having run off to get help for her friend, Warren returned and witnessed the terrible sight of Hannah Richardson, a huge gash on her neck, 'crouching up by the house' and bleeding profusely. Hannah's final request was for a drink of water, which Daphne Warren quickly granted. Warren later recalled that Hannah Richardson's injuries were so severe that as she drank she bled. Warren then helped to carry Hannah inside the house onto a bed where she died approximately five minutes later.[74]

Several hours after the murder, a post-mortem examination was conducted by two Chatham medical practitioners, Dr Daniel Gailbraith and Dr Irvine Wiley. Hannah Richardson's 'head and neck were terribly swollen.' Gailbraith described her as a 'quadroon woman'[75] approximately '45 years of age well developed, healthy and about 5 ft 4 in height and well nourished.' Her breastbone had been broken and it was surmised that her injury must have been caused by a very severe blow from some blunt instrument, and there was also a great deal of bruising on her neck and head. A rupture of her thyroid gland was deemed to be the immediate cause of her death. Dr Wiley's assessment mirrored Gailbraith's.[76]

'Fiendish Behaviour' or 'Mad Acts'?

These grisly and unsettling tales of murder, along with the post-mortem examinations of Martha Veney and Hannah Richardson, point to the hypervisibility and centrality of the Black female body in the trials that were to follow. However, while the Black female body was at the centre of these powerful, almost dramaturgical,[77] stories, the trials were ultimately forums for competing truth claims about Black masculinity and its association with violence. Whether Veney's or Richardson's actions were understood as the 'fiendish behaviour' of vicious patriarchs or as the 'mad' handiwork of inferior or mentally deranged men, stereotypes of Black males as petty patriarchs within their own households drew upon the well-worn notion that such men, victimized by the wider society, could direct their fury towards their wives and children. Indeed, while Black men and women alike had to endure White supremacy, Black men enjoyed relative power and privilege. This preoccupation with codes of Black masculinity meant that the Black female body came to occupy an unstable and interstitial space, resting at the interstice of hypervisibility and invisibility, the centre and periphery. Because these Black women were dead and their husbands were on trial for their murders, their stories were subsumed beneath and marginalized by a set of rhetorical strategies, tropes, and imagery which increasingly came to deal with the issues of Black male subjectivity, masculinity, and madness. By contrast, as we shall see in the next two chapters, the profound racial and sexual anxieties produced by interracial gender conflict meant that (White) womanhood remained central in discussions involving gender conflict across the colour line.

Discussions of Black masculinity quickly came to dominate the Veney trial. The prosecution predictably sought to establish that Anderson Veney was a disreputable man with a long history of cruelty towards his wife. The defence, by contrast, argued that this history of cruelty was the mark of an irrational mind, an outward manifestation of mental illness. For both sides, then, as the case progressed, Anderson Veney came to occupy centre stage while glimpses of Martha Veney became increasingly fleeting.

The prosecution argued that Anderson Veney's motive was that of 'determined jealousy'[78] and that Veney's cruelty, jealousy, and bouts of anger were so well entrenched that even a hardworking and respectable Black woman like Martha Veney was not exempt from his rage. When Hattie Primeaux was asked to comment on the state of the relationship between Veney and his wife prior to the crime, she informed the court that Martha Veney was 'always a lady' but nonetheless was constantly subjected to a litany of verbal abuses – including accusations of 'imputed indecency' and infidelity.[79] Primeaux also heard Anderson Veney constantly making death threats towards his wife. This verbal abuse was accompanied by a campaign of physical abuse. On several occasions, Hattie Primeaux had seen Martha Veney in various states of physical distress; eight years earlier, in a fit of jealous rage, Anderson Veney even threw Martha Veney down a flight of stairs.[80] Others corroborated Hattie Primeaux's testimony, surmising that Veney's motive was jealousy. One even went so far as to say that Veney boldly admitted to this after killing his wife.[81]

Veney's defence was conducted by two attorneys: Malcolm Cowan of Belleville and, most notably, Delos Rogest Davis. Anderson Veney's access to the reputation and professional accoutrements of this Black male trailblazer must have lent him an air of class and respectability. Davis's distinguished career as a jurist also served as a counterweight to the negative images of Black men that infused the trial. Davis and Cowan had few options in constructing a defence for Anderson Veney. The unusually high number of first-hand witnesses meant that the defence's only credible strategy hinged on making a case for Anderson Veney's madness. Defence counsel's cross-examination of Chief Constable Lewis Lemay sheds light on this strategy:

Q: Had you known the prisoner long?
A: Since we were little boys.
Q: What kind of character did he have?
A: I cannot put a straw in either one of their roads.
Q: Neither he nor his wife?
A: No, sir.
Q: *We have no desire to so far as she was concerned.* He had always been that kind of a gentleman?
A: As far as I can [say,] a gentleman in manners.
Q: A sociable fellow?
A: Yes.
Q: Was he inclined to be of a quiet disposition or rather the reverse?
A: Jolly.
Q: Always jolly, a goodhearted fellow?
A: Yes, sir.[82]

A range of defence witnesses – nineteen in all – were called forth in support of Veney's defence and to support the story of a 'jovial' and 'good hearted' fellow who had fallen mentally ill. Similar themes characterize their testimony – all part of a plan to create a narrative of Veney's insanity. What is particularly striking is that both non-medical and 'expert' medical testimony was deployed to delineate the contours of Anderson Veney's madness; this conformed to a general pattern that has been observed in studies of similar trials in nineteenth-century Ontario.[83] Most of the testimony came from people who had known the accused for some time and could thus comment on his descent into abnormal behaviour. Roman Smith, a man who worked with Veney as a steward on the lakes,[84] testified that in recent years Anderson had often looked 'wild and starey ... like a man who was going insane,'[85] and that their relationship began to sour when Veney began acting 'very queer and entirely different to his old-time actions with me,' which included Veney accusing Smith of kissing his wife.[86] Another witness testified that, although she and Veney generally maintained a cordial and social relationship, he recently passed by her house several times without so much as a nod in her direction, and on the day in question he had a 'wild distressful look.'[87] Still another woman, who claimed she had known Anderson Veney for about twenty-five years, told the court that although he was usually 'gentlemanly' and 'polite' in nature, on one occasion Veney 'look[ed] rather strange' and 'simply spoke to me and did not shake hands [although] he was always a polite person.'[88] Similarly, William H. Brown, an African American minister of Amherstburg's African Methodist Episcopal Church, told the court of an instance when Anderson Veney was to be 'received' into the church. The custom was for prospective members of the congregation to extend a hand to the minister, a ritual that was tantamount to accepting the church's 'invitation,' which then led to being 'received and registered' into the church membership. Veney, however, made a curious spectacle of himself: 'Instead of joining or giving his hand or anything of that kind he knelt at the pew with his back to me, his back was to me and there was not much expression on the part of myself or anyone and in a few moments he rose up and said to me, "happy"; that was of his own accord and that was about all that transpired at that time.'[89] Veney's despondent and lethargic state in prison – he had little appetite and often spent hours resting his head against the cold concrete walls – was also cited as evidence of his mental illness.

The medical experts delivered important testimony. Dr Thomas Hobley, an Amherstburg physician, examined Anderson Veney a few weeks prior to the murder and treated him for insomnia and a great deal of 'misery in the head.' Hobley attributed these symptoms to a 'congestion of the brain,' saying that Veney's 'intellect was weak.'[90] Dr James Sampson, a medical practitioner from Windsor who visited Veney in prison a week before the trial, noted that the prisoner would not answer any questions and 'assumed a very unnatural and feeble attitude, looked exceedingly stupid and absolutely unintellectual.'[91]

The prosecution tried to challenge the testimony of the medical experts, as indicated by its cross-examination of Dr Sampson. In the context of the crown's effort to disprove the doctor's claim of Veney's insanity, the White supremacist tropes of blackness which had implicitly shaped the trial came bubbling to the surface:

Q: What do you say in regard to the odour or the breath or skin of insane persons?
A: There is an insane odour not easily mistaken for any other, not always easily discovered on one single patient, easily discovered on a group of patients.
Q: I am instructed that the breath and odour was entirely sweet, that his peculiar odour is entirely absent?
A: All the time or now?
Q: When he was examined. Have you any knowledge you can impart to us with reference to that point?

A: I have a very fair nose and I do not want to swear to its entire absence nor that I discovered a marked absence. His race are subject to a peculiar odour ...

Q: You say that an insane man patient has a certain distinct odour that [can] be recognised by an expert. You are familiar with that odour, at least you have discovered it at times?

A: Yes, but you understand that a man in his ordinary practice is brought in contact with that very seldom.

Q: Would you expect to find the odour in one prisoner in the cell among a lot of other prisoners, a ventilated cell, a colored man, would you be astonished if you did not find the odour there?

A: No, I would not be astonished if I did not.[92]

This exchange graphically illustrates that White supremacist imagery shaped 'expert' knowledge about Black masculinity. The prosecution sought to undermine the testimony of the defence's expert witnesses by raising the issue of whether the odour given off by a Black male body could be readily distinguished from the odours emanating from the 'diseased' bodies of the mentally enfeebled.

The effectiveness of the prosecution's cross-examination of Dr Sampson was augmented by the testimony of other medical experts. Dr Richard Morris Bucke, superintendent of the London Ontario Asylum, stated that four examinations, consisting of physical examinations and interviews, had convinced him that Veney was sane. Two of these examinations were even conducted in the company of Dr Sampson. Dr Rémi Cosgrain, Amherstburg's jail surgeon, concurred. He, like Dr Bucke, could find no compelling evidence of Veney's insanity. While under examination, Cosgrain expressed the belief that Veney may have suffered from a kind of 'simple melancholy,' but he insisted that Veney's despondent and morose conduct was a sign not of madness but of a man in a deeply repentant state. Veney's demeanour, argued Cosgrain, was 'attributable to ... [his] brooding over what he had done and the enormity of it. I asked him why he did it and he said, well, because I was bad; the devil got hold of him and made him do it and that he was sorry for it.'[93] At the close of the trial, the jury, unpersuaded by the insanity defence, sided with the prosecution. Anderson Veney was sentenced to death, with a jury recommendation for mercy.

The Hiram Richardson murder trial followed a similar trajectory. The graphic nature of the eyewitness testimony and the post-mortem examination upon Hannah Richardson's body was all the prosecution felt it needed to secure a conviction. As in the Veney case, crown counsel M.G. Cameron shifted the focus from the terrain of Hannah Richardson's body to the 'fiendish behaviour' and/or 'mad acts' committed by Richardson. Under cross-examination by defence counsel W.J. Elliot, Mary Richardson testified to her father's inexplicable and erratic behaviour. She recounted this incident: 'He once took all the furniture and clothing – he was in a passion the night before and threatened mother; he killed our pig and threw it in the river and wrung the chickens' necks and threw [them] in the river and the corn and the meat in the house.' She also testified that her father would routinely destroy the family's possessions, and on one occasion he even 'split up the bedstead and burned it.' Enmeshed in a peculiarly destructive cycle of behaviour, Hiram Richardson would spend brief stints in Michigan, only to return home to 'buy new things and then after a while ... destroy them and go away again.'[94]

Hiram Richardson also testified at his trial and corroborated his daughter's testimony; he admitted to often destroying his family possessions, although he claimed that he could not remember any of these incidents. In addition, Richardson offered his own theory regarding the roots of his proclaimed madness: he traced back it back to a specific episode twelve years earlier when he 'was thrown from a wagon.' Before that he and his wife 'were always peaceable but for the last five years we were not so.' Richardson stated that he 'felt different after the accident and sometimes felt myself dangerous.'[95]

Several witnesses testified that they had witnessed Richardson exhibiting signs of madness. James Richardson, Hiram Richardson's older brother, also pointed to Richardson's accident as the beginning of a pattern of odd behaviour: 'After the accident he appeared to act like a crazy man – his temper seemed worse. He used to go away for half a day and come back at night; he used to appear to be talking to himself at times and throwing his arms about. He used to get angry at times ... I don't think my brother has been sane since the accident.'[96] Others told similar tales of Hiram Richardson's strange behaviour. Richardson's employees, co-workers, and long-time acquaintances recounted various incidents, including seeing Richardson doing field work and talking to himself, moving his arms about, and exhibiting uncontrollable fits of temper – often with little or no provocation.[97]

There was, however, little medical testimony in support of Hiram Richardson's insanity plea. One doctor was willing to say only that 'a severe injury to a head would weaken the man mentally.' Yet, under cross-examination, this witness also stated that 'from his observation in the jail and the conduct of the prisoner in court he would believe him to be sane.' Two other doctors testified at the trial. One testified that, while Richardson's actions might be classified as a kind of 'impulsive insanity' or a manifestation of an 'ungovernable impulse,' conversations with Richardson in the gaol, coupled with general observations of him, convinced this doctor that the defendant was 'perfectly sane.' And Dr R.J. Bray, gaol physician and coroner, stated bluntly: 'I haven't seen or heard anything to lead me to the belief that [Hiram Richardson] is not sane.'[98]

Richardson's claim to madness was also undermined by his very own words. At his preliminary trial in front of Justice of the Peace Robert P. Wright, approximately six months prior to the trial, he was asked if he wished to say anything on his own behalf. Richardson replied, 'All the trouble arose through his wife associating with the Warrens and others who wanted [us] to go to Detroit and spend [my] money as [I] earned it.'[99] At his trial, Richardson similarly told the court about having 'found Warren in the house and [hearing] her proposing to my wife to go to Detroit and make money easy. I spoke to my wife and forbade her to have anything to do with them [the Warrens] again.' Richardson's explanation of the immediate motive for his crime made him sound little like a man driven by a kind of impulsive insanity[100] and it did not convince the court; no grounds for an impulsive-insanity defence existed in Canadian criminal law. He was found guilty of manslaughter and sentenced to life in the Kingston Penitentiary.[101]

Hiram Richardson's verdict of manslaughter, rather than murder, was perhaps a subtle articulation of male privilege. The jury, while it was not swayed by Richardson's insanity plea, was ultimately unwilling to sentence him to death for taking the life of a Black woman. Anderson Veney, who was guilty of the same crime but enjoyed a relatively elevated status in the community, unlike Richardson, faced a death sentence. A critical factor was the presiding judge, Malcolm Street. When instructing the jury, he expressed his opinion that 'a great deal of the evidence was given on the part of the defence, which you have heard, but which did not seem to me to bear very materially upon the real question.' Indeed, Justice Street also bluntly expressed his view that 'there is no evidence ... to show that [Veney] was ignorant of what he had done, or that he was ignorant of it being a matter for which he was subject to punishment.' Street believed that Veney 'knew that he was arrested for having killed his wife, he knew that he killed her, and he appears to have regretted that he minded, as he said, outside talk and letters.'[102]

Anderson Veney's death sentence was, however, soon overturned. Three petitions were submitted to the minister of justice on Veney's behalf. The petitions were signed by many of Amherstburg's elite, including the mayor and ex-mayor, a banker, a broker, and a bailiff. These petitons represented an effort to rearticulate the defence's contention that Veney was essentially a 'respectable' man who enjoyed the 'esteem of all classes of our population.' They described Veney as a man of an essentially 'harmless character' who had gradually succumbed to periods of 'mental aberration' which, in turn, compelled him to murder his wife. His actions, maintained the petitioners, were inconsistent with their 'previous knowledge of his character.'[103]

Medical evidence of Anderson Veney's rapid physical and mental dissipation also played an important role in the outcome of this case. After the end of the trial, Dr Sampson, a key defence witness, wrote a letter to defence counsel Malcolm Cowan. Sampson was utterly convinced that Veney was insane and a 'pitiful picture of mental instability.' In Sampson's view, if Veney were sentenced to death, this would constitute 'a scandal' and as 'ghastly a spectacle as was ever witnessed at the gallows.' Veney was re-examined by two physicians: the Amherstburg gaol physician and the Ontario's inspector of prisons and police institutions. The former held to his opinion that Veney was 'sane and conscious.' The inspector of prisons, however, claimed that although Veney was sane when he killed his wife, 'brooding' over his crime coupled with his confinement had created a change in his condition. The inspector believed that Veney was suffering from a softening of the brain and that, whether confined to prison or an asylum, he would not live past two months. This led to the commutation of his sentence to life in prison at the Kingston Penitentiary. In fact, though, the commutation of Veney's sentence mattered little. He died in the prison hospital before a year had passed.[104]

Conclusion

The cases explored in this chapter illustrate how 'residual patriarchy' characterized Black men's partial access to the social fiction of masculinity. Offering poignant glimpses of domestic, familial, and gender relations, they show how Black men were simultaneously the beneficiaries of dominant codes of masculinity – against which and through which they were also measured – and 'Othered.' The case of George and Eliza Ross is a rare example of a case of property theft that tells us much about the unequal gender relations in nineteenth-century Ontario and the role of the law in, ultimately, firming up Black male privilege. One sees a similar pattern of the law reinforcing male privilege in the instance of the Jonathan George murder case. The rape cases of Jonathan George and Allan Saunders suggest that when Black men raped Black women they benefited from the insouciance of the court or, at the very least, the imposition of sentences that were in line with broader sentencing patterns. As feminist scholars have reminded us, these sentences have frequently served to reinforce male privilege. In this sense, these cases of intra-Black sexual assault were a marked departure from those across the colour line.

This chapter has also shown that Black patriarchal power was not absolute in cases of spousal murder. These Black men were privileged in the sense that the victims – their wives – were obscured and marginalized. Post-mortem examinations placed the bodies of these women victims at the centre of the discourses of these trials, but, because the trials focused on the motives, proclivities, and dispositions of the men who murdered them, the women were barely visible. In these instances, however, race was also on trial and a racial subtext emerged that was a function of *whom* these men had murdered. As we will see in the last two chapters of this book, had they harmed or murdered White women, their victims would certainly not have suffered this kind of invisibility.

The process of rendering Black women invisible revealed a subtle articulation of Black male privilege. These Black men enjoyed a certain power over their spouses, but that power was more tenuous and ambiguous than the power Black men exercised in other kinds of cases. In the trials examined in this chapter, it is evident that there were complementary constructions of Black masculinity at work. Black men were deemed particularly prone to commit acts of violence and, simultaneously, owing to race, mental weakness, or a mixture of the two, unable to control their passions and appreciate the severity of their actions.

4

Tales of a 'Peculiarly Horrible Description': Archetypal Rape Narratives

We still have retained the punishment of death for rape ... We have thought it well ... to continue it on account of the frequency of rape committed by negroes, of whom we have too many in Upper Canada. They are very prone to felonious assaults on white women; if the sentence and imprisonment were not very severe, there would be the great dread of people taking the law into their own hands

– John A. Macdonald, 1868[1]

The Black male rapist and his White female victim is an archetypal image of sexual danger. In reality, these cases were very rare. Indeed, one study found only one such case in York County, Ontario, between the 1880s and the 1930s.[2] Out of all the (non-property) cases mined for this book, only a small fraction – 5 out of 77 or 6.4 per cent – featured the rape, sexual assault, or sex murder of a White woman at the hands of a Black man. These cases are not statistically significant, but, because they embodied the archetype of sexual danger, they attained the status of spectacles and so are important in understanding the widespread anxieties about Black-White sexual contact in Ontario and beyond. The Canadian government's refusal to remove the death penalty from its list of capital offences in 1868 (following the British example) because of the supposed sexual threat Black men posed to the country's White women is a poignant example of the power of this cultural script of sexual danger.[3]

Legal cases involving Black men who allegedly raped White women show the complexity of discourses of blackness and sexual danger. Predictably, some of the cases offer stock characters and narratives: White elites imposing harsh sentences on ruthless Black men convicted for the sexual violation of helpless White women. However, the two capital cases explored in this chapter, which are more richly documented than the others, reveal a more nuanced picture. Although legal officials believed these cases were of a 'peculiarly horrible description,' we can detect ambivalence towards the Black men who committed the deeds. The archetype of sexual danger did not prevent discussions among legal elites of the importance of showcasing British justice and fair play. Nor did these cases preclude the possibility of merciful overtures to the Black men who, lawyers, judges, doctors, and other experts argued, could do little to control their passions. Under the British flag, Black rapists who violated White women were not doomed to get the rope at the hands of an angry mob. If Black rapists of White women were to hang in Canada, it would be courtesy of the state, not lynch law, mob rule, or the vigilante justice of the United States. Negative representations of U.S. race relations served the self-perceptions and interests of Canadian judicial elites and their nation-building ambitions.

Oxentine and Harris

In the fall of 1858, Mary Ann Lawrence, the wife of a Sandwich innkeeper, gave a sworn statement in the crown's case against Daniel Oxentine, a Black male and one of her employees, for the rape of another employee, Isabella Steinhoff. According to Lawrence, one morning Oxentine, Steinhoff, and Lawrence were all present in the Lawrence family home. Lawrence testified that she sent Isabella Steinhoff berry picking with her son John and Daniel Oxentine. Lawrence joined the group a little later and Oxentine left the group shortly after she arrived. After Oxentine's departure, Lawrence, likely wary of the potential sexual danger Oxentine might pose to a young (White) woman, admonished Steinhoff not to go with Oxentine unless his daughters accompanied them. Nonetheless, Lawrence's deposition suggests that what took place between Oxentine and Steinhoff – if anything – may have been consensual.[4] Lawrence testified that, upon the return of the berry pickers at about two o'clock that afternoon, Isabella Steinhoff showed the berries she had gathered to Oxentine and boasted to him that she 'had picked more berries than the rest of them.' Lawrence also said she 'washed the same clothes that Isabella wore ... on that day ... [and] discovered no stains of blood upon them or any other thing which would lead me to believe she had been [assaulted].' In spite of testimony that, at best, might have cleared Oxentine of wrongdoing, or, at the very least, raised questions about the validity of the charge made against him, Oxentine was charged, found guilty, and sentenced to death, the only available sentence for rape at this time.[5]

Far better documentation exists for a similar case that took place in the fall of 1859. A Black man named Levi Harris was charged with assault and attempted rape of Jane Ruttle.[6] In court, Ruttle dramatically reconstructed what occurred between her and Harris during the night of this alleged incident. Levi Harris was cast in the role of the dark, foreboding stranger, while Jane Ruttle, a respectable married woman, took the part of the virtuous White matron.

The case file contains two accounts of the events. The first was presented in a statement of information given to magistrate J.P. Houston on 16 September 1859. Ruttle stated that, while walking with a horse-drawn cart, a coloured man riding a 'Grey Beast' told her 'he would have what he wanted of me.' It was at this moment, testified Ruttle, that Harris got off his horse and started towards her. 'I fell on my knees,' Ruttle informed the magistrate, *'and begged him not to touch me.'*[7] At this point, continued Ruttle, it appeared that Harris was prepared to grant her request. As she turned to her horse, however, she discovered that Harris was coming after her. It was then, testified Ruttle, that she 'let the Horse go and [ran] as fast as I could and he overtook me and seized hold of my hands and I fell and he grabbed hold of me and [took me to] a crop in the road.' At this moment, Ruttle stated, a man (read White man) dramatically came to her rescue. When he asked her what was the matter, she responded *'I was murdered.'*[8] In response, Ruttle's chivalric rescuer 'started in the woods after [Levi Harris].' Ruttle's highly racialized physical sketch of her attacker described an intimidating figure, 'not very large' but 'very dark' and with 'large eyes and large lips. I would know him if I saw him again.' Moreover, perhaps in an effort to dispel any whiff of impropriety surrounding the identity of the man who saved her, she concluded her testimony by saying that she 'did not know him either.'

A little over a week later, Ruttle testified in front of J.P. Houston again. This time she provided an abbreviated but slightly embellished account of the events she had recounted earlier. She also constructed an even more terrifying image of Harris than she did on the first occasion, leaving no doubt that her ordeal embodied the epitome of sexual danger. Ruttle told the court that the indignity she allegedly suffered at Harris's hands was further compounded by the fact Harris had said he was 'very sorry he did not stop my mouth for [I was] a [G.D.] White Bitch.' She added that she was 'almost insensible at the time,' and that she 'had nothing more to say [than what] I gave in the information.'

Indeed, Jane Ruttle did not need to say much more, given the hyperbole surrounding the coverage of the trial in the press. The case, constructed as a spectacle of unparalleled sexual danger, was offered up for Chathamites' consumption. The headline in the 20 September 1859 issue of the *Tri-Weekly Planet* reported: 'A DREADFUL AFFAIR – A RESPECTABLE WOMAN ASSAULTED ON THE HIGHWAY – OUTRAGEOUS TREATMENT – LIFE DESPAIRED OF.' The piece went on to describe this encounter as a 'most shocking outrage' causing 'the greatest state of excitement.' The description of Ruttle was infused with a language of respectability. She was 'the wife of Mr. John Ruttle, a highly respectable farmer of the Township of Chatham.' Harris, predictably, was constructed as the antithesis of respectability, 'a scoundrel,' and 'a colored man ... aged some 21 years, of very dark complexion, low sized and possessing, it is said, a most unprepossessing visage.'[9]

Two additional aspects of this case make it particularly fascinating. First, the accused made a brief statement on his own behalf, and, second, the Black leader Josiah Henson became involved in the proceedings.[10] This case file contains a statement by Harris which is, in effect, an admission of his guilt. When asked whether he wanted to respond to the charge made against him, Harris candidly replied: 'The woman present is the very identical Person that I offered the assault upon. I never saw the woman to my knowledge before that time. I have nothing more to say.'[11] Harris's confession may be explained by Josiah Henson's involvement as one of the witnesses in this trial. Henson's role was quite significant; he informed the court that Harris had compliantly 'delivered himself up to [Henson],' and that he 'committed [Harris] to the gaol.' Extended newspaper coverage of Henson's testimony provides some startling answers to why Henson came to play such a pivotal role in this case.

Henson told the court that, about six days after the alleged assault, he 'knew the boy [Harris] had disappeared from his home.'[12] Henson next saw Harris between ten and eleven at night when Harris appeared at his door asking for something to eat. When Josiah Henson called out 'who's there?' he received no answer, but when he took a few steps from his home the prisoner responded 'it's Levi.' When Henson asked 'What Levi?' the voice said 'Levi Harris. *Father Henson, I came to see if you would give me something to eat.*'[13] Henson agreed and told Harris to enter the house. Locking the door after Harris entered, Henson declared, 'Before I give you something to eat, you are aware that there is a very bad report abroad about you, and before I do that, you know it is the duty of every man who loves his country and freedom to detect any person who might do wrong.' Cloaking himself in the mantle of national duty, the elderly Henson 'at once seized the prisoner' and, enlisting the help of his sons, began 'springing upon the prisoner like a tiger.' After giving Harris his supper, Henson and his sons brought him to the gaol, despite Harris's insistence that he was not guilty of the charge. According to Harris, he 'had met a woman, spoke to her [as] she was walking, driving a horse and cart, and [she] got frightened and ran away.' Moreover, Harris maintained that the only reason he had been hiding in the days following the alleged assault was that many people were 'after him.' In the end, Harris received a sentence of ten years in prison. This sentence was lighter than those the courts meted out for other sexual conflicts across the colour line. Perhaps the perceived valour of Josiah Henson convinced the court to spare Harris an even worse fate. Nonetheless, the sentence was rather stiff given that the charge was attempted rape and that the attempt didn't seem to have gone very far.

Samuel Merriman

The Samuel Merriman rape trial, before the High Court of Justice at the 1885 Essex spring assizes, also fits an archetypal narrative of sexual danger. Belle D., a fourteen-year-old White girl, testified that she and a nineteen-year-old male companion named Joseph M., with whom she was 'just taking a walk,' were surprised by 'two colored men.' Belle D. testified that the men 'came up and [said they] would shoot me.' She was certain of the danger they posed, she added, because one of these men 'had a revolver – I knew it because I saw it.'

Contrary to contemporary dominant codes of White male chivalry, Belle D.'s companion 'ran away,' leaving her alone at the mercy of her two attackers. In graphic detail, Belle D. gave her version of what then occurred, prompting the London *Advertiser* to describe Samuel Merriman as a 'brutal offender.'[14] Belle D. told the court that 'the prisoner held me by the back of the neck [and] held a revolver to my face ... I did not holler or make a noise ... I was too much afraid[.] I said to him for god sake let us go.' Merriman then 'threw me down [and] he pulled my legs open and the other man held the revolver to my face. I tried to keep my legs shut,' she added, but Merriman 'tore my drawers and then got on top of me[.] I didn't see his naked person I was lying on my back ... [and] I was fighting all the time.'

Belle D. further stated that the 'other man' also violated her and they told her they would 'get [Joseph M.].' When Belle D.'s companion did reappear, she tearfully told him what happened. When she returned home, she told her mother, Delila M., who testified that Belle was crying and appeared 'pale and weak.' Delila M. brought her daughter to see the chief of police that night and both adults were certain that Merriman was one of the men involved. Delila M. testified that, when a police sergeant came to her home with Merriman in tow, she told her daughter, 'Come into the sitting room.' Upon entering the room, Belle D. 'drew back' and said 'that is the man.'

The police sergeant testified that he 'knew the prisoner' and arrested him around half past twelve on the night of the alleged incident. Upon arriving at Delila M.'s home, the sergeant informed her that he 'wanted to see the daughter.' Belle D. 'appeared frightened' but nonetheless appeared to be 'very confident' in describing her first attacker. She also mentioned that he wore a 'red handkerchief that came to his chin.' The evidence is incomplete, but it appears that at the time of his arrest, Merriman may have had a red handkerchief concealed beneath his shirt. The next day, Delila M. brought Belle D. to a doctor who concluded that '[Belle D.'s] private parts had been penetrated and the hymen was ruptured.'

At the trial, Belle D.'s testimony did not go unchallenged. She was pressed particularly hard with regard to whether she could be certain that she had correctly identified her attackers. She told the court that she 'saw the prisoner ... in the store a week before at my corner,' and further, that although she did not know his name she 'knew him by sight ... [as] I said at the other court. I had seen him before but not sure how many times.'

Ultimately, however, it was the use of strong racial rhetoric that made Belle D.'s testimony quite difficult to challenge. For example, Belle D. told the court that she was certain that Merriman was the man who attacked her first not only because she 'knew him by sight,' but also because she 'saw him a week before beating a white woman.' Belle D. also told the chief of police that 'a nigger had done something to me – I said two niggers I never saw the other man before I saw [the] two niger [*sic*] in gaol.'

Joseph M. told the court that he was sure he had 'looked in their face' and thus was certain that one of the prisoners was one of the men. He further testified that he 'had no doubt' as to the identity of the prisoner when he later saw him in court in Windsor. But, when pressed under cross-examination, he admitted, like Belle D., that 'it was very dark' and that there was 'no moon' that night. Joseph M. also admitted that he could not be entirely sure if the two men who stood accused were the ones who assaulted his female companion because he 'didn't know the prisoner before and there are lots the same color.'[15]

Race was aggressively expressed in the press coverage of this case, which conveyed a sense of revulsion that was no doubt shared by most of Windsor's Whites. Curiously, at first readers were given no indication that this was not an 'ordinary' rape case. The accused man's race had not been revealed when the *Advertiser* announced Samuel Merriman's trial. On 9 April, however, the full details of the case became clear in a short but revealing description. The *Advertiser* reported that Merriman 'outraged' Belle D., who was described as a 'poor girl,' with the 'assistance of another colored man ... who in turn outraged [Belle D.] with the assistance of the prisoner.' The *Advertiser* told its readers that Merriman was 'a person with more the appearance of an animal than a man.' Hence, in the view of the *Advertiser*, it was only fitting that Merriman, being a 'brutal offender,' should receive a stiff penalty for his deed.

Such sentiments might help to explain why Belle D.'s character was never questioned during the trial. No one seemed troubled by the credibility of the testimony of a young unmarried woman who kept the company of young men at night, a scenario that certainly harmed more than one White woman's charge of rape against a White man.[16] Moreover, the doctor's examination results – that is, the evidence of bruised and bloody genitals as well as a ruptured hymen – could have well been the result of a sexual encounter with Joseph M. rather than sexual assault. At the very least, this is a point that likely would have been raised had the defendants been White.[17]

The defence did not challenge Belle D.'s story. What might have prevented it from doing so? We have, admittedly, only the limited evidence of a judge's bench book with which to form a reply. But it does appear that the defence chose to argue that this was a case of mistaken identity, perhaps because the case's stock characters, two animalistic and highly sexed Black men, were simply too compelling to suggest the crime had never taken place at all. The defence's strategy was to maintain that the wrong two Black men were on trial. It suggested that Black faces and bodies all look the same when concealed by the dark – a point that the defence even managed to get Joseph M. to concede. Hence, this strategy was used as attempt to exonerate Merriman and his accomplice without necessarily invalidating dominant fears of Black male sexual danger. In the end, Merriman was sentenced to twenty years in the provincial penitentiary. His use of a gun, no doubt, played a role in the severity of the sentence; but so too did the race of his victim.[18]

Frank Roughmond

A generation later, in the spring of 1909, hundreds packed the Stratford courtroom to see Frank Roughmond, yet another Black suspect who was dubbed a 'negro tramp,' tried for the rape and murder of Mary Peake, the elderly wife of a local farmer, for which he was found guilty. The Stratford *Daily Herald* dramatically reported that 'it seemed as if half the countryside had come into the city so dense was the crowd in the vicinity of the court house.' The *Herald* placed the story on the front page, along with a dark and blurry picture of Frank Roughmond. A detailed account of the trial was provided for the city's residents; even Roughmond's arraignment hearing was served up as the stuff of high drama for Stratford readers.[19]

The hyperbole of the newspaper reports contrasted with the dry legal formalism of the prose that jurists employed to summarize the case. Even they, however, could barely conceal their contempt for the accused. In a departure from the formulaic legalese that typified case summaries, they noted: 'This is a case of murder of a peculiarly horrible description as it was combined with rape, the prisoner being a negro.' What made the crime 'peculiarly horrible' was that it was a story of sexual violence and murder across the colour line, the archetype of sexual danger.

On the day of the murder, Roughmond was discharged from the Stratford gaol after serving a sentence for using 'obscene language.' A 'strolling vagabond living on his wits as a fortune teller and palmist,' Roughmond wandered throughout Stratford during that morning. After being refused a drink at a local bar for lack of funds, Roughmond later managed to procure a beer and gin at another bar called the Queens. Shortly after, he was spotted on the edge of town heading west, wearing a 'policeman's overcoat' he had apparently stolen from the Police Court while the chief of police was at dinner. Meanwhile, Mary Peake was alone in her house on the Peake farm, about two and a half miles west of Stratford, where she was busily engaged in her domestic duties. Her sons, John and George, had been placed in charge of the farm by their father, William Peake, who left early that morning. John broke his pitchfork in the field and went home to repair it.

When he entered his home, 'it occurred to him to go down to the cellar and get a drink of cider.' As he arrived about 'half way down the cellar,' he 'saw a negro, the prisoner, lying on his back close to the stairs and another figure further over.' He called out to his brother, who left the scene to report the crime to the police.

Robert Fuller, a neighbour, later testified at Roughmond's trial that he was responsible for the 'hunting and securing' of Roughmond aided by several others who lived nearby. They tied Roughmond's hands and guarded him until the police arrived. In the interim, however, a lynch mob began to take shape. Fuller had allegedly sent some of the men to check on Mary Peake, and when they reported that she was dead, Fuller angrily told Roughmond that 'they ought to put a rope around his neck.' Terrified, Roughmond responded to the mob's outrage by employing a strategy that he would use, albeit unsuccessfully, throughout the various stages of this case. Pleading for his life, Roughmond beseeched the mob to recognize his humanity. Imploring them to live up to the dominant rhetoric of British justice, Roughmond told his would-be lynchers that he, like them, was a Canadian, born in the Gaspé, and, further, that 'we [have] a law in this country and a King.' When the police arrived, Roughmond was promptly arrested and spared the mob's wrath.

On the next day, two doctors, Dr D.B. Frasier and Dr David Smith, conducted the post-mortem examination of Mary Peake. They found she had been 'ravished before death' and they found 'marks of violence' on her body which seemed to indicate that 'her mouth had been held forcibly closed, to prevent her from screaming.' They also found abrasions on the nose and cheek; a deep wound in the centre of the upper lip; a jagged wound on the lower lip; a tooth broken; a mark on the chin as if made by teeth or something sharp; bruises on the neck; face covered with blood; and blood from mouth and nose. In addition, the doctors were of the opinion that Mary Peake's death had 'resulted from the shock' of seeing a 'negro' – an assessment that reveals much about the racial attitudes that permeated this community.[20]

A panoply of adjectives was used to draw explicit links between blackness and Black masculinity and savagery. Words like 'husky brute,' 'big negro,' 'burly negro,' and 'inhumane monster' were frequently used to describe Roughmond.[21] Another similarly compelling example of the power of racial rhetoric was the testimony of Dr David Smith, one of doctors who examined Roughmond in the gaol and who also participated in the post-mortem examination. The general consensus was that, while the victim's 'weak heart' made her particularly vulnerable to illness, her medical condition was exacerbated by the mere sight of Roughmond. Significantly, J.J. Coughlin, the defence attorney, argued that Peake died before she was ever touched by Roughmond. His substantive defence was that, upon seeing Roughmond, she died 'of shock.' If Mary Peake died of 'shock,' according to this line of reasoning, Roughmond's mere presence provoked sheer terror. Mary's 'look' at a Black male was the catalyst that triggered the events which led to her death; this look had such a deleterious effect on the body that it was akin to physical violence. Indeed, only in conjunction with the shock triggered by the sight of Roughmond were Peake's injuries considered serious enough to actually kill her:

Q: Would you agree, I suppose, Doctor, the cause of death was shock?
A: Yes sir.
Q: And you would agree with Doctor Fraser in the statement she had a diseased heart?
A: Yes, we found that.
Q: And you attribute the diseased condition of her heart as being the cause why the shock which she sustained killed her?
A: Partly so, yes.
HIS LORDSHIP [Justice W.R. Riddell]: Take an old woman of her years and the condition of health she appeared to be in and taking these physical injuries that you saw – were those physical injuries likely to produce in such a woman – even if she did not have a weak heart – were they likely to cause death?
A: I think so under the circumstances.
HIS LORDSHIP: That is usually the test.
MR. COUGHLIN: What do you mean by the circumstances, Doctor?
A: I mean by that that the presence of a man as we have heard evidence given, with the fright associated with it.
Q: The presence of an evil looking man?
A: Yes, sir.

Q: A negro?
A: Yes, sir.
Q: You think that she, not being accustomed to the sight of negroes, would naturally be frightened?
A: Yes.
Q: Particularly on finding him in a cellar there?
A: Yes.
Q: And it is taking all these things into account you think it would be natural for an old lady to receive such a shock?
A: I do.
Q: From that and the physical injuries – these were not such as likely to lead to death?
A: The physical injuries were such as to produce excruciating pain and that pain is one cause of shock and there might be pain enough there be the physical injuries that we found to produce shock enough to cause death.

Coughlin continued this strategy in his cross-examination of the coroner, Dr Joseph Dunsmore Monteith. In his direct testimony, Monteith had emphasized the importance of physical evidence at the scene of the murder, such as bloodstains, bruises, and marks, the kinds of things that had been 'described by medical men which were apparent to the eye.' Coughlin attempted to counter by re-emphasizing that there was another explanation for the victim's death:

Q: You would attribute the cause of death in this case to shock, I understand, Doctor?
A: Well, yes, shock was the cause of death.
Q: A shock which might have been produced by fright?
A: Well, judging from the evidence that I have heard the medical men give, I would come to the conclusion that death would be the result of shock from the two causes, physical and mental.
Q: The mental cause being fright?
A: The mental cause being fright.
HIS LORDSHIP: And the physical injuries you have heard described were not such as in themselves would naturally cause death – for instance the indentations – the bruising of the lip that you have heard described by the Doctors are not such as in themselves would cause death?
A: Not such as we generally would expect would cause death, but what might cause it under certain conditions.

Q: You say they might under certain conditions, but you do not look for them –?
A: Under ordinary conditions we would not expect the evidences as shown on the body from physical violence to be liable to cause death, under ordinary conditions.
Q: How do you explain that in this particular case that they do have some bearing in your opinion, in causing death?
A: The circumstances surrounding the case, the conditions that would be present at the time that the physical violence was expended, creating –
Q: Particularly with the diseased condition of the heart?
A: Well, more susceptible, although at the same time the conditions were present, that the deceased was exposed to, might also cause death even if the heart had been normal.
Q: I suppose one of the conditions would be the appearance of a man of a Black race?
A: Yes.
Q: A thing which is apt to frighten a woman? [*sic*] confronted in a place like the cellar?
A: Yes, fright.
Q: And the prisoner here is not a good looking man, even for a negro – that would be something more?
A: That would likely have some factor in causing fright – it would be a factor in causing fright.

This kind of stark and overtly racialist discourse was juxtaposed with other kinds of language, such as medical language, which also pointed to the complex web of racial feeling that characterized the Roughmond case. The judge's charge was expressed in the rhetoric of British justice, with traces of White paternalism, and a disquieting White male (homo)eroticization of the Black male body. After congratulating defence counsel Coughlin for skilfully and ably defending Roughmond on such short notice (Coughlin had only one day to prepare), Justice Riddell also addressed the jury directly, stating that in his view, the office of the 'common juryman' was the 'highest office' which a 'British freeman' (read White) could occupy. Turning his thoughts towards Roughmond, the judge delivered a lengthy discourse on the tradition of British fair play:

[Frank Roughmond] is not of our race. That is no fault of his. Whether it be a misfortune it may be a matter of opinion. His people were not brought here at their own instance or desire. His ancestors were forced from their native home, brought here to this land, no doubt against their will. He is not to blame ... he and I and you and I have this satisfaction that the colored man, the negro has precisely the same rights in a British, a Canadian Court of Justice that the purest blooded white man could have. He must receive fair play and you must give this man in the dock precisely the same even handed justice which you give to the wealthiest and purest blooded white man in the nation, but no more ... You must cast aside from your minds any prejudice or feeling which you may personally have against this prisoner or his race.

While this rhetoric of British justice and fairness ostensibly gestured towards the ideal of equal treatment under the law, Riddell's invocation of a member of the respectable citizenry also served to emphasize Roughmond's 'Otherness,' and just how far he was located from this ideal.

An underlying White paternalism undergirded these high-minded notions of British justice, though, significantly, the judge also cautioned the jury against letting their pity for the 'unfortunate' Roughmond cloud their judgment: 'You will also, cast out of your minds at the same time any feeling of sympathy or pity for a man placed in his position which this unfortunate Black man is placed, unfortunate he is, be he guilty or innocent. There is no place in the jurybox, no room in the juror's oath for pity.'[22]

Paternalism was an important element of Riddell's attitude towards Blacks. Scholars have noted that Riddell, a self-styled expert on Black Canadian history, fancied himself a progressive when it came to his racial attitudes. Riddell took great pride in the accomplishments of the White abolitionists who had worked to free Blacks from slavery in Canada. He also believed that Blacks had been particularly in need of Whites' largesse because they were distinctly inferior, 'incompetent,' and 'uncivilised.'[23]

Riddell's views about Blacks also contained the powerful dominant sexual mythologies of the day, which stressed the abnormally large sexual appetites of Black men. His attitudes offer an example of the eroticization of Black males. Consider Riddell's instruction to the jurors that they 'consider the facts of this case as they now appear.' These 'facts,' as Riddell saw them, included the essential truth that Roughmond was a Black man who had been imprisoned for about twenty days and thus 'had been deprived of any sexual gratification with the opposite sex.' Riddell also instructed the jury to 'ask yourselves if he is not a strong lustful looking man ... a strong lusty young negro, just out of jail, found with an old woman who had been raped.' This, combined with the fact that Roughmond's glasses and knife were found lying near the victim, was evidence that simply could not be overlooked, particularly by 'honest men with a strong sense of duty.'

The jury deliberated quickly and delivered a guilty verdict, after which Roughmond vehemently professed his innocence.[24] As Riddell passed Roughmond's death sentence, he told the prisoner: 'You were quite right, whether you were Canadian or not, to say, that in this Canada of ours we are governed by a King and a law which is higher than the King himself.' The judge also added that Roughmond was correct in suggesting that 'no man had a right to put a rope around your neck unless and until you had been found guilty in the regular administration of the law. I am glad,' Riddell continued, 'that my people, my Canadian people had that self restraint which is characteristic, I think, of our people.' Riddell told Roughmond that his case was a 'great object lesson to other peoples by whom your people are less humanely treated.' In conclusion, said Riddell, 'you differ from most of us in blood, in race, but no man can say that you have not had a fair trial.'[25]

Riddell was alluding, of course, to the United States and lynch mobs. The lynching of Black men for real or imagined transgressions against White women in the American South was offered by Justice Riddell as a powerful cultural script against which to affirm the more humane nature of British justice and Canada's national character. Yet its unchallenged assumptions are flawed for two reasons. First, as Martha Hodes has argued, in the antebellum South, lynch mobs for Black male sexual transgressions of this nature were rare. Class boundaries among Whites meant that dominant ideas about the dissolute sexual mores of poor White women could mitigate the criminal responsibility of accused Black rapists. Also, the fact that most Black men in the antebellum era were property 'meant that white Southerners had a stake in protecting their human chattel from extreme violence or murder.' Black men who committed (or were accused of) sexual indiscretions against White women did not necessarily fall victim to mob violence, nor did they necessarily receive the death penalty in the post-bellum South. Lisa Linquist Dorr's study of twentieth-century Virginia rape cases suggests that, when Black men were accused of sex crimes against White women, various factors were at play and different outcomes were thus produced. Indeed, Dorr found that White Virginians were reluctant to impose the death penalty in most of these cases and that three-quarters of the Black men accused of rape were neither lynched nor executed. Race, gender, and class, argues Dorr, worked in concert to produce complex results, and, often, White men 'counteracted segregation's tendency to assert race over gender by occasionally uniting with Black men and shoring up masculine privilege.'[26]

Roughmond was sentenced to be hanged on 28 June 1900. His only chance of escaping the penalty of death was to employ a reference made during the trial that he may have been 'weak minded' at the time that he committed the crime. On two separate occasions, two alienists, Dr C.K. Clarke and Dr Bruce Smith, went to visit Roughmond as he awaited execution. They prepared reports for Justice Riddell, apparently to determine his mental state when he committed his crime. These psychiatric assessments of Roughmond are fascinating textual artifacts which illustrate early-twentieth-century eugenicist theories of racial hierarchy and racial discourses concerning the diminished and unstable character of Blacks.[27]

The first report, a curious mix of biographical sketch, psychiatric (and corporeal) assessment, and socio-legal commentary, was written on 7 May 1909 and outlined the details of the initial visit. Here, Roughmond is described in somewhat contradictory terms, both as a 'well developed negro, apparently in the very best of physical health,' with normal eyes and 'no hallucinations nor does he show many of the ear marks of mental disease,' and, conversely, as having a high palate 'with a marked central torus' and decayed teeth. The authors of the report added that Roughmond 'received us in an affable way and was anxious to give us any information that we desired.'

These alienists were also very interested in Roughmond's personal history. He informed them that he was born in 1875 in the Gaspé, received a 'fair' education between the ages of eight and twelve, and then 'farmed at home until he was 16 years of age.' Like many of his Black male contemporaries in Canada, he worked as a porter on the railroads and in hotels, and still later he hunted and fished to support himself. Roughmond's 'excuse' for leaving the railway was apparently 'the development of rheumatism.' As he wanted to avoid the discomfort of railway work, hunting 'moose caribou ... for himself not others' was how Roughmond supported himself, and he led a solitary life. Roughmond also supported himself by telling fortunes. He apparently believed that his ability to 'gull the public,' as the doctor's report put it, was the 'genuine thing' and an 'unusual gift.'

The tone of the alienists' report betrayed their contempt for Roughmond. However, references to the prisoner's sexual history showed none of the charged quality that was evident during the trial. His examiners merely noted that Roughmond 'had not been irregular in his sexual life.' They ended their report on the 'affable' subject/object of their inquiry by stating that the prisoner was 'nothing more than a man of low type who is somewhat addicted to the use of alcohol, and who belongs to the very large class of tramps found wandering about the country.'

By contrast, the narrative of the alienists' second visit, on 26 May 1908, showed little trace of the 'affable Negro' of the first account. The depiction of Roughmond that appeared in this text much more closely resembled the portrait that appeared in newspaper accounts of his trial: that of a dangerous 'negro.' The alienists reported that during the second examination 'it came out that he was not at all truthful, and when closely questioned admitted that he had not told us the whole truth at the first examination.'[28] For example, Roughmond's inquisitors stated that he denied that he had ever been a porter on the railway. Moreover, they now portrayed him as 'a shiftless character all his life, and no doubt has done considerable tramping.'

In the second examination, Roughmond also spoke out about his treatment in court, eloquently enough that Clarke and Smith agreed that he did so 'intelligently.' Roughmond complained about not having been 'allowed to go into the witness box' or make clear that 'some of the evidence had been manufactured.' Alluding to the inadequacy of his legal representation, Roughmond stated further that 'his trial must have been convincing to any jury, as the evidence was put in such a way that there was little or no chance for him.'

Perhaps with his death imminent, this insolent and less deferential Roughmond was prompted now to speak so freely. The absence of the acquiescent, affable Sambo-like figure from the alienists' second report might also explain their hardened attitude towards Roughmond, whom they portrayed in unflattering and starkly racialist language. 'We believe,' concluded the report, *'that he conforms to the ordinary type of common negro, and is probably a man of brutal instincts; he is also superstitious and ignorant.'*[29] This dominant racial trope of the 'ordinary common negro' with 'brutal instincts' ultimately sealed Roughmond's fate, thereby extinguishing any faint hope he had of escaping death. Government officials decided to go ahead with the scheduled execution on 28 June.

William McCathern

The central protagonists and themes in the case of Alice McColl and William McCathern in Chatham, Ontario, in the 1920s bear some striking similarities to those in the Roughmond case. Like Roughmond, McCathern was arrested for the rape of a well-known and respected elderly White woman. Both cases were widely reported, and both provided a microcosm of early-twentieth-century notions of illicit Black-White sexual contact and conflict. In both cases, White paternalistic impulses rested alongside racialized deployments of race, class, sexuality, and gender. There were also important differences: Roughmond was charged with both rape and murder whereas McCathern was charged with rape. This had an influence in the outcome of the McCathern case and was the single most important factor in the commutation of William McCathern's sentence: by 1920, the practice of meting out the death penalty for rape (as opposed to murder or rape coupled with murder, as was the charge in Roughmond's case) had long ceased. In addition, as we shall see, racialized images of the Black brute or sexual predator worked in McCathern's favour.

The chain of events that led up to McCathern's arrest and the subsequent drama that unfolded in the courtroom was particularly unsettling to contemporary observers. On the night of 29 October 1926, Alice McColl retired to bed at around nine or ten o'clock. A restless sleeper, McColl as usual had a hard time falling asleep that night. Awaking at approximately two o'clock in the morning, she left her room and then returned. She then turned out the light and tried to go back to sleep. McColl barely got settled when she heard a 'terrible noise' in the bathroom – the sound of 'something heavy falling.'

She turned on the light and opened the bathroom door; standing there, testified Alice McColl, was William McCathern, rifle in hand. Pointing the gun at McColl, McCathern marched her from her bedroom, through the dining room, and into the kitchen, at which point McColl called out to her sisters for help. Angered by this, McCathern struck his victim, and proceeded to 'outrage' her. McColl testified that she was beaten for the better part of an hour and then choked until unconscious. She was then dragged back through the dining room and into her bedroom and hoisted onto her bed where, once again, McCathern allegedly attempted to 'outrage' her. He then turned out the bedroom light and began to rifle through McColl's bureau drawer, giving Alice McColl the chance she needed to escape. She ran to the front door, unlocked it, and ran across her wet lawn, eventually reaching a neighbour's house. Finding no response there, or at the next house, McColl kept moving down the street until a neighbour heard her cries of distress and took her in. There she was able to recover under the care of a doctor and a nurse for three or four days. The next time McColl laid eyes on William McCathern, he was in the Chatham jail, where police asked her to identify him as he stood amidst three other prisoners, one Black and two White.

Once the theatre of conflict shifted to the courtroom, the trial became a microcosm of the sexual anxieties that lay just below the surface of Black-White social relations in early-twentieth-century Chatham. These anxieties reflected the dominant culture's views of the insatiable sexual desires of Black men and the predatory nature of Black masculinity/ sexuality. McCathern's location as a poor, itinerant, unskilled worker also placed him at a grave disadvantage. By contrast, neither the character of the victim nor her mental competency were on trial. Neither, for that matter, was McCathern's guilt or innocence; his guilt, it seems, was never questioned. What was on trial instead was McCathern's morality and, perhaps most important, his very humanity.

The fact that Alice McColl was a respectable citizen of Chatham helped the crown mount an effective prosecution. All nine witnesses called to testify in the trial, including McCathern's own brother, were called by the prosecution. Conversely, William McCathern's defence was almost wholly inadequate. His attorney, V.T. Foley, was hastily procured only a day before the trial with the help of a sympathetic local Black minister. Moreover, Foley's relative unfamiliarity with the particulars of the case, his decision not to put McCathern on the stand, and his unwillingness to cross-examine the prosecution's key witness – Alice McColl – meant that McCathern had little hope of being acquitted.

Notwithstanding the considerable amount of testimony from prosecution witnesses and the fair amount of physical evidence against him (though much of the evidence that was presented was also circumstantial), McCathern's fate was influenced by the prosecution's ability to tap into the contemporary fear and loathing of interracial sex and sexual violence, as well as dominant notions of Black sexuality. Like its American counterpart, White middle-class Canadian society adhered to the view that any form of Black-White sexual contact was inherently repulsive and inherently taboo. Throughout McCathern's trial, he was constructed as the classic 'Black brute' – a licentious, subhuman, libidinous creature who showed little regard for human life, a sexual predator, and a threat to the weak and helpless. In addition, the prosecution was able to conjure up the powerful imagery of the Black male's insatiable craving for White women. Prosecuting attorney Hugh J. Macdonald's carefully chosen words – for example, 'a more horrible case of rape could hardly be conceived' – played upon racialized imagery, as did his assertion that, as far as he was concerned, 'if there was a case in which the extreme penalty for a crime of this kind could well be imposed ... it is this case.'[30] The jury evidently concurred with the prosecution's construction of McCathern; perhaps this is most clearly indicated by the fact that it took them only nine minutes to reach a guilty verdict, an astonishingly short period.

Rape cases often were characterized by sentiments of outrage and revulsion. One example is the infamous 1926 St Catharines rape case of four White men: Frank De Young, Richard Darling, Walter G. Liddiard, and John Robert Gough. This was a case that McCathern's attorney knew well. In almost every respect (save for the intersection of race and sex, and the outcome), it was similar to the McCathern affair. The men were all convicted of the brutal gang rape of a young White woman. The presiding judge at this trial acknowledged that the crime was 'about as horrible a crime of rape as could be committed.' Yet he had decided 'not to impose the longest term that the law permits.' Interestingly, the judge found it difficult to satisfy himself that he was 'not doing something a little weak in refraining from passing a sentence of imprisonment for life.' The death penalty, then, was not even a consideration. Nevertheless, none of the defendants received a penalty nearly as harsh as that meted out to McCathern. De Young, Darling, and Liddiard each received fifteen years apiece while Gough was handed a sentence of ten years.[31] The appellate court later added twenty lashes to the sentences of the first three at the behest of the attorney general, who 'hardly expected' the death penalty to be passed in this case but felt that the sentences were not sufficiently harsh.[32]

In the McCathern trial, Justice Fisher told the jury that British justice mattered more than race, yet his assertion highlighted race. He informed the court that, although McCathern is 'coloured[,] it [makes] no difference in the administration of justice [because] ... a British court recognises neither colour nor creed. He has had a fair trial; it makes no difference who he is or *what he is*.'[33] The words 'what he is' implicitly called McCathern's humanity into question, situating him in the realm of the subhuman. Furthermore, the judge prefaced his sentencing decision by praising the 'law abiding citizens of Chatham for their *restraint'*[34] in not tearing McCathern from the 'strong arm of the law' and burning him alive. 'Thank God,' Fisher went on to add, that 'in this country there is no law for, or practice of permitting the disposal of any crime, no matter how serious by mob violence, lynching, or burning at the stake.'[35]

The language of mob violence, burning at the stake, and lynching illustrates how racial imagery and the positioning of bodies was constructed in juridical discourse. Justice Fisher's reference to lynching was no coincidence, but part of a discernible pattern (evident in the Roughmond trial and many others) by which White Canadians engaged in the pornographic display of southern U.S. lynching rituals. As Grace Hale has noted, in the United States there was a ceremonial element to the spectacle of the lynching of Black men. This helped to create a sense of shared identity, a means through which to 'make whiteness' among White witnesses.[36] As we have seen, White Canadians were well aware of the frequency of these practices south of the border. Moreover, as the indignant tone of Fisher's remarks suggests, they used it to assert their moral superiority twice over, as Whites and as Canadians. They smugly believed that they were more tolerant of Blacks – even transgressors like McCathern – than Americans.[37]

Fisher called McCathern's conduct 'diabolical' and 'fiendish' and said that the punishment had to fit the extreme nature of the crime. Despite the recent occurrence of similar crimes committed by Whites, Fisher insisted that he 'never heard of a more extreme case that the one [McCathern] had been found guilty of, and he could not imagine one.' However, the construction of McCathern as a morally degenerate and irredeemably savage brute was most clearly evident in Fisher's statement that McCathern's 'fiendish and murderous conduct stamped him as a libertine and outlaw from Christian civilization.' He then gave McCathern the harshest penalty allowable under the law for the crime of rape. It reflected the court's chivalrous desire to protect the province's girls and women from harm. McCathern was sentenced to death. This sentence was extraordinarily harsh, and in the 1920s it clearly flew in the face of judicial convention, but the death penalty for rape was technically still allowable under the law and remained so until 1954.[38]

Reconfiguring Black Masculinity

William McCathern's sentence was appealed on the basis of the harshness of his sentence, an argument that Roughmond, a convicted murderer whom the experts had deemed sane, could not make. In addition to compelling legal grounds for appeal, it is clear that social factors also provided ammunition for McCathern's appeal, that is, the racialized image of the 'libertine' or 'brute' that shaped the McCathern rape trial. However, this is not to suggest that racial representation was static or immutable. Indeed, in large measure it was another portrayal of McCathern that enabled him to escape the gallows. A contesting image emerges in McCathern's appeal to the appellate court. It is not that the idea of brutishness disappears, but more that it is tempered or mollified by a different image, also driven by very specific racialist assumptions and racial representations of blackness. It illustrates that the constitution of colonized subjects was characterized by ambivalence. The image that spared McCathern's life and mollified his initial association with an image of unequivocal savagery was that of a poor unfortunate creature or stupid animal – innately brutish but also the victim of a harsh environment. Hence, McCathern was to be regarded not only as a brute but as an almost infantile object of pity. This played an important role in his sentence being reduced to twenty years and twenty lashes.

William McCathern's precarious position as a Black labourer placed him at a disadvantage in the trial. Yet it allowed for the construction of an alternative image which saved his life. Ten signed affidavits from various individuals were presented to the appellate court on McCathern's behalf. Three members of McCathern's family, his mother, father, and younger brother, gave statements in support of clemency.[39] Six Whites also gave statements in support of a reduced sentence for McCathern: two doctors, a clergyman, two farmers (both of whom were former employers of McCathern), and a labourer who was one of McCathern's associates. The local Black clergyman who earlier secured McCathern's legal counsel also gave a statement to the court.

From the narratives constructed in the affidavits it is clear that McCathern's life was the epitome of a marginal existence. His mother testified that, after having served in the Canadian Army in France during the First World War, her son returned to Canada to find that the only occupation he could get was 'that of a labourer doing such odd jobs as is possible for a man such as him to procure.'[40] Similarly, George Yott, a Chatham farmer, stated that he 'knew [McCathern] to be an illiterate man who has apparently not had any educational advantages, religious or otherwise.' Yott also commented on the harsh reality of Chatham's racially stratified labour market, saying that McCathern's occupation was 'that of a day labourer doing such jobs as was possible for a coloured man to [do] in this community.' Dr James Walter Coulter agreed, stating that in his view there was a 'notable absence of opportunity for the people of the coloured race in this community.'[41]

Another revelation that came out of the affidavits and contributed to McCathern's mollified image was his addiction to an intoxicant called 'canned heat' (a form of alcohol). Several of the affidavits presented to the court mentioned McCathern's addiction to alcohol and its effect on his mental state both well in advance of and during his commission of the crime.

Coulter's statement best illustrates how even medical evidence was instrumental in McCathern's construction of an alternate image for the purpose of the appeal. It was still wrapped in the same racialist imagery that infused the trial. Coulter attributed much of McCathern's behaviour to his alcoholism and harsh environment. However, he also argued that these external factors explained McCathern's innate nature: 'The moral and social deviations, and the level to which an alcoholic sinks, depend on [his] original mental make up and environment. When individuals who are by nature crude and ethically defective have their inhibitions removed by deadly alcohol, such as "Canned Heat," the underlying criminalistic tendencies and brutality appear in aggravated form. Thus, weaklings and mental deficients naturally succumb most rapidly to pernicious and atrocious influences.'[42] This testimony had a huge impact on the decision of the appellate court. It was effective in large measure precisely because it did not challenge, undercut, or disrupt dominant discourses of blackness.

Also notable in the affidavits presented to the court were arguments citing the importance of recent legal precedent and the issue of racial discrimination. One affidavit, in particular, presented on behalf of McCathern's father, alluded to the 1926 rape case in St Catharines, pointing out that the sentences meted out to those White defendants were far more lenient than that meted out to McCathern. William McCathern, Sr's affidavit expressed the opinion that 'naturally ... the ends of justice would have been satisfied if my son had received the same penalty that the prisoners in the aforementioned cases received, or in any event punishment proportionately in accordance with the comparison of the evidence in my son's case, and said cases.'[43] This injunction, couched in common-sense terms and calling for the equitable deployment of legal punishments for equal crimes, was a strategy that challenged the lofty ideal of colour-blind British justice.

William McCathern, Sr's affidavit also more overtly blamed White supremacy for his son's harsh sentence. He did not want the court to feel that he was suggesting that because his son was 'of the coloured' race that this was 'taken into consideration.' The carefully worded nature of this passage in the affidavit employed a rhetorical tactic that made a reappearance in a subsequent passage. Both passages dealt with the underlying discrimination that informed McCathern's sentence by gesturing to race while still, in effect, dancing around it – thereby posing no threat to the dominant rhetoric on the impartiality of British law.

In commuting the sentence to twenty years and twenty lashes, the appellate court relied on several points related to the procedural imperatives of British justice and to White paternalism. Reflecting a desire to uphold the imperatives of due process and legal precedent, the court ruled that the death penalty in this case was 'manifestly excessive, having regard to the evidence,' and, moreover, 'manifestly excessive having regard to the punishment imposed for similar crimes in this Province, and does not tend towards the standardization of sentences as is the policy of the law.' In addition, the appellate court ruled that the trial judge was remiss in neglecting to exercise 'judicial discretion, having regard to the evidence,' and had not inflicted punishment 'commensurate with the offence and all the circumstances of the case.' Indeed, it was the view of the court that 'in similar recent Ontario cases' the punishment had been imprisonment, on evidence more revolting than the evidence in this case. The court also concluded that the fact that McCathern did not testify was important. If he had, reasoned the court, the jury might have found that McCathern was 'guilty only of an attempt to commit the crime charged.'[44]

Paternalistic portrayals of McCathern based on phenotype and environment also played a prominent role in the court's decision. Thus, McCathern's war record, the 'absence of moral and religious training' in his upbringing, his 'general home environment,' his condition of mind at the time of the commission of the crime resulting from the use of intoxicants and poisons, and, lastly, the cumulative effect of the use of these intoxicants and poisons over a prolonged period of time were considered to be important factors.[45]

Two of Chatham's more prominent crown attorneys were incensed at the appellate court's decision to reduce McCathern's sentence. A memo from the deputy attorney general to the attorney general perhaps best explains the appellate court's decision. Paternalistic legal officials explained McCathern's pathology as the product of both environmental and biological/racial determinants. This saved McCathern from death.

The deputy attorney general wrote: 'They will do what they will do quite irrespective of any special material and [the] question which will present itself to them to my mind will be whether this particular class of offence should be punished by death and if so whether a low class negro is a good subject to begin with when men of whom much better might have been expected have not been sentenced so drastically.'[46]

As even the deputy attorney general (unwittingly) recognized, there is, at best, only an ambiguous line of demarcation between the construction of Black brutishness and Black infantilism. The prosecution and the defence shared common assumptions about McCathern's humanity or lack thereof. Both felt that McCathern was essentially a 'low class Negro.' Measured against a constructed and reified notion of White male respectability, 'men of whom much better might have been expected,' McCathern's war record was thus more than evidence of his service to the state; it was also an indication that even a man like him could aspire to transcend his lowly station and behave in accordance with the expectations of respectable manhood.

Conclusion

The cases explored in this chapter epitomize the dominant culture's worst fears about the sexual dangers Black men posed to White women. The sentences these men received were born of the interplay of social, cultural, and legal factors. Cultural and social dynamics in these trials revealed the ambivalence that characterized the dominant culture's views of such crimes. Were the perpetrators of these acts the antithesis of the 'Other,' antithetical to the very nature of the nation, or, by contrast, did these cases provide an opportunity to showcase the superior nature of British justice, the celerity of the rule of law over the mob?

These social and cultural questions were debated in concert with the imperatives of the law and legal procedure, which had their own internal logic with regard to sentencing. Sentences, in the main, reflected the nature of the crimes in a technical sense according to the provisions of the Criminal Code. Nonetheless, judges were given some discretionary power over the sentences they handed down and they were not immune from the broader social currents and cultural lenses through which these cases were refracted.

The cases of Oxentine, Harris, and Merriman illustrate this dynamic at work. Oxentine's death sentence was the only one allowable under the code but it was based on less than compelling evidence and there is no evidence that he was given consideration for commutation. In the case of Harris, a ten-year sentence was rather harsh given that he was charged for attempted rape and there was not, in fact, much of an attempt. As for Merriman, a ten-year sentence represented a straightforward response in accordance to both the law and conventions in sentencing; however, the details of the case, though fragmentary, suggest that he was harshly convicted on similarly weak evidence. Merriman was alleged to have used firearms, a fact that on the surface means his sentence was in line with the code. Yet one wonders whether a conviction would have been found against him had he been a White man attacking a White woman. Aspersions would have been cast upon his victim's character whether or not that would have made a difference. Indeed, given what we know about the history of sexual violence in Canada, there is a fair chance that he would have been acquitted.

Lastly, the cases of Roughmond and McCathern are powerful examples of the dominant culture's fear and loathing of interracial rape, violence, and murder at the hands of marginal and dangerous Black men. In almost every respect, both of these cases were the embodiment of the epitome, the archetype, of sexual danger in twentieth-century Ontario and the crimes involved were seen as a threat to the moral order. Conversely, these tales of a 'peculiarly horrible description' also provided White elite jurists with a rare opportunity to showcase the superiority of British justice.

Yet again, with these cases the internal logic of the law and legal procedure mattered too. Both Roughmond and McCathern were sentenced to death. Roughmond was hanged. McCathern was spared the rope. Roughmond had no supporters willing to petition for clemency. Nor did he have solid legal grounds for an appeal, nor a compelling social or political reason (i.e., White paternalism) that may have been cloaked as a technical legal argument. McCathern's case was considerably different from Roughmond's in this regard. McCathern's death sentence, while technically allowed under the law, was deemed excessive. The appellate court argued that the sentence was an aberration from the general principle of standardized sentences for crimes of a similar nature. The court's decision was clearly a check on the social and cultural anxieties at the heart of McCathern's death sentence. The appellate court judges felt it was too harsh. Nonetheless, a sentence of twenty years and twenty lashes sent a stern message to racial and sexual transgressors such as McCathern. His sentence demonstrated that British justice was firm, but fair, and represented a triumph of the racial liberal order.

5

Race, Sex, and the Power of Dominant Rape Narratives

The previous chapter looked at rape cases involving Black men and White women and argued that the courts' response was shaped by the parameters of the law and the peculiar alchemy of racial stereotypes of Black men and the dangers they posed to White womanhood; these cases embodied the archetype of sexual danger. I will continue with that theme, but it is joined by others. This chapter examines cases of assault, robbery, and murder that in one form or another involved sexual contact – criminal or consensual – that crossed the colour line. The archetypal image of the particular sexual danger posed to White women by Black men rarely figures directly in these cases, but it was always there as subtext, determining the views and actions of members of the dominant culture be they police, jurors, prosecutors, judges, or ministers of justice. The courts handed down stiff penalties for such transgressions while, conversely, White men who assaulted Black women were treated with a considerable degree of leniency.

The dominant culture's anxieties about the sexual dangers Black men represented to Canada's White women and the nation spanned the nineteenth century and survived well into the next. In the early twentieth century, a moral panic coalesced around African American migration to the Canadian west. In 1910 an eleven-year-old White girl in Edmonton was allegedly assaulted by two Black men, one of whom was charged with robbery. Although there was no sexual assault, the crime represented the sexual threat that Blacks posed to Canada's White women. An editorial in a Lethbridge newspaper lamented that the crime was evidence of a 'Black Peril' brought by recent African American migrants from Oklahoma. The editorial voiced particular concern for the safety of White women left alone on homesteads. Similarly, in 1911 the Imperial Order of the Daughters of the Empire circulated a petition and immigration report which expressed the view that African American migration to Manitoba would 'scare farmers' wives.' The petition declared that there would be 'no guarantee that our women would be safer in their scattered homesteads than white women in other countries with a Negro population.'[1]

But the matter was not always clear-cut. Some cases in my sample were characterized by a certain ambivalence that reflected the instability of racial boundaries and the difficulty of policing them. Moreover, in others, the issue of nationhood became an important theme, which significantly changed the discussion of race and sex. Despite fears that sexual encounters with Black men constituted the ultimate violation of White womanhood, at times efforts to assert the superiority, beneficence, and tolerance of White Canadians could work in favour of the Black defendant and to affirm Canadian national identity. The eight cases studied here are all violent crimes that involved interracial gender conflict. However, only three cases resulted in formal charges alleging some form of sexual assault. A close reading of these case files reveals that normative and hegemonic attitudes towards race and sex were more important and certainly more complex than formal legal categories. This chapter grapples with the ways in which shared cultural assumptions about Black male sexual danger were shaped by what one cultural theorist has called the 'functional overdetermination' of overlapping discourses of race and sex.[2] In turn, we will see how these cultural assumptions shaped these cases.

Crossing Racial Boundaries

On 7 March 1880 a case came before a Windsor justice of the peace involving two men, Peter Hines and William Beatty – the former Black, the latter White and middle class. They went to Margaret Murton's house under the pretext of selling whisky.[3] Murton was sexually assaulted by both men, who were convicted and sentenced to seven years in prison. This was a relatively short sentence for the Black perpetrator in particular given that his victim was White. Why was his sentence so light compared to other Black men who committed similar crimes?

The facts are these. On the morning in question, William Watson answered the door of his home but refused to purchase liquor. One of the men then attempted to force his way in. Maria Smith, presumably a neighbour (who also testified in this case), convinced the prisoners to leave. Maria Smith told the court that a short time later she heard the cries of Margaret Murton. Watson testified that he heard Murton shout 'don't kill me.'[4]

Margaret Murton – the victim in this affair – testified that early that morning she heard a 'tapping' at her door. Moments later, the 'lock and bolt and hinges was all broke in and the door falling on the floor.' Following this, she continued, 'the coloured man,' Hines, came in and struck a match. Murton asked Hines what he wanted, and an unresponsive Hines 'came then and took hold of me[.] I screamed ... he put a hand on my mouth and grabbed my throat with the other and said make no noise or I will Murder you.' After a brief struggle, Hines had 'carnal connection' with Murton, who lamented that she was 'almost dead' when the men left her. Hines's accomplice, William Beatty, also raped her. She said she was 'bruised and broken down' and had to stay at a neighbour's house as she was now 'afraid for my life that they would murder me.'[5]

Murton was certain that it was Hines who first assaulted her. After he finished, 'the other one came and said Peter come away and leave her,' while Murton exclaimed 'for the [mercy] of God help me up.' Then, said Murton, 'the other one [presumably William Beatty] came and had connection with me as well.' She was less certain of the race of her second attacker.

Confusion around the racial identities of the culprits was a central theme of this case. Racial boundaries in the case were porous, as revealed by the testimony of police officers Robert Craig and Donald Graves. Craig told the court that he first saw the two men about half-past four. Both, according to the officer, were 'up to some devilment,' and William Beatty in particular appeared to be 'about half drunk.' Shortly after six o'clock, the constable saw Margaret Murton, who informed him that 'a couple of coloud [*sic*] men had been at her house and had ravished her.' Thus, she had essentially identified her White attacker as Black. According to Craig, when he asked Murton to give him a description of the men who assaulted her 'as near she could,' she told him that 'one was a tall slim darky that worked around the Lumber yard.' When asked how she could be certain of the identity of her attacker (or at least one of them), Murton replied that 'he lighted a couple of matches' so she had a good look at his face. The other man had stood close to the door and had hidden his face from her.[6] William Beatty's concealment within the darkness of the room had resulted in his corporeal blackening. He became, figuratively and literally, 'black' in Margaret Murton's testimony.

The testimony of the second officer, Donald Graves, bears out this point. Murton also told Graves that she was attacked by two coloured men, only to say also that 'she was sure one was colored but not so sure of the other.' Once again, Murton described one of her attackers as 'a tall slim young man[,] a coloured man and said she had known him before.' Constable Graves actually tried to clear up the problem by telling the court that 'Beatty's face that morning appeared as if he had been using coal dust from the spots from his face and as if he had not been washed for a week,'[7] an image that was evocative of the intersection of blackness and lower-class whiteness embodied in White working-class occupations like coal stoking and forms of cultural expression like blackface minstrelsy.[8]

The racial ambiguities that characterized the trial also emerged in the newspaper coverage. On 9 March 1880 the London *Daily Advertiser* ran a story on the trial but gave no indication that Murton had mistaken one of her attackers, the White man, as Black. Only in the newspaper coverage, however, is there any allusion to the crucial role that issues of class and character, in concert with notions of respectable whiteness (and gender), played in influencing this case. The *Advertiser* called the sexual assault of the 'lone widow' by two men at three in the morning in her own home a 'horrible outrage.'

This particular imperilled White woman was, however, jeopardized by her class position. Articulating class in terms of geography, the *Advertiser* referred to Margaret Murton's dwelling as a 'shanty' and its location as being 'on the lumber yard at the west end of Windsor.' This signalled her lowly class status. The relative squalor of Margaret Murton's living conditions, and the relative ease with which her attackers broke down her door, heightened her vulnerability and lowered her respectability.

In the press coverage of William Beatty, class relations were also articulated in the language of race. Beatty seemed in danger of falling from his privileged perch of respectable middle-class White masculinity. During the preliminary hearing, Police Magistrate Alex Barttle, after informing Beatty and Hines that the evidence was very strong against them, turned to Beatty and, as the *Advertiser* reported, 'expressed his great regret that a man [who was] the son of one of Windsor's old[est] citizens and who had a wife and family of his own should be guilty of such a heinous crime.' The paper reported that, while signing his commitment forms, Beatty 'trembled like a leaf.' As if to signify the ever increasing dissolution of Beatty's once respectable whiteness and masculinity, the paper went on to note that he also 'showed signs of continued dissipation.'

Racial ambiguity marked this case to a large extent, but, while Hines's testimony placed him in the stereotypical role of a Black predator, a different picture of Hines appears in the newspaper reports. In the *Advertiser*, Hines, 'the negro,' is described as a 'harmless looking fellow, who appears full of school-boy mischief.'[9]

At the centre of this case stood the victim – Margaret Murton – a sixty-four-year-old White woman who was taken by surprise in the dead of night and assaulted by an unknown Black male in her own home. In that regard, the story fit the classic tale of a dangerous Black male and a vulnerable White woman. But there is also the involvement of William Beatty, in effect a 'fallen' White male, as a co-defendant, and the marginalized social status of the victim. Furthermore, in this case we also see the unusual depiction in the press of Hines not as a predator but as a 'harmless looking fellow.' The narratives that make up this case – in both the criminal case file and the newspaper coverage of the trial – reveal how widespread ideas about rape and Black male sexual danger could be slightly altered when the female victim belonged to the lower class and one of the perpetrators was a middle-class White man who had fallen into a state of degradation. In the end, the porous nature of racial boundaries, the importance of race and space in articulating class relations, and contradictory representations of Black masculinity meant that the outcome of the trial differed from that of other cases involving Black men and White women. In the result, both men – White and Black – received only a seven-year sentence, blurring the racial boundaries of this case.[10]

The Freemans: Murder, Bastardy, and Miscegenation

The late-nineteenth-century trial of the Freeman family elicited much attention and had all the elements of a high drama: sex, murder, bastardy, and miscegenation. The Chatham *Daily Planet* greeted its readers on the morning of 8 October 1893 with news of the trial, heralded as no less than 'one of the most Notable Trials in the Criminal Annals of

Canada,' and provided ample and hyperbolic coverage of the 'Heinous Crime.'[11]

A small rural township just outside of Chatham, Raleigh was steeped in Black Canadian history.[12] In the late 1840s the township was the site of an all-Black agricultural settlement run by a White philanthropist, abolitionist, and Presbyterian missionary named William King.[13] King, a former slaveowner who later became a staunch opponent of slavery, proposed to establish a settlement, the Buxton settlement, based on the principles of 'independence ... self reliance on a homestead, and literacy.'[14] When Whites in Raleigh learned of King's proposed scheme, many objected. They drafted a strongly worded petition, signed by 377 residents, asking the Toronto Presbytery not to introduce a 'Colony of ... Vicious Blacks' into the midst of an old, 'Well established Township' to which 'Moral, Industrious, and Intelligent' White residents had given 'Years of Toil.' Another petition, similarly 'anti-Negro' in its character, was adopted by the Raleigh town council. It suggested that 'a poll tax should be levied against American-born Negroes, that the vote, public schools, and jury service should be denied them, and that Negroes should be forced to post bonds for good behaviour as under the Black codes of Ohio.'[15]

Five decades later, the descendants of King's Black settlers found themselves at the centre of a sensational murder case. What marked this 'tale of horror' most profoundly was George Freeman's alleged sexual relationship with a young White girl named Ida Jane Lizzart, and the murder of a White police officer.

Scandal ripped throughout Raleigh when word spread that Ida Jane Lizzart, who had been living with George Freeman and his wife for two years, gave birth to a Black child. Most people suspected that the father of the child was George. The relationship between George and Ida Jane was of such great concern to Raleigh's White community that a local doctor insisted that charges be brought against George Freeman.[16]

On the basis of the information presented to the justice of the peace, George Freeman was charged under the Charlton Act and a warrant was issued for his arrest. The Charlton Act was the work of a Norfolk Ontario MP named John Charlton, an entrepreneur and financier, whose political career spanned the late nineteenth and early twentieth centuries. Charlton was concerned with many aspects of moral regulation, including Sabbath observance, temperance, censorship of 'obscene' literature, and opposition to abortion and birth control.[17] What interested Charlton most, however, and the issue that marked his public life, was the regulation and criminalization of seduction. In 1886 his seduction bill became law and, as a result, the concept of seduction – the impossibility of consent in certain non-violent sexual situations – formally entered Canadian criminal law. Generally speaking, the law criminalized heterosexual liaisons where the girl was between fourteen and sixteen; where the woman was under the age of twenty-one and was given the promise of marriage; and where the woman was under the age of twenty-one and was the ward or employee of her seducer. In all cases, the law applied only to women of 'previously chaste character.'[18]

On 23 January 1893 County Constable Alexander McDonald took the warrant and, in the company of another man, Harry Best, went out to the 'Freeman Colony.' This term would be used repeatedly. It served both to racialize and to spatialize the Freemans' land, making it a kind of 'interior frontier,' to borrow a concept from critical anthropologist Ann Stoler. The concept of interior frontiers, notes Stoler, has contradictory connotations. Frontiers indicate sites of passage and exchange on the borders and edges of territories, nations, and empires. When the word 'frontier' is coupled with the word 'interior,' interesting contradictions arise. Interior frontiers mean that nations have internal borders as well as external ones, that 'the purity of the community is prone to penetration on its interior and exterior borders.'[19]

The authorities charged George Freeman with seduction and with the crime of having carnal knowledge of a girl under the age of consent (statutory rape). The *Planet* described George Freeman as 'a big strapping fellow' and reported that on the day of his arrest he 'stoutly resisted being taken.' The initial attempt to bring Freeman into custody was ultimately rebuffed by his wife, who 'came to her husband's defence and hacked at the officer with a hoe until he was obliged to release his grip and beat a retreat.' Constable McDonald, determined to apprehend Freeman, resolved to return later – with reinforcements.[20]

McDonald returned to the Freeman place with police constables Bob Rankin and Peter Dezelia, two city officers enlisted to apprehend 'the miscreant.'[21] These officers were not working in cooperation with the crown attorney and there was some question about whether permission was granted by the chief of police for the employment of city officers in this case (an issue that would later be of some importance in how the trial unfolded). The second confrontation between George Freeman and the police was much more violent; at the end of it, Constable Rankin lay dead.[22]

Constable Dezelia was the first to recount a version of the events that transpired at the Freeman place. Dezelia, coincidentally, occupied something of a mythic stature and was part of the local lore of the Chatham area. Twenty-one years later, he was still a member of the Chatham force and was known as the 'man who never forgot a face.'[23] According to Dezelia, the police arrived at the Freeman place at about four in the afternoon of 24 January 1893. George Freeman, seeing the police approach his house, ran yelling 'murder!' through the side door of his house and into a field towards his father's house (50 rods or 275 feet away), while the police and a 'posse of citizens' (which the defence later contended looked like a lynch mob) chased him.[24] Constable Rankin was leading the charge when 'the door opened and out came six colored men, yelling at us to go away or they would shoot.' According to Dezelia, he told the Freemans that the posse 'was not going to hurt them' and implored them to 'listen to reason,' but his pleas fell on deaf ears and the Freemans began shooting. In the ensuing melee, Rankin was chased behind a cookhouse; one of his pursuers was armed with an axe, the other with a grub hoe. In dramatic fashion Dezelia reported that he 'felt a bullet strike my belt[,] another one went through the tail lapel of my overcoat and another passed between my legs, grazing the skin near the knee.' The bullets also passed near my head, and, in fact I smelt the smoke of the gun, and the powder of it flew into my face so close was the man. Hearing Bob call "Pete!" I ran in his direction.'

Dezelia continued with his reconstruction of events, using overtly racist language. 'As I got on the fence,' said Dezelia, 'I saw the blacker one of the two who had followed him knock him down with a blow from behind, which broke the handle. The other man attacked Bob with his axe. I fired as the first one struck Bob, and the coon fell.' While firing and missing yet another shot, Dezelia allegedly witnessed Rankin suffer a 'frightful blow' from an axe. Dezelia's narrative ends by underscoring the extent of George Freeman's barbarity: 'George,' said Dezelia, 'taking advantage, drove me back, after which he hurried over to where poor Rankin lay and lifting a huge billet of wood, brought it down with terrible force upon Bob's head. That was the last I saw.'

Dezelia concluded by emphasizing that County Constable McDonald, unarmed, was 'chased away by two fellows during this confrontation.' Indeed, according to Dezelia, not only were there no firearms available for the posse but a request to nearby 'millmen' for help in apprehending George Freeman initially fell flat. The millmen said that they would instead 'get a rig and go over later and get Rankin.' These

THE CHATHAM DAILY PLANET

ON TRIAL

For their Lives at London.

THE FOUR FREEMANS

Are now before Judge and Jury.

A "True Bill" for Murder

Has been Returned by the Middlesex Grand Inquest.

PROGRESS OF THE CASE IN COURT.

His Lordship, Mr. Justice Falconbridge on the Bench.

Mr. Lount Prosecutes, and B.B. Osler Defends.

COURT-ROOM THRONGED WITH DEEPLY INTERESTED PERSONS.

Full Particulars of the All-engrossing Procedure.

WHAT WILL THE VERDICT BE?

THE PARENTS.

JEREMIAH FREEMAN. (since deceased.)

CELIA FREEMAN.

THE PRISONERS.

GEO. FREEMAN.

ALEX. FREEMAN.

LITTLE LOCAL LINKS

Chatham *Planet*, 9 October 1893. The Freemans stand trial in Middlesex County.

millmen did finally agree to lend their support to the cause; according to Dezelia, 'seven millmen finally went over to the old man's house, but were shot at and scared away.'[25] George Freeman was finally apprehended. Along with family members Lemuel, Alex, and William Henry, as well as his aging parents, Jeremiah and Celia, George Freeman stood charged with murder. The stage was set for the trial. Jeremiah would die of 'grief' before it began.

The Trial

The Freemans stood trial amidst a throng of 'deeply interested onlookers,' as well as a mob of Whites standing outside the courthouse, in neighbouring Middlesex County.[26] The atmosphere was racially charged, but the Freemans were skilfully represented. No less than the high-profile lawyer Britton Bath Osler, one of the most respected lawyers of the day, was in charge of the defence. The records are silent about how this case came to Osler's attention. Osler served as a crown attorney of Wentworth in 1874 and was made a provincial QC in 1876 and a federal QC four years later. After leaving his position as crown counsel and joining a prestigious Toronto law firm, Osler successfully defended the interests of the Grand Trunk Railway. In fact, according to his biographer, Osler acquired such an impressive knowledge of the technical aspects of these cases that he became an associate of the Canadian Society of Civil Engineers.[27] Osler was also known both for his startling physical presence – he sported a prominent facial scar incurred through an accident that left him burned – and for his brilliant oratorical skills. His superior grasp of legal arguments often overwhelmed both juries and courtroom adversaries. His first case to garner national attention was the trial of Louis Riel in 1885, where he assisted the crown attorney.

In the Freeman trial, both the defence and the crown, headed by William Lount, a well-respected lawyer in his own right (who would five years later prosecute in the case of M, the peg-legged murderer of a police officer in London; see chapter 2), crafted divergent accounts of what transpired on the day of Constable Rankin's death. In his opening address to the jury, Lount, predictably, echoed Dezelia's testimony, calling the crime 'outrageous, high-handed, and a cruel taking of life.' Lount also pontificated on the subject of George Freeman's guilt, stressing that he resisted lawful authority. Moreover, Lount believed that all the Freemans were 'equally guilty' since they were all 'gathered together to help George in his armed resistance of the law.'[28]

The difficult task of refuting these accounts led defence counsel Osler to employ a number of strategies, the internal contradictions of which reflected the dominant culture's ambivalence towards Blacks. Osler attacked the credibility of the police force and the reliability of physical evidence presented at the trial, and introduced the testimony of witnesses who constructed a narrative counter to the press account. An important element in this rhetorical project of constructing counter-narratives was an emergent discourse of 'respectability.' Even during the preliminary stages of the case, Ida Jane Lizzart emerged as a fallen White woman with a murky sexual past. This was to prove problematic for White elites who staked out the sexual violation of this woman as the terrain upon which they sought to persecute the Freemans. In contrast to the portrayal of the Freeman colony as a kind of internal frontier, Osler sought to construct its inhabitants as 'model' members of an industrious and hard-working family compound, who had attempted to defend themselves from a near lynching. He sought to use this image of Black agrarian industriousness and pastoral harmony to discredit the terror and the 'un-Britishness' and 'un-Canadianness' of mob violence and the lynching ritual. North of the 49th parallel, lynching discourse served as a site for the performance of White masculinity but it also played an important role for Canadians who wished to deal with miscegenation in a country where no formal legal prohibitions were in place to prevent sexual liaisons between Black men and White women.[29] At the same time, however, lynching rhetoric in Canada also signified American racial disharmony and was used to firm up the border, inscribing the Canadian nation by declaring such practices un-Canadian and un-British.[30]

Along with the issue of mob violence, Osler turned his attention to the physical evidence. Osler challenged the Chatham city police chief's credibility. He questioned the chief's assertion that he could positively identify the blood and hair of the victim on a murder weapon that in all likelihood could have belonged to others at the scene of the crime, and he noted that the 'red appearance' of the gun could well have been rust and dirt, not blood. Osler also placed Justice of the Peace McNaughton and Constable McDonald under scrutiny, suggesting that the two were involved in corruption. Osler asked Chief Young if he was aware that McDonald employed himself by 'hunting up county cases.' The chief denied having any such knowledge, but Osler persisted, asking the witness if he was aware that McDonald and McNaughton were engaged in corruption or 'work[ing] into each other's hands,' an activity for which the constable was apparently under investigation. Osler suggested that the officers had been working outside their jurisdictions to increase their fees, often issuing arrest warrants where they should not have. Constable McDonald, argued Osler, was a constable not for Kent County but for Dover Township. Osler thus held that the 'tragic result' of this police corruption was the fact that the 'greed of one man' – Alexander McDonald – ultimately led to Freeman's arrest for 'an offence against a girl he did not know[,] for an offence of the circumstances of which he had no knowledge.'[31]

This was an exaggeration, for the nature of the relationship between Ida Jane and George was, at best, ambiguous. Nevertheless, if, as Osler argued, the original premise upon which George Freeman was arrested was suspect, the charge against him was invalid. Although Ida Jane was called to give a deposition at the police magistrate's hearing in

January, she was not called as a witness during the trial at the Assize Court in the fall. Her statement to the police in the January inquiry into Constable Rankin's death must have proved problematic for the White elites of Raleigh. Not only did Ida Jane's testimony make it difficult to discern the true nature of her relationship with George, but the question of her age also raised problems. Finally, and perhaps most critically, Ida Jane's reputation as a fallen and 'dissolute' White woman made it increasingly difficult to establish that a real transgression ever took place.

Ida Jane testified that she was indeed 'living at the prisoner George Freeman['s],' and that she was there 'the day and night before [the murder].'[32] She informed the court that she had a room of her own in George Freeman's house and one could access it 'from the kitchen into the front room and from that to my room to get where I was.'[33] Little else, however, could be deemed a certainty from Ida Jane's statement to the court. No doubt it distressed George Freeman's accusers that Ida Jane could not even accurately remember her own age. When asked to do so in the preliminary hearing, her response was, at best, equivocal: 'I must [be] fourteen years I think ... I do not know my age [I] may be eighteen.'[34] Further, Elizabeth Freeman's statement cast ambiguity on the specific nature of George's relationship with Ida Jane. When asked if she 'knew the girl who lived with George,' Elizabeth said Ida Jane Lizzart. However, when it came to the crucial question of Ida Jane's age, Elizabeth Freeman stated unequivocally that the girl was sixteen or seventeen years old. Equally important was Ida Jane's reputation. Some indication of its importance can be gleaned from Elizabeth Freeman's assertion that Ida Jane 'bore the worst of characters.' This image of Ida Jane as a White woman of questionable character was one of the key reasons the discourse of Black male sexual transgression of White womanhood was ultimately abandoned. Ida Jane's murky sexual past and her (seemingly consensual) concubinage with a Black man proved to be too shaky a foundation upon which to build a case against George Freeman.

Indeed, by the time that the case made it to the Assize Court, discussion of interracial sex was driven underground, relegated to the realm of silences and subtext. Instead, the prosecution focused more narrowly on the death of Constable Rankin and the premeditated and collaborative nature of the crime. The defence, by contrast, sought to fit this case squarely within a much broader context, constructing a counter-narrative of what transpired on the Freeman place that challenged the prosecution's image of Black violence inflicted on a White officer of the law. In so doing, the defence also drew on paternalistic representations of hard-working and respectable Black farmers who feared vigilante justice and the violence of White mobs.

Seizing upon the powerful discourse of the lynching ritual, the defence contended that the Freemans faced the very real fear of mob violence, and that this explained their actions. George Freeman's testimony is a case in point. He steadfastly maintained that, on the morning of the incident, he was home when the men came to his farm and that he 'did not know they were constables.' Freeman further contended that these two men, whom he could not definitively identify as officers of the law, 'kept coming' and 'shot and shot' as he tried to escape to the safety of his father's dwelling. George did admit under cross-examination that one of the men who came for him that morning 'had blue clothes and brass buttons on his coat and I think a club at his side' and that he knew such clothes were worn by policemen. An indication of George Freeman's fearful state of mind, however, is that he believed that these men 'might have been disguised to murder me.'[35]

Accordingly, a crucial element of George Freeman's defence was the assertion that he had been 'in terror' of mob violence when he shot the police. Testimony from certain witnesses seemed to support this claim. For example, in the preliminary hearing, Elizabeth Freeman stated that she 'heard threats against George for keeping this girl in his house,' and, moreover, that 'they were going to take him out and tar and feather him ... this was done by the mill hands.'[36] Ida Jane Lizzart also told the court she overheard members of the posse say that George Freeman was to be tarred and feathered. Jessie Freeman was similarly concerned for George Freeman's safety. He told the court that he, as well as Alex and Lemuel Freeman, worried that 'there was somebody going to mob George out.'[37]

It seems that George Freeman did not show quite as much concern for the other members of his family during this ordeal. Under questioning during the Police Court proceeding, he admitted that a murder had taken place on the Freeman compound, but he absolved himself of any personal responsibility for the melee and said that his brothers William Henry and Alexander had 'fought with the man who was killed.'[38] At trial, Osler claimed that George's statement was evidence of his distressed state of mind and moved to have it thrown out on the basis that it was 'irregularly and improperly taken.' The statement, according to Osler, 'was procured when the prisoner was in terror and not responsible for what he said and any use made of his alleged confession would not be proper.'[39] Under direct questioning, when asked to relate the 'circumstances under which you made the statement,' George replied, 'I didn't want to make one, but when I began to cry, a man in the police office said to me now was the time to make a statement. I told him I wanted to see Mr. Pegley [his lawyer] first. I was crying, and didn't know what I said. When I was coming along the road to the police court, I heard threats that [they] were going to kill me. I was very much scared.'[40]

In North America, Black men suspected of harming White women had reason to fear for their lives, for the threat of the lynch mob was always present in such cases. Osler pushed this very point: that Freeman was in fear of his life. He strengthened his argument in an examination of Deputy Crown Attorney George B. Douglass, who had much to do with the initial charges brought against George Freeman:

Q: Did you not think the prisoner made this statement in terror of his life? Don't you know that threats were made to lynch him?
A: I do not.
Q: Didn't you know that the warden of the County had to protect the prisoner from a mob when he was being brought to the police station?
A: No, I never heard of it.
Q: The prisoner made his deposition in fear didn't he?
A: I scarcely think so, there were tears in his eyes as he spoke. He seemed very sorry.

In the end, Osler ignored this testimony. In his summation to the jury, he stated that there was evidence to support the position that George feared mob violence 'such as we have read of in the papers on the other side – fortunately not in this country.' The lynching of Black men served as a signifier of the U.S. race problem and thus framed the discursive contours of Canadian nationhood.

In his closing, Osler drew upon two other dominant images of blackness, couched, as the Chatham *Planet* put it, in terms of 'an appeal on the grounds of Justification and Humanity.' Osler portrayed the Freemans as a 'respectable' hard-working family, while at the same time drawing upon a second image: paternalistic notions of the moral and physical weaknesses of Blacks and their inability to control their passions, particularly under terrifying circumstances. He declared: 'What we have here is a settlement of men living peaceably and orderly and quietly together. A man of high moral character, Jeremiah Freeman had raised his family and had them grouped about him; William Henry living in the house, Alexander settled in the house west of him, George settled in a house on the other side, the homestead between them, the family at once united in their work free from the courts, free from all criticisms, hard-working, industrious, not in any way quarrelsome.' As Osler continued his address, the rhetoric of the respectable and hard-working family bled into more pervasive paternalistic representations of blackness: 'And as out of a Black cloud the lightning comes and strikes. This unfortunate family are all stricken down. Poor old Jeremiah, in his old days, charged with this murder and dies from the result, and the other men of the family are before you on trial for their lives, and the weeping women and children waiting for the result.' Hence, the police, argued Osler, were the evil interlopers who disrupted a scene of Black rural domesticity, docility, and tranquillity. However, even if one could make an argument for this portrayal of the police/posse, the defence still had to grapple with the violence of the attack upon Constable Rankin. To do so, Osler drew upon coded notions of Black incivility and savagery: 'Say what you will about it ... impressively, the brutal fighting instinct of man is the basis, the bottom of the race. If not, the race doesn't exist. Civilization veneers over it for the use of the community, they respect it and give it place when provocation brings it out.' While this statement situated the Freemans in particular and blackness in general in the context of a shared 'humanity' and 'civilization,' it also covertly signified that within 'the race' Blacks were more susceptible to 'the brutal, fighting instinct of man' and thus belonged at civilization's 'basis,' its 'bottom,' a position that, to a large extent, Osler tacitly argued, mitigated their criminal responsibility.

The rhetorical strategies employed by Osler were noteworthy both from a tactical point of view and for what they revealed about the complex and contradictory impulses evident in legal expressions of blackness. The defence's use of powerful White paternalist sentiment in particular was also mirrored in the judge's charge. Alongside familiar rhetoric espousing vaunted notions of colour-blind justice, the judge warned against the dangers of misguided White paternalism: 'The prisoners are people of another race and color from yours and mine. The Counsel for the Crown has disclaimed any appeal to you to allow any sympathies for them on the one hand or any prejudice or dislike against them on the other hand to weigh with you in considering this case; and that is the way in which you are bound to view it upon your oaths. The prisoners come to you as citizens of the province and of the community upon the same plane as any other individuals and you will deal with them exactly as you would if they were of the Caucasian race.'

In the end, the tacit fear of the power of paternalistic sentiment, which surely led some White elites to fear the Freemans' possible acquittal and informed the discursive strategies of the crown and the judge, was, at least in part, unfounded. After a brief deliberation, the jury acquitted Lemuel and Celia Freeman. The jury did find George, William Henry, and Alex Freeman guilty – but of the lesser charge of manslaughter rather than murder. While White paternalism spared the Freemans from the gallows, it did not completely absolve them of responsibility. During sentencing, the judge made it clear that he considered the jury's verdict a merciful one. Indeed, he proclaimed that he 'would have no fault to find with the verdict if it had been for a higher crime, for a more cruel case of killing short of murder has never been tried in my experience ... if I had been called upon to impose the death penalty I should have held out no hope whatever.'

Though the Freemans' sentence – life in prison – was the maximum allowable under the law, it was, nonetheless, couched in the rhetoric of mercy. Newspaper coverage claimed that the prevailing sentiment of the citizens (read White citizens) of Chatham and Raleigh was that the Freemans 'got off easy.' Indeed, a Chatham *Planet* headline on the day of sentencing read: 'The Debt Cast on the Whites by Centuries of Oppression of the Blacks.' On one level, this interpretation of the verdict was typical of the kind of overblown rhetoric common in newspaper coverage. But it also suggests that, to some, the sentence reflected more than a run-of-the-mill paternalism; it reflected a heightened historical sense of racial justice that was an important element of (White) Canadian nationhood. Yet a more menacing and unsettling White supremacist discourse also emerged from the newspaper coverage, barely concealed beneath the humour it purported to espouse. The *Planet* reported that, in the aftermath of the trial, Lemuel Freeman, leaving court as a free man, was approached by a reporter. 'That ought to be a lesson for you, Lem,' the reporter remarked, 'to show respect for the law.' To this the 'colored man' allegedly replied, 'You're right boss. It will do me all the rest of my days. I'll never meddle in no such trouble again, you bet!'[41] The Freeman trial was a showcase for the celerity of colour-blind British justice, where the even-handed nature of the law was cause for celebration. However, this did not signify a change in racial attitudes, for a racist lampoon of stock Black characters punctuated the final pages of coverage of the trial.

The Freeman case also revealed much about existing anxieties around miscegenation. This trial's place as one of the most 'significant in the annals of Canadian history,' as well as the community violence that visited Raleigh and surrounding areas, meant that it was marred by serious tensions and contradictions. As Robin Winks notes, at the same time as 'anti-negro fever' took hold in Raleigh, the school board of the city of Chatham desegregated its schools by admitting African Canadians.[42] The decision was made only a few weeks following the trial.

Frank Turner and Urban Sexual Dangers

While the tale of Ida Jane Lizzart and George Freeman sheds light on the rural history of race and sex in Ontario, the Ontario Supreme Court case of Frank Turner, tried in 1920s Chatham, illuminates urban spaces where race and sex mixed and comingled.[43] On early Christmas morning 1928, Turner was arrested on a charge of robbery with violence and assault causing bodily harm upon Willa Arnold, a fifteen-year-old working-class White girl. In the preliminary hearing at Police Magistrate's Court, Willa Arnold gave her version of the events. She testified that, on her way home from an evening of work at a Chatham bookstore, she stopped at her aunt's house for a brief visit. After about twenty minutes, her arms filled with a bundle of packages, she continued on her way home, at which point 'a colored man stepped out in front of me' and asked 'if I would like a ride home.' She agreed, and took a seat beside Frank Turner in his large late 1920s model Chevrolet 'touring car,' replete with running boards and fancy side curtains. Significantly, Willa Arnold evidently entered Frank Turner's car voluntarily, an act that, as a working-class woman, very well could have placed her claim to White respectable womanhood in jeopardy. Predictably, the prosecution's strategy was to turn the seemingly consensual site of this 'miscegenetic' encounter into something sinister, as evident from the transcript:

Q: Well, how did you happen to get into the car?
A: Well, I don't know unless I was frightened. That is the only thing I can say.
Q: What do you mean by being frightened?
A: I was surprised when he stepped out in front of me.
Q: I see. Well, now, then, the man, – was there anyone else in the car besides this colored man and yourself?
A: No.

Q: Did you know this man?
A: No.[44]

Like the rest of her narrative, Willa Arnold's suspect explanation – that it was a visceral sense of fear that compelled her to get into a Black man's car – fits perfectly with the dominant racist paradigms which held that interactions between Black men and young White girls endangered White women. According to Arnold, Turner said he 'was a stranger in Chatham and asked could he relieve me of my parcels and he put my roaster in the back seat.' Turner then drove beyond Chatham's city limits though he had earlier asked his passenger, who lived on Wilson Avenue, where the street was located. When she told him that they had long passed Wilson Avenue, Turner ignored her and kept driving farther and farther from the centre of town. Now panic-stricken, Arnold told the court that she began to cry out 'Help, help!' – whereupon she received a blow to the head. She went on to say that her only recollection after receiving the blow was 'a girl's voice' which said, 'Now, tell us where you live.' This was likely the voice of Mrs Ellen Rankin, who found Willa Arnold unconscious in the middle of the road.

In the face of such damning testimony, the defence attempted to counter the ominously racialized narrative of a dangerous stranger by showing that Willa Arnold had in fact known the defendant for quite some time prior to the night in question:

Q: Now how long have you known Frank Turner?
A: Just since this accident.
Q: Quite sure you didn't know him to see him before?
A: No.
Q: He lives close here to you, doesn't he?
A: Yes, he does.
Q: And he tells me he used to go by here working, teaming or something. Have you ever seen him before? Is there a Mr. Porter near here?
A: Yes, there is.
Q: Ever see him driving a team for Mr. Porter?
A: I can't remember ever seeing him.
Q: So, according to your story the man was a stranger that came up to you?
A: Yes.[45]

This line of questioning was not very aggressively pursued, though it might have gone a long way to explaining why Arnold appeared to have voluntarily accepted Turner's offer of a ride. Perhaps realizing that there were limits to how far they could question the extent of Arnold's familiarity with a Black man in a highly charged atmosphere, the defence switched to another tactic. It now wanted to suggest that it was difficult to distinguish one Black from another, a fact that made positively identifying one of them difficult:

Q: Isn't it true that you weren't able to tell the police anything about your assailant or the sort of car you were in even that night when you were asked?
A: Well, I told them it was a touring car, and I said I couldn't remember anything, see, except on the one side, but I couldn't see out on the other plain [*sic*].
Q: I see. Now, I suppose it was dark on this street?
A: Yes, it was.
Q: And you [had] never seen Mr. Turner before[,] Miss Arnold[,] had you?
A: No.
Q: And will you agree with me that colored people are similar in looks?
A: Yes, I would, but anybody that had that experience, I think would always remember.
Q: But you had no occasion to – You only saw the man once on a dark street, isn't it possible, Miss Arnold, isn't it possible you made a mistake in the matter?
A: I suppose it is possible but I think I could remember any body that ever had an experience like that. I think I could remember all my life.[46]

The court concurred with Willa Arnold and the sentence meted out to Frank Turner was harsh. The *Border Cities Star* made this story front-page news. A bold headline trumpeted: 'EIGHT YEARS, TWENTY LASHES IS TURNER'S SENTENCE: FOUND GUILTY OF ASSAULTING GIRL, CHATHAM COLORED MAN ROUNDLY SCORED BY JUDGE FOR DISGRACE TO RACE IN ATTACK ON WHITE WOMAN.' The case had 'aroused wide interest,' and, in the midst of a crowded courtroom, Justice Fisher, presiding judge at the assizes, 'severely lectured' Turner during sentencing. He said that the accused, as evidenced by his 'past record,' had 'contempt for Canadian law,' and he criticized his 'seeming indifference to what might have happened to Miss Arnold if things had not turned out as they did.'[47] The judge further decried 'the frequency with which men pick up young girls and young women for *licentious purposes* and having *appalling results*.'[48] In addition to the jail sentence and despite the defence protests to the contrary, Fisher decided to grant the prosecution's desire to add whipping to the jail sentence, reasoning that 'whipping is an excellent deterrent to crime [and] ... a proper punishment for crimes of a serious nature, particularly for crimes against the female sex.'[49]

Typically (and tragically), the defence counsel, bereft of many options at this point in the case, had little room to manoeuvre in its request for leniency. Thus, a feeble attempt was made to argue for a reduced sentence on the paternalistic grounds that Frank Turner 'is a colored man and only three or four generations removed from slavery. His humble surroundings, lack of opportunity, and environment caused his downfall and he is only 28 years of age.' As we have seen, such paternalist sentiments could result in the reduction of harsh punishment. But in this instance the court was unmoved. Most strikingly and disturbingly, however, Justice Fisher went so far as to tell the accused that he *'might as well kill a girl as rape her.'*[50] It is worth recalling that Frank Turner was not charged with rape but he was convicted of robbery and assault. Justice Fisher's words are, in sum, a poignant illustration of how dominant rape scripts – and dominant representations of the Black male sexual predator – determined this case from the beginning. The sentence imposed upon Frank Turner thus served as a reminder of what lay in store for those Black men who dared transgress the boundaries of race and sex.

White Men, Black Women

The evidence, albeit fragmentary, suggests that the courts' adjudication of White male sexual violence against Black women was quite different from their adjudication of cases where Black men committed violence against White women. These cases are much more difficult for the historian to find because court records tend to list the race of the accused rather than that of the victim. Yet those that can be located serve as telling counterpoints to the cases explored above since they contain a different articulation of race and sex. Two cases, one in the late nineteenth century, the other at the turn of the twentieth, give a striking indication of how inverted tales of race and sexual conflict across the colour-line diverged from their antitheses – the 'tales of a peculiarly horrible description' and the 'archetype of sexual danger' that featured so prominently in the discourses surrounding the threat that Black men posed to White womanhood.

One case that appeared before the Kent County fall assizes demonstrates the difficulties Black women faced when seeking justice from the courts for sexual violence at the hands of White men. In 1884 the Chatham *Tri-Weekly Planet* reported this Raleigh case with far less fanfare or hyperbole than it would the tale of Ida Jane Lizzart and George Freeman nine years later. The *Planet* stated that the trial of *Queen v. Charleston* involved a 'defendant ... accused of committing an indecent assault upon a young girl (colored).' The article informed readers that 'about a month ago, she was visiting friends, named Kersey, at which place [the] prisoner also was. Upon going home [she] alleges that the prisoner met her in the woods and committed the assault set forth in the indictment.'[51] The indictment was noteworthy in terms of the charge brought against James Charleston. He was charged with indecent assault, not with the much more serious offences of attempted rape or rape; it was alleged that he 'unlawfully and indecently did assault [Arabella Jackson] and did then beat wound and mistreat – and other wrongs to the said Arabella Jackson.'[52]

The information was brought to a justice of the peace by Arabella's uncle, a man named Marcellous Green, who was present when Arabella first told her family of the assault. According to Green, he confronted James Charleston's father with the news that his son 'had tried to take advantage of [Arabella], and then issued a formal complaint in front of a magistrate.'[53] The complaint offered graphic detail alleging that Charleston 'unlawfully did make an indecent assault upon the person of Arabella Jackson, by taking hold of her in a rude manner and throwing her down and thrusting his hand up her clothes.'[54]

Arabella informed the court that, on the day of the incident, she visited the Kersey place at Mr Kersey's invitation and 'left there about two minutes past six in the morning.' As she started home, she decided to 'walk on the railway track as it was drier walking.' It was then that she noticed Charleston had 'come up behind her.' For reasons that are unclear, Charleston allegedly told Arabella that the people with whom she was staying in Buxton 'would not let me in [so therefore] I could go with him and stay with him.' Arabella also testified that Charleston claimed that since '[another man] had screwn me ... [and] I might as well do it with him as to do it with another fellow [and] said if I would he would give me a dollar bill.' Arabella concluded: 'He took hold of me and threw me on a pile of logs and put his hands up my clothes as far as my knees, I put my hand down and took hold of his to prevent him. I struggled with him about ten minutes – and got away from him. He followed and asked [me] not to tell and he would give me a Handkerchief. I told my Grandmother and my Uncle when I got home the same evening. I was not willing that he should put his hand up my clothes.'[55]

Under cross-examination Arabella did not waver from her story, telling the court that she neither asked James Charleston to go home with her nor consented to sexual contact with him. She added that she told her attacker to 'leave go my arms.' Unfortunately for Arabella (and her uncle who brought the complaint before the magistrate), the White elites and White law officials were not willing to give her much support. A Kent County officer told the court that, when he went to arrest Charleston for his deed, 'the prisoner made his escape by running away' and that he, the officer, did not attempt to arrest Charleston before he ran. In the end, Arabella's word was not enough to stand against that of her White male attacker. The jury found James Charleston not guilty of the charge of indecent assault.[56]

A higher-profile case occurred at the turn of the century in Glencoe, a small town just outside London. The 'Glencoe Outrage,' as the case came to be known, occurred in April 1900. Sarah Dorsey, described as 'colored, 38 years of age and ... employed for several months at the McKellar house,' was the victim of a brutal sexual attack at the hands of six White men: Montgomery Golding, William Orr, Arthur Monk, James Kelley, Archie McCallum, and Nathan Fillmore.[57]

On the night of the assault Sarah Dorsey decided to go to London on the 11 p.m. train. She purchased a ticket at the Glencoe village station and waited for the train to arrive. She was met by a local young man, Arthur Monk, who told her the train was half an hour late. He suggested they might pass the time by taking a walk. [58] Soon after leaving the train station, 'the couple took a drink from a bottle of whiskey which [Sarah Dorsey] had purchased and later they took a drink from a bottle which the man had produced.' From that time on, reported the Glencoe *Transcript*, 'the woman was unconscious of her movements.' After suffering her assault, Dorsey lay in a state of unconsciousness for nine hours. In a development that surely pointed to the degraded status of Black womanhood in turn-of-the-century Ontario, she was 'locked up in a box stall at a hotel stable, from which she was released into the street.' Sarah Dorsey's employer found her some time later 'suffering intensely from cold' and wearing clothing which was 'badly torn.'[59]

The preliminary hearing was held in May and it garnered a great deal of attention among members of the Glencoe community, who crowded the courtroom. The interest generated by the spectacle of such a trial was tempered by a sense that the town's moral standing had been affected by the incident. As the *Transcript* put it, there was a 'feeling of satisfaction now that there is ground to hope that the parties guilty of the outrage are likely to be punished as they deserved and the name of the village vindicated.'[60]

The hopes of those who wished to see the good name of the town restored rested upon Nathan Fillmore – dubbed 'young Fillmore' – a stable boy of sixteen years of age who, also charged with assault, turned queen's evidence and gave an eyewitness account of Dorsey's assault and the involvement of the other accused men. Not only was Fillmore able to provide the crown with crucial evidence of the assault, but, in the words of one newspaper report, the defendants were 'identified in many places by other witnesses whose stories fit in with that of Fillmore.' Indeed, the article suggested that the prisoners would find the evidence arrayed against them a challenge.[61] In light of the convincing evidence in the crown's possession, it is perhaps not surprising that 'no evidence for the defence was offered.'[62]

Yet, in the patriarchal White supremacist society within which the trial unfolded, strong evidence was not enough to shield Sarah Dorsey from scepticism. The press reported that her evidence 'was practically of no consequence.'[63] Even worse for Dorsey, her character did not stand up to scrutiny during cross-examination. According to press reports, she could remember only having left the railway station that evening in the company of Monk. Under cross-examination, Dorsey also 'admitted to buying a bottle of liquor ... and taking a couple of drinks therefrom.' Defence counsel managed to get Dorsey to admit she had been arrested for drunkenness several times and also convicted of vagrancy while living in Toronto. Finally, it was also revealed that Dorsey had previously spent six months in the Mercer Reformatory in Toronto, an institution founded in 1874 for female law offenders.[64] Understandably, she had been quite reluctant to admit it.

Of the six men charged with assaulting Dorsey, three were granted bail while three – Montgomery Golding, William Orr, and Arthur Monk – were confined to the Glencoe jail until the start of the Middlesex fall assizes about six months later.[65] By then, it seems that the mood of the town (which had wanted to see the 'name of the village vindicated') had softened. Now of great concern was the fact that one of Dorsey's attackers, William Orr, 'was very sick during the greater part of his incarceration, his condition so bad that he was removed to the hospital for a couple of weeks.' The illness from which Orr suffered was apparently consumption, but by the time of the trial he had evidently improved and could 'climb the court house stairs unaided.'[66]

This rather sympathetic report of the deteriorated physical status of one of the participants in the 'Glencoe Outrage' case signalled a change in public sentiment. The Middlesex grand jury made a finding of 'No Bill' in this case, that is, it incredibly found that there was not sufficient evidence against the accused to proceed to a trial at the assizes before a petit jury. Perhaps in the end the Middlesex grand jury felt that six months of incarceration in the Glencoe gaol and Orr's deteriorated body signified that the men had suffered enough and that it was time to put the whole sordid affair behind the town. The six men, after being arraigned and discharged, were reportedly warned by Justice Hugh Edward Rose 'to behave themselves, as they might find themselves in a more uncomfortable position if they appeared before the bar of justice again.'[67] The assault of Arabella Jackson and the 'Glencoe Outrage' are Canadian illustrations of what has been well documented by U.S. scholars of the history of race and sex: Black women in North America lived under the ever-present threat of rape by White men and the reality that they would very rarely see their attackers punished. The dominant image of the oversexed libidinous Black woman, a vestige of the slavery era, meant that the very notion of raping a Black woman was a highly dubious one in the minds of many Whites.[68]

'Unfortunate Familiarities'

The final section of this chapter turns to a vexing issue that confronted the criminal courts: the issue of White women and Black men who entered into consensual and relatively long-term sexual unions – whether 'legitimate' or 'illegitimate.' Mixed-race sexual relations were, of course, always highly charged, as the U.S. scholarship well documents.[69] Ontario was no different; twentieth-century Ontario death-penalty cases include instances where Black men were sentenced to death for the murder of White women who were their lovers or spouses. Dominant assumptions about the sexual danger that Black men posed to White women infused and informed these cases, though to a less explicit degree than other cases in earlier sections of this chapter. The fact that these women were killed by their Black male lovers served as a kind of cautionary tale of the inexorably tragic consequences (mainly for White women but, as we shall see, also for White men) of such 'unnatural unions' and 'unfortunate familiarities,' to borrow the language of one judge.[70] In most U.S. states, interracial marriage – not only Black-White but Indian-White and White-Asian – was illegal until the 1950s and 1960s. In Canada, interracial marriages were never illegal, but on several occasions the federal government did consider proposals to amend both the Criminal Code and the Indian Act to outlaw them. Outside the law, in both the United States and Canada, interracial sex was a social and cultural taboo.[71] Consensual sex between Black men and White women threatened White masculinity and in particular the 'natural' unions between White men and White women.

'Taking the Chance of Marrying a White Woman': Race, Sexuality, and Nation in the Fountain Case

The dominant culture's anxiety around consensual interracial relationships could also be extended to the institution of marriage. These anxieties were crystallized in the 1919 Fountain murder in the town of Stamford, just outside Niagara Falls. On 19 February, Fred Fountain, a native of the Bahamas, murdered his White wife and their two children while they slept. This case does more than illuminate how archetypal rape scripts informed and determined consensual illicit sex. Fountain's status as a racial 'Other,' or, as one immigration official labelled him, a 'deportable immigrant,' reveals the complex articulations of race, sex, and nation that marked interracial unions.

Fountain was twice tried for the murders during a period of a little more than two years. The first trial was held on 15 October 1919. In a memo to the minister of justice in Ottawa, Justice Alexander Logie, the presiding judge in the first trial, constructed a deceptively straightforward account of the trial proceedings. Logie described Fountain as a 'West Indian (Coloured) from Nassau in the Bahamas. His murdered wife was an English woman. Both were ... in the employ of the American Consul in Nassau and were married there.' Along with their two children, Logie continued, Fountain and his wife moved to Niagara Falls, Ontario, taking up residence in a rooming house with two other families. 'On the [e]arly morning of 19th February last,' wrote the justice, 'following a small celebration of the murdered woman's birthday the wife and two children had their throats cut by the prisoner and died from haemorrhage.' Espousing the line of argument advanced by the prosecution, Logie continued: 'The prisoner was jealous of his wife which was the only motive for the murder.' His wife's open display of affection for another man at her birthday party was seen as the most likely source of his jealousy. Evidence presented at the trial to support this motive was two letters by Fountain 'confessing the crime,' one written to his mother and the other to a tenant in the same apartment house. These letters were used at both trials by both the crown and the defence – the former, to make the case for his culpability; the latter, to make a case for the irrational workings of a mind marked by a debilitating bout of melancholia. It should be noted, however, that one of these letters also pointed to the importance of race in this trial: 'Dear Momma: I am sorry to say that Rosey had a party on her birthday and it turn out to be an engagement with a man by the name of Frank Owans. She has been acting foney for sometime towards me ... so I kill her and the children and myself for I cant stand such things going on in my sight ... All this was cause by Dasey Gallivan didn't want me in the family as I was a darky, so she tried to make a brak[e] in [t]he family a month ago ... Dasy Gallavan and Will Gallavan [*sic*] brought the boy by the name of Frank Owans to my house.'[72]

Logie was unconvinced that the letters revealed melancholia or dementia, and declared: 'I have no recommendation to make. The murder was cold blooded and the prisoner tried, not too strenuously, to commit suicide after the deed was done ... he said he wished to join his dear ones, *perhaps* he will.'[73] This statement alluded to the guilty verdict and death sentence, which was to be carried out on 17 December 1919. Far from bringing the Fountain case to a resolution, however, this verdict and the sentence was only the first chapter of a case that would not be ultimately resolved for six years.

After months of correspondence regarding Fred Fountain's mental competency and criminal culpability, on 11 December 1919 (just six days shy of Fountain's date with the hangman), the minister of justice ordered a new trial. He did so on the grounds that two medical experts, Dr Harvey Clare, the medical director of the Ontario Hospital for the Insane, and Dr Alex MacKay, had each made a convincing case that the 'prisoner's mind was so clouded from his mental disease that he had no knowledge of the deed he committed' and thus was 'not responsible at the time of the deed.' The medical language was buttressed by paternalism; Clare's letter to the minister described Fountain as a 'poor unfortunate.' The diagnosis of these two medical experts was corroborated by Dr J.M. Forester, the medical superintendent for the Hospital for the Insane in Toronto. Particularly disturbing to Clare and MacKay was that, even though they were in attendance at the first trial, neither was called on to give evidence.[74] Moreover, as the minister stated in his decision to grant Fountain a new trial, the defence counsel was unaware of this medical evidence. Predictably, both the Ontario attorney general and crown counsel in the first trial strenuously objected to the minister's decision; their protests, however, were summarily dismissed.[75]

Armed with this new evidence, at the second trial, held on 30 and 31 March 1920, defence counsel contended that the murders were the result of Fountain's mental derangement, which manifested itself in a kind of 'jealousy without cause' brought on by a severe bout of Spanish influenza. The prosecution was now faced with the testimony of three medical experts (doctors MacKay, Forester, and Clare), who were willing to testify on behalf of the defence for the mitigation of criminal responsibility. The prosecution argued that Fountain's behaviour did not fit the legal definition of insanity as defined in section 19 of the Criminal Code.[76] The judge in the first trial maintained that Fountain's main motive for the crime was jealousy driven by a very specific cause, resulting in a murder of very specific intent. More important, Justice Houghton Lennox's charge in the second trial indicated that the court was not swayed by an insanity defence – even in the wake of compelling 'expert' testimony. Rather, the judge's charge shows how dominant tropes of Black sexual danger could effectively diffuse even the testimony of respected psychiatric experts. Couching his assessment of the trial in the language of 'common sense' knowledge, Justice Lennox told the jury: 'This man was jealous, if you take the ground work of the Defence. He is a coloured man, he is not responsible for that, but he is responsible for taking the chance of marrying a white woman. The result was that he was probably much more violently jealous and much more suspicious than if they had been differently mated. That I think is common knowledge.'[77]

Lennox's comment clearly dismissed the main arguments put forth by the defence and instead made sense of Fountain's crime by invoking common-sense notions of the 'violently jealous' nature of Black men. It also suggested that the problem was compounded by his 'taking the chance of marrying a white woman.' Had Fountain been 'differently mated,' his insecurities would be held in check, sparing people 'one of the worst murders in the history of the County.'[78] His wife's flirtation with another White had unleashed a jealous rage, because Fountain could never attain the masculinity represented by a White man.

Lennox's assertion that Fountain 'was not responsible' for being 'a coloured man' tells us something about the White paternalist gaze. If the jury was to sympathize with Fountain, it was because of the tragedy inherent in his 'Otherness,' his blackness. While presumably the court believed that Fountain was in control of his mental faculties during the commission of the crime, his blackness, a signifier of the cruel and capricious nature of fate, was certainly beyond his control and, thus, certainly worthy of sympathy. Fountain's location as 'Other' was underscored by the fact that Justice Lennox asked whether the prisoner, born on a Caribbean island that was a British possession and a colonial outpost of the British empire, spoke English.[79]

Paternalistic sentiments were also evident in Lennox's sentencing statements. For example, he told Fountain that 'I think that it is quite possible that when [your wife's] relatives came out here they resented their sister marrying you. But they had no reasonable ground for that. Your wife had the right to decide whom she would marry, and there is a great probability that you would have made her a good husband. The distinction in colour is made by a higher power than ours, and we have no right whatever to take matters into our own hands.'[80] Lennox continued: 'You are peculiarly situated here among people of a different origin, and you had less opportunity to do well than some other people have had. I sincerely sympathise with you in the position in which you are now placed, and I think there is a great deal to be said in mitigation of what you have done.'[81] Ultimately, however, Justice Lennox maintained that the evidence showed 'nothing in the final sense of the extenuation of the crime you have committed. The law is inexorable in that respect.'[82] For the second time in a little over a year, Fountain was sentenced to death; this time the sentence was to be carried out on 16 June 1920.

Roughly a week before Fountain's scheduled execution date, the Department of Justice commuted his sentence to life imprisonment. Paternalist portrayals of Fountain figure prominently in two key representations made on his behalf in the weeks prior to his execution date. One letter, authored by Richard Hardcourt, Welland MP, who purported to speak for a large number of 'thoughtful and responsible men' in the city, described Fountain as 'an unfortunate man, who is demented and was so at the time of the murder.' This fact, Hardcourt said, was 'a very strong case for life imprisonment.'

Under Section 19 of the Criminal Code, the legal definition of insanity rested upon three points. First, a person was deemed legally insane if, at the time of committing an offence, he was suffering from a diseased mind rendering him incapable of appreciating whether the act or omission was wrong or appreciating both the nature and quality of the act. Second, a person under delusions while committing an offence was not to be acquitted. The only exception to this principle was if the specific nature of the delusion led an offender to believe that there was a justification for his actions. Third, there was a presumption of sanity in the commission of a crime unless it could be proved otherwise.

The second letter on Fountain's behalf was written by Dr Harvey Clare. He acknowledged that 'according to the legal definition of insanity the Jury believed that he understood the nature and character of the act, and knew it was wrong' and 'consequently were compelled to bring in a verdict of guilty.' Regardless, Dr Clare believed that the legal definition of insanity was too narrow to adequately explain Fountain's mind state, and he remained resolute in his position that Fountain 'was insane at the time of the act.' Clare went further, suggesting that both the defence attorney and even the prosecuting attorney in the second trial 'will be anxious to say a word on behalf of *this poor chap*.'[83] Indeed, attitudes towards Fountain apparently softened to the point where the Remission Branch of the Department of Justice went so far as to recommended that Fountain be considered for release after a period of approximately ten years.[84]

These paternalist sentiments, however, were mingled with, and indeed eventually trumped by, disavowal. Not long after the commutation of Fred Fountain's sentence, an official with the Department of Immigration and Colonization wrote to the chief of the Remission Branch of the Department of Justice. His letter pointed out that Fred Fountain was 'subject to deportation' and that 'under the circumstances, there will probably be no difficulty in the matter of arranging for the return of Fred Fountain to the Bahamas, should his release for that purpose ever be directed.'[85] The chief of the Remission Branch responded favourably to the news that Fountain was a 'deportable immigrant' and agreed to place the letter on file so that 'if [Fountain] should be released at any time ... arrangements can be made to have him sent back to the Bahamas Islands, *to which he belongs*.'[86]

By November 1922, Fountain had been transferred from the Kingston Penitentiary to the Mental Disease Hospital for the Insane at Guelph, Ontario.[87] In January 1923 the superintendent of penitentiaries requested permission to deport Fountain.[88] Nonetheless, in March 1924, Fountain was still languishing in Guelph, a situation that the inspector of prisons and public charities for the province of Ontario found intolerable. 'Your Department,' wrote the inspector in a letter to the

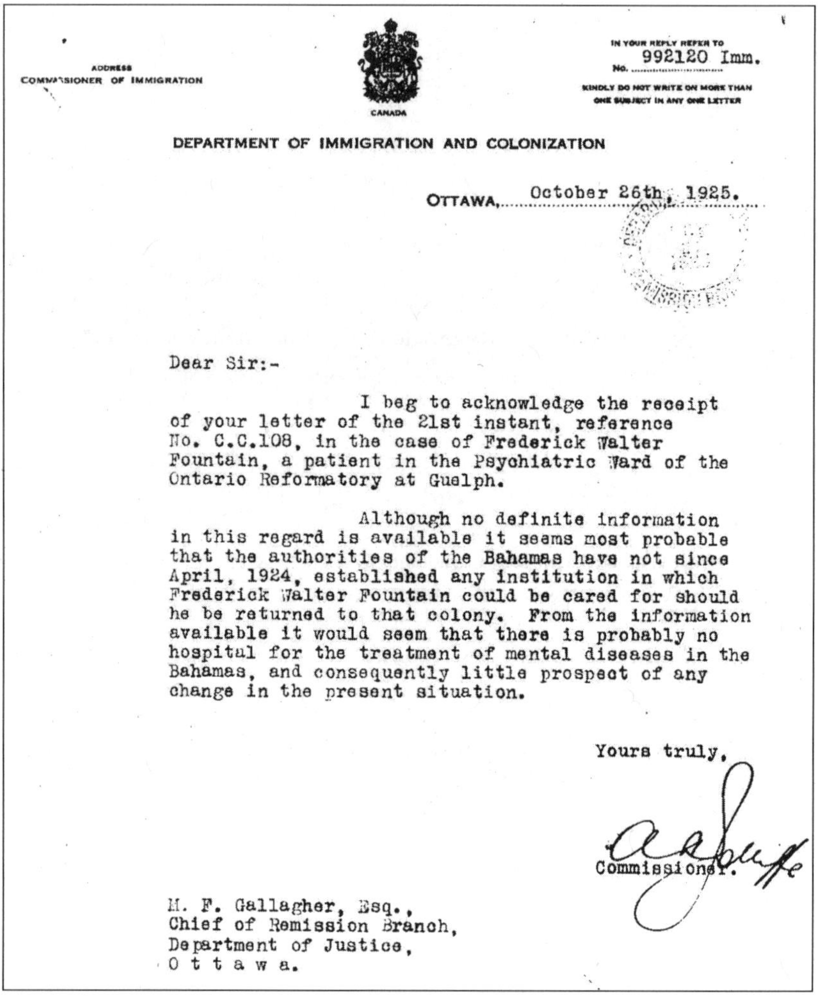

ADDRESS
COMMISSIONER OF IMMIGRATION

CANADA

IN YOUR REPLY REFER TO
No. 992120 Imm.

KINDLY DO NOT WRITE ON MORE THAN ONE SUBJECT IN ANY ONE LETTER

DEPARTMENT OF IMMIGRATION AND COLONIZATION

OTTAWA, October 26th, 1925.

Dear Sir:-

I beg to acknowledge the receipt of your letter of the 21st instant, reference No. C.C.108, in the case of Frederick Walter Fountain, a patient in the Psychiatric Ward of the Ontario Reformatory at Guelph.

Although no definite information in this regard is available it seems most probable that the authorities of the Bahamas have not since April, 1924, established any institution in which Frederick Walter Fountain could be cared for should he be returned to that colony. From the information available it would seem that there is probably no hospital for the treatment of mental diseases in the Bahamas, and consequently little prospect of any change in the present situation.

Yours truly,

Commissioner.

M. F. Gallagher, Esq.,
Chief of Remission Branch,
Department of Justice,
O t t a w a.

Fred Fountain, government correspondence, 26 October 1925, Library and Archives Canada, RG 13, vol. 184.

minister of justice, 'is now paying at the rate of $1.50 per day for keeping this man.' Invoking a discourse of race and nation, the inspector expressed the view that Fountain 'belongs to a class of foreigners who should never have been allowed into this country, and whether he is sane or insane, he is an undesirable acquisition to our population and

ADDRESS
COMMISSIONER OF IMMIGRATION

CANADA

IN YOUR REPLY REFER TO
No. 992120 Imm.
KINDLY DO NOT WRITE ON MORE THAN ONE SUBJECT IN ANY ONE LETTER

DEPARTMENT OF IMMIGRATION AND COLONIZATION

OTTAWA, November 12th, 1925.

Dear Sir:-

Referring to telephone communication from your office of the 10th instant with Inspector Reynolds concerning the case of Frederick Walter Fountain, your reference C.C.108, from the information available in this Department ~~there~~ would appear to be little prospect of ever being able to make arrangements for the suitable care or confinement of Frederick Walter Fountain on return to the Bahamas.

In December, 1922, the Governor of the Bahamas advised that as Frederick Walter Fountain was a native of the Bahamas there could be no objection to his return there, but as you are aware objection was later made to his return upon the ground that there was no suitable institution in which he could be kept under supervision and provided with proper treatment. Under all the circumstances there does not appear to be any ground for the authorities of the Bahamas refusing the return of Frederick Walter Fountain, notwithstanding his mental condition, and it would seem that there must be some provision in the colony for care of the insane.

Further representations will therefore be made to the Department of External Affairs with a view to ascertaining if some arrangement cannot be made with the authorities of the Bahamas with a view to having Frederick Walter Fountain received and cared for should his deportation be effected at an early date. Upon receipt of further report your Department will be notified.

Yours truly,

Commissioner.

The Chief of Remission Branch,
Department of Justice,
O t t a w a.

Fred Fountain, government correspondence, 12 November 1925, Library and Archives Canada, RG 13, vol. 184.

his presence here for the balance of his life is not only a bill of expense against the Dominion Government, but it is demoralising, and there is no reason under the sun why this country should keep this type of foreigner and support him in the balance of his days.' The time had come, he concluded, 'when we should reserve our public institutions for our own citizens and not for foreign criminals.'[89]

Officials in the Bahamas initially baulked at the idea of taking Fountain, arguing that there was nowhere in the colony where he could get suitable treatment.[90] By January 1926, however, the government of the Bahamas had changed its mind and agreed to place Fred Fountain in the Bahamas General Hospital.[91] A month later, the Department of Justice recommended that Fountain be released to his own country.[92] It instructed the superintendent of the Guelph Hospital for the Insane to 'deliver Fountain into the custody of the officer appointed by the Deputy Minister of Immigration and Colonization to see to his deportation.' Fountain thus received the same treatment that the Canadian state gave other 'dangerous foreigners.'[93]

The Harry Lee Murder Case

Finally, the sensational murder trial of Harry Lee in 1950s Hamilton also illuminates attitudes towards consensual sex between Black men and White women and the potentially tragic consequences of such unions.[94] Lee, a 'mulatto,' was charged with the murder of his paramour, Mary Rosenblatt, a married White Jewish woman. The case was a convoluted affair with many twists and turns. Mary Rosenblatt was regularly employed on a part-time basis as a waitress at the Scottish Rite Masonic Hall in Hamilton as well as at various synagogues in and around the area. On the day in question, Rosenblatt finished her cleaning at a synagogue in Westdale (a Hamilton suburb) and took a taxi in the late afternoon to Cannon Street in the city of Hamilton, where Harry Lee resided with his landlady. Several hours later, Rosenblatt was seen dead in the passenger side of Harry Lee's car with two bullet wounds in her chest.[95]

The defence presented in this case was neither terribly compelling nor convincing. Moreover, the defence counsel for Lee clearly had the burden of struggling within a broader cultural context in which pervasive ideas about the sexual wantonness of Black men were widely circulated.

Harry Lee contended that two 'armed thugs,' whom he believed belonged to a gang, entered his home, forced him to tie up his paramour with twine, kidnapped them, and took them on a 'wild ride' across southwestern Ontario. Rosenblatt, said Lee, was eventually shot by these two 'mysterious men.' People generally held Lee's story to be a 'fantastic tale.' It was a source of entertainment for the Hamilton media, and strained the limits of credibility.[96]

Whiteness also figured prominently in this trial, as did doubts about the definition of White racial identity. The case demonstrated discomfort with the idea that a White woman would voluntarily take a Black man as a lover. Rosenblatt, however, was not unambiguously 'White.' Indeed, she was a Jewish woman at a time of pervasive anti-Semitism in Canada. As the historical scholarship well documents, Jews still faced myriad restrictions and barriers in Canadian society in the late nineteenth and the early twentieth centuries; they struggled against de facto social restrictions, including exclusion from country clubs and resorts, and faced restrictive quotas in universities, professional schools, and various occupations. Moreover, the influx of Jews to Canadian cities in the early twentieth century had provoked an anti-Semitic backlash and produced a fair amount of hand-wringing over the deleterious effects that such an allegedly inferior and 'clannish' people might have on the national character.[97] Rosenblatt's Jewishness was never explicitly made an issue in court, though, as we shall see, at one point in the trial it perhaps inadvertently challenged her White racial status.

Even though Mary Rosenblatt was alleged to have taken a Black male lover, her character barely came under scrutiny. A frank acknowledgment of these kinds of openly transgressive sexual practices would surely have resonated beyond these particular cases, having profound implications for White manhood as a whole. That dominant tropes of White female virtue were not seriously or directly challenged in this trial spoke to a general unease over infidelity. This general unease was punctuated by the reluctance (or outright refusal) of White male elites to entertain fully the notion that respectable White women would voluntarily forsake their husbands and actively seek out the forbidden pleasures of the Black male body. And yet, as the U.S. literature shows, throughout the nineteenth and twentieth centuries, White men often feared that 'their' women desired Black men.[98]

Throughout, Mary Rosenblatt was constructed as a respectable, if perhaps misguided, woman. The claim that she had sexual trysts with a Black man was probably true but no one seriously entertained the idea aside from Lee and his defence counsel. At the very least, however, it was tacitly believed that her failure to adhere to dominant and recognized codes of White female domesticity, that is, to remain in the safety and sanctity of the domestic sphere, started a tragic trajectory of events which inevitably led to her downfall. Mary Rosenblatt was described as a housewife residing with her mother and two infant children in Hamilton who *'chose to augment the family income by occasional and part time work as a – waitress ... though her husband could afford to support the family.'*[99] The references to Mary Rosenblatt's respectability in the case file were much more overt, and more pointed. For example, a condensed summary of the case prepared for the minister of justice contains a brief profile of Lee, who is constructed as a racial 'Other,' and Rosenblatt, who is portrayed as a respectable middle-class woman – a married mother of two children.[100]

The fact that Rosenblatt's relationship had been shrouded in secrecy made it easier for White elites to dismiss the possibility of consensual interracial sex. This underlying theme was embodied quite poignantly in the police report, which confidently concluded that there was 'no doubt that Mary Rosenblatt knew Lee probably [but] in an innocent although foolish way was friendly with him.'[101] Thus, Lee's actions were deemed the result of Black male sexual frustration, a kind of 'thwarted passion.' While there was an active disavowal of mixed-race sex, Lee's crime was, nonetheless, highly sexualized. Consider, for example, the closing arguments of the crown attorney, who contended that Lee 'wanted [Mary Rosenblatt] ... [a]nd wanted her to abandon the family she loved. He wasn't satisfied with what he was getting – if he was indeed getting anything.'[102]

This tension between sexual disavowal and hypersexuality was apparent in the testimony that was brought into evidence. For example, a key medical witness, Dr W.J. Deadman, gave expert opinion on the cause of Rosenblatt's death, and was recalled by the prosecution, over the defence counsel's objection, also to give evidence pertaining to the 'condition of [Rosenblatt's] genital.' The defence's objection was based on the position that this had 'no relationship in this particular case when the cause of death was something other than having to do with the genitals.' The judge, however, was of the opinion that this was relevant. Dr Deadman stated that, during the course of his examination of Mary Rosenblatt, he could find no evidence of 'trauma ... that, is, injury.' He 'examined the fluid, microscopically, from the private parts and was not able to find any evidence of seminal fluid.' He concluded on the basis of this examination that the 'parts' were not different from the parts of a 'normal married woman.'[103]

Thus, the doctor's testimony could rhetorically evoke the image of Black male sexual violence upon the bodies of White women while repudiating the very repugnant idea of consensual interracial sex. The fact that there was no evidence of 'trauma' or 'injury' (heavily loaded tropes and metonymical signifiers of Black male sexuality) meant that there was little possibility of any sexual contact between Lee and Rosenblatt. Had there been such contact, Rosenblatt's genitals presumably could not have resembled those of a 'normal married woman.' The lack of evidence of trauma was considered sufficient to disavow consensual miscegenous sex, which in turn served to bolster the prosecution's assertion that Lee's crime was the manifestation of an unrealized or 'thwarted' passion.[104]

Significantly, G.M. Kennedy and J.L. Argo, the defence counsel, sought to challenge the doctor's testimony by wading into what was dangerous sexual and racialized territory. Kennedy suggested that there was indeed evidence of sexual contact between the two, and that the doctor had distorted the facts by concluding that sex between a Black man and White women could signify only 'rape.'

Q: Did you have occasion to make a swab test?
A: I made a swab test, yes.
Q: What was the result of your swab test?
A: The result was I looked carefully for spermatozoa, the sperms which are the known presence of seminal fluid and I was not able to find any.
Q: Is it quite possible that the spermatozoa, if any, present, could be missed?
A: That is possible.
Q: I suggest to you further, doctor, that the fluid which you examined microscopically might not have been in contact with the spermatozoa so it would not show?
A: Well, any fluid in the vagina is quite likely to be in contact with spermatozoa should they be introduced into the vagina.
Q: Supposing, doctor, that the normal act of intercourse had occurred some forty-eight hours prior to death, would there be any spermatozoa present in the fluid?
A: I wouldn't expect to find any, no ... I would not expect to find them twelve hours after intercourse in the normal case.
Q: Supposing, doctor, that a person had taken a vaginal douche some time subsequent to the intercourse. Would there be any likelihood of spermatozoa being found?
A: There would be very little likelihood of finding any after a douche.[105]

Allusions to racialized sexuality as rape situated Black male sexuality as the very antithesis of White masculinity. Moreover, this kind of discourse also highlights another key theme that emerged in both the Lee and Fountain cases: competing masculinities and sexual contests between Black men and White men.[106]

In addition to the frequent and vehement disavowals of consensual sex across the colour line, the trial was also marked by a concern for the White man directly implicated in this sordid tale as well as a much broader concern for the damaging effects that miscegenation might have on White masculinity and the White patriarchal family. This masculine contest was articulated through the competing testimonies of a Black male paramour and a White husband – each seeking to configure and reconfigure a White female subject/object, each seeking to claim the 'undying' love of the dead White woman.

The testimony of Charles Rosenblatt, Mary Rosenblatt's husband, was one of the key moments in the case. On the stand, Rosenblatt sought to portray himself as a good husband and father in a domestic and familial context characterized by harmony while also jealously guarding his wife's reputation. When asked whether a note allegedly written by his wife, and stating that she and Harry Lee were 'both crazy in love with each other,' was authentic, Charles Rosenblatt replied that the note was simply 'ridiculous':

Q: Would you tell his Lordship and the jury why that is ridiculous?
A: Well I don't think Mary was going around with anybody. I did not then, and I still don't.
Q: Did you ever throughout your whole period of years of married life have any reason to suspect the conduct of your wife?
A: No, I didn't. I think any man – any woman that is running around her husband would suspect it, would be the first to suspect it, or vice versa ...
Q: So far as her attention to yourself, her children and her home, were they anything different to what a faithful wife should be?
A: No, that is all she ever thought of.[107]

Defending Mary Rosenblatt's respectability also involved defending her White racial status. One of the investigating officers was asked to comment on the quality and authenticity of pictures taken by the chief inspector of Mary Rosenblatt's body at the crime scene and in her burial casket. The pictures also included a glimpse of the inspector. The subsequent exchange between the attorney and the inspector inadvertently challenged Mary Rosenblatt's whiteness, pushing her body to the margins of the fragile, tenuous, and porous racial boundaries which policed this case. The discussion began with a photo presented to the officer. In the photo, Rosenblatt's body appeared to be quite a bit darker than Inspector Wannell's. The defence counsel asked whether marks shown on the body appeared darker than they should have been. The officer answered 'no.' He was then asked if he himself appeared too dark in the photo. The officer agreed. This gave the defence counsel the opportunity to suggest that the pictures were overdeveloped. The officer rejected this suggestion, and the exchange ended by raising questions about whether Rosenblatt occupied what David Roediger and James Barret have called an 'inbetween' racial status:[108]

Q: I suggest to you, Constable Rallo, these pictures were over-developed.
A: No, if that was the case it would make the whole picture much darker.
Q: Then I take it that in Exhibition No. 29 the top of the casket there in the background is pure white satin?
A: Offhand I cannot say if it was white or not.
Q: You don't remember?
A: No.
Q: Does it look like a pure white satin background in that picture or is it somewhat grey?
A: It looks a bit greyer on this due to the fact of the flashbulb.
Q: I suggest to you, Constable, that if a picture is overdeveloped the skin texture or any marks will be shown up quite a bit darker?
A: Yes, but at the same time the whole picture will be darker.
Q: Yes, and particularly the marks?
A: Yes, if they are dark marks to begin with, yes, that will show a little darker.
Q: These marks on Mrs. Rosenblatt's arms are quite dark?
A: Yes, but if you will notice, the face is exactly *flesh tone colour and possibly could not be any way than what it is.*
Q: I show you Exhibit No. 2 showing the face of the deceased. Would you take a look at those two pictures and tell me whether or not there is quite a considerable darkening of the picture?
A: Yes, but the pictures were taken at two different times.[109]

If these darkened pictures served to 'blacken' Mary Rosenblatt's corporeal whiteness, metaphorically, they could also potentially threaten her 'White' interiority, her respectable subjectivity.[110] The blackened representation of Mary Rosenblatt's body in these photographs has striking resonances with the film-noir tradition, which puts into play shades of light and dark in order to exhibit people who become 'black' because of their 'shady' moral behaviour. As Eric Lott has argued, in this way racial imagery is used to show Whites' moral weaknesses. This process disrupted dominant tropes of Black male sexual transgression, which may well have been on shaky ground because of Rosenblatt's Jewishness. When the prosecution recalled Charles Rosenblatt, he was asked only one question – 'Your wife is what colour?' He answered, 'White.'[111] This brief exchange signified the seriousness of what was at stake. Recognizing the possible destabilizing effects of the darkened representations of the White female body in these photographs, the prosecution sought to firm up and reinscribe the racial demarcations which marked the trial. It may well have also been true that this exchange was a manifestation of Rosenblatt's less than full access to White skin privilege. In effect, Rosenblatt became White during the trial, or at least her whiteness was confirmed.

In the aftermath of the Harry Lee trial, the defence tried to employ various strategies in order to secure a commutation of his sentence. One argument cited by the defence was that the length of the jury's deliberations (four hours) suggested a deep ambivalence about the verdict it eventually meted out. In addition, the defence cited the results of a psychological assessment of Lee at the behest of his attorneys which said that Lee suffered from 'a paranoid type of mental illness.' These findings were corroborated by a physician hired by the Department of Justice.[112]

What is most striking, however, is the oppositional discourse that emerged outside the legal and medical arenas. The sheer number of people who showed Harry Lee support in his last days is striking. Many simply did not believe that he could have committed such a crime. A letter to the minister of justice that expressed this view also invoked the rhetoric of Canadian nationhood. Penned by a self-described 'Canadian citizen, taxpayer,' the letter protested 'the discrimination used in dealing out justice in Canada (yes there is discrimination in Canada).'[113] The letter further decried that 'tax money [was] being spent at one thousand dollars a head to a hang man who brags about the amount he gets, and the numbers of victims he has had since Christmas also the numbers of victims in the future. A man of this mentality,' the letter continued, 'should be thrilled at doing the job Gratis, the money saved could be used to procure *qualified* lawyers for those without means.'[114] Others closer to Lee also pleaded for his life. Lee's childhood Sunday school teacher asked the minister 'to be merciful unto [Lee] and to allow him every opportunity to prove himself innocent.' Another Hamilton resident asserted that 'there is a widespread feeling in the city that [Harry Lee] is not the real murderer and if any evidence should arise later that he is innocent something could be done about it if Harry Lee were still alive.'

In another impressive show of support, a petition organized by Lee's church, the Pentecostal Assemblies of Canada, contained 450 signatures.[115] Indeed, the churches showed the strongest degree of support, much of it spearheaded by the Reverend Sidney Kerr of the Galt Forward Baptist Church and the Reverend J.H. Blair of the Central Gospel Tabernacle. These two Black leaders worked tirelessly to attain a reprieve for the condemned Lee, organizing petitions, writing letters, and, in the case of Kerr, even discussing Lee's case over the phone with an aide to the minister of justice. The minister was unmoved by these efforts and Harry Lee's sentence was carried out.[116]

The space that Harry Lee occupied in the imaginary of the Black community and even among other non-Black members of the Pentecostal Church was different from the position he held in the mind of the larger society.[117] If the dominant culture constructed Lee as the epitome of danger to White womanhood, a passionate 'mulatto' driven by his lust for the White female body, the Black (religious) community's portrayal of Lee emphasized the perils and the temptations that White women held for respectable (and near-White) Black men. In a letter to the minister of justice, the Reverend Blair made it clear that Lee transgressed the boundaries of respectable Black manhood. He wrote, 'I do not endorse his actions in associating with a married woman,' but he stressed that 'I am not convinced he is guilty of the murder. He has not had any past criminal record. Our people are law abiding citizens and have no desire to pervert justice.'[118]

This condemnation of Lee's sexual relationship with Mary Rosenblatt was thus in some ways eerily congruent with the dominant culture's anxieties regarding miscegenation. It is also evident, however, that many people in and around Hamilton, both Black and non-Black, understood Lee's transgression differently – as the result of a tragic fall from a life of pious religiosity – thus eschewing the dominant discourse of a highly racialized White supremacist notion of Black male sexual depravity.

Thus, Lee's story was also appropriated by the reverends Blair and Kerr for their own purposes. A morality tale of sorts was constructed out of the case for the congregations of the Forward Baptist Church and

WHAT GOD DID *for* HARRY LEE

An amazing story of the Grace of God toward the man who was

HANGED IN BARTON STREET JAIL
HAMILTON, *Ontario, February* 3rd, 1953

Pamphlet: *What God did for Harry Lee.* Forward Baptist Church and Central Gospel Tabernacle, Hamilton, 1953. Library and Archives Canada, RG 13, vol. 1711.

the Central Gospel Tabernacle. A fascinating document titled 'What God did for Harry Lee' chronicled Lee's story in a highly dramatized fashion. The three-page tract traced Lee's beginnings from a boy 'born of humble, honourable negro stock' to his ignoble fall from grace and years as a 'backslidden believer,' and to his eventual redemption as the reverends Blair and Kerr ministered to him in Hamilton's Barton Street Jail in his final moments. He was executed on 3 February 1953.[119]

Conclusion

The cases discussed in this chapter show that the history of race and sex in Ontario has been fraught with peril, particularly when it involved sexual contact between White women and Black men. The case of William Beatty and Peter Hines did involve sexual violence between a Black man and a White woman. In that sense, it most closely resembles the cases examined in chapter 4, those that fit the archetype of sexual danger. What makes the Beatty and Hines case different from the archetypal script of sexual danger, however, is that, unlike the stark Black/White binaries that shape stock tales of race and sexual danger, Hines's accomplice was a White man whom his victim thought was Black because he was concealed by the dark and covered with coal spots. Beatty, a middle-class White man, was sharply reprimanded for his crime. His sentence, seven years in prison, would have been much stiffer had he actually been Black. His Black accomplice, Hines, was given the same sentence – far lighter than was the norm for Black men who committed similar crimes against White women. The working-class status of his victim and the middle-class status of his accomplice were factors in Hines's relatively light sentence. So too was the sympathetic treatment he received in the press.

Whereas the Hines and Beatty case demonstrated that racial ambiguity could characterize cases involving race and sex, the other cases involving Black men and White women in this chapter were marked by the ways in which they were determined by dominant ideas of the dangers Black males posed to White womanhood. When Ida Jane Lizzart bore George Freeman's child, he was immediately suspected of statutory rape. The preliminary hearing proved that he committed no such offence but the attempt to bring him to justice resulted in the killing of a police officer on his family farm. Freeman and his brothers were sentenced to life in prison for manslaughter, a sentence that was couched in the rhetoric of mercy and superior British justice. But, if not for the moral panic engendered by George's relationship with Ida Jane, his family would never have been on trial. These sorts of anxieties were also prominent in the case of Frank Turner, who was sentenced to eight years and twenty lashes for attacking a young White girl to whom he had offered a ride; the presiding judge lamented that Turner had raped his victim although he was never charged for the crime of rape. As this chapter has shown, the court was far more lenient, even insouciant, when it came to instances where White men were charged with assaulting Black women.

Lastly, cases of Black men murdering White women were held up as examples of tragically doomed 'unfortunate familiarities.' These stories were held up as cautionary tales for White women who chose Black male lovers or husbands, or who became otherwise overly familiar with Black men. Both Fred Fountain and Harry Lee were depicted as having killed these women out of the frustration of their not being able to measure up to the standards of White masculinity. If Fountain was driven to commit murder when his wife began to tire of him and show (natural) affection for a White suitor, Lee was depicted as a pathetic figure driven to commit murder out of his 'thwarted passion.' Both cases were fuelled by stock images of the rape archetype: violent Black men who could not control their insatiable desire for White women.

Conclusion

When Blacks were on trial in Ontario's criminal courts, race was on trial too. Black defendants tested the limits of freedom in post-slavery Canada. They experienced a social order that was far from the celebratory rhetoric of equality found in abolitionist broadsheets of the mid-nineteenth century, with their routine portrayal of euphoric ex-U.S. slaves kissing British soil as they crossed the border. This rhetoric has been emblematic of the Black experience in Canada, and has become a deeply embedded part of the national psyche. The myth is grounded in more than a kernel of truth, but, like all myths, it is too simplistic. Scholars have challenged it for decades though, stubbornly, it still endures. From the mid-nineteenth century until the mid-twentieth century – the cusp of the modern civil rights movement – Blacks found that their reality was an expression of 'race' in a liberal racial order. Theirs was a life characterized by the contradictions of formal legal equality on the one hand and profound legally supported social inequality on the other: immigration restrictions, discrimination in the labour market, and a Canadian version of 'Jim Crowism.'

This book has explored myriad dimensions where race was on trial in the history of Black criminal defendants. Criminal cases of property crime and interpersonal conflict featuring Black defendants are suggestive of the tensions at the heart of this racial order. Cases of property crime give us a window on the harsh realities of Black life in the nineteenth century, both the material deprivations that many Blacks faced and, in some instances, the harsh sentences that resulted. At the same time, as we have seen, as citizens Blacks often turned to the law to help adjudicate disputes within their communities in some instances and resisted its authority in others.

The death-penalty cases involving Black defendants examined in this book are particularly demonstrative of the tensions at the heart of the liberal racial order. They are statistically few but qualitatively rich. At the heart of these cases was the push and pull of the rule of law and broader dominant conversations about Blacks' place in Canada. In instances of both intraracial murder and murder across the colour line, were Blacks to be executed or were these sorts of cases to be an opportunity for White jurists, through the prerogative of mercy and/or paternalistic and racialized exculpatory arguments, to showcase the superiority of British justice? The outcomes of these cases were the result of the interplay of legal factors and social attitudes, the tension between the veneer of the rule of law and biologically and culturally rooted ideas about race in Canada.

Race was also on trial in instances of gender conflict among Blacks. Cases where Black men harmed or murdered Black women show that Black patriarchy was conferred on Black men both in terms of legal procedure and in terms of broader cultural forces. In cases of property crime, rape, and murder, there is compelling evidence of the patriarchal privilege enjoyed by these men, and this is in large measure due to the race and gender of their victims: Black women. Nonetheless, death-penalty cases involving Black men who murdered their spouses provide less clear-cut evidence of the privileges enjoyed by Black men. Discussions about Black men's inability to control their passions dominated these cases, an inability that was said to be a function of 'race,' madness, or both.

The cases in this book involving gender conflict across the colour line were perhaps the most incendiary. These cases were statistically few but nonetheless loomed large in the imaginations of Canadians. In 1868 the federal government decided to retain the death penalty for rape in Canada explicitly because of the conviction that Black men were prone to committing assaults upon White women. The death penalty for such crimes, John A. Macdonald believed, would serve as a useful deterrent and a necessary tool. In addition, Macdonald surely wanted to assure White Canadians that they need not resort to U.S.-style mobs to deal with such crimes. This was to be the prerogative of the state. In a few of these cases, the threat of mob violence – lynching in particular – was present but was not acted upon. In William McCathern's trial, the judge celebrated the nation and congratulated residents of Chatham, Ontario, for not burning the defendant alive, for respecting the principles of British justice. Frank Roughmond, the vagabond, was confronted by a mob and threatened with a lynching when he was found unconscious beside his victim. But he lived to see his execution date.

These were also cases where race was on trial, of course, but here the rule of law was put to its most extreme test given the revulsion and outrage sparked by such crimes. Running through all of them was the archetype of sexual danger, epitomized by the predatory Black male rapist of a White woman. It was also at work when Black men committed violence against White women with whom they were involved in 'unfortunate familiarities,' such cases being held up as cautionary tales for White womanhood.

Though this book is based on extensive research, in truth, it represents a modest beginning in the intersection of Black Canadian history, Critical Race Studies, and the law. There is much more Black Canadian history in the legal archives precisely because the law has had a central role in creating this history. The law, from the days of slavery to the difficult days of freedom, has profoundly shaped the Black experience in Canada. This book is a call for scholars of Black Canadian history to pay more attention to what the law can tell us about the complex and fraught histories of Blacks in both pre- and post-Confederation Canada. The central contradiction that framed the Black Canadian experience was legal freedom and legally supported social discrimination. The essence of the racial liberal order was the dynamic tension represented by Blacks' formal equality before the law and their racial inferiority – expressed in both biological and cultural terms – in the minds of those who were the architects of the legal system and of the social and economic systems that existed outside the walls of the courtroom but not beyond its purview. This book's exploration of Black criminal defendants, it is hoped, contains an important piece of the puzzle as we try to understand how race was expressed in the Canadian context and to comprehend the Black Canadian past on its own terms.

Notes

Introduction

1 See Robin Winks, *The Blacks in Canada*, 2nd ed. (Montreal and Kingston: McGill-Queen's University Press 1997), chapter 10, and James W. St G. Walker, *Racial Discrimination in Canada: The Black Experience*, Canadian Historical Association, Booklet no. 41 (Ottawa: Canadian Historical Association 1985).

2 Archives of Ontario (AO), Records of the Attorney General of Ontario, RG 4–32, Stephen Leacock to Edward Bayly, December 1929.

3 AO, RG 4–32, Bayly to Leacock.

4 According to Walker, 'only if someone were affected, and others not, would the law be classified as inequitable, according to this logic, or if some other party gained an unfair advantage from it ...' James W. St G. Walker, *'Race,' Rights and the Law in the Supreme Court of Canada* (Waterloo, Ont.: Wilfrid Laurier University Press 1997), 308. Canada also had its own version of Jim Crow. While it was legally supported in Canada and part of social customs, it was not legally codified as it was throughout the southern United States and parts of the north and the midwest. In an essay in a collection on the history of human rights in Canada, I argue that Canada's ties with the British empire, which increasingly embraced what I call (drawing heavily on the work of Ian McKay) a liberal racial order, influenced how Jim Crow was expressed in Canada. Jim Crow here reflected pervasive beliefs about the biologically rooted and intractable nature of

Black racial inferiority within the context of a liberal order which was based on ideas of formal legal equality and a belief that the lower races could be advanced under the right conditions of tutelage. See Barrington Walker, 'Finding Jim Crow in Canada,' in Janet Miron, ed., *A History of Human Rights in Canada* (Toronto: Canadian Scholars Press 2009), 81–98.

5 Kenneth Stamp, *The Peculiar Institution: Slavery in the Ante-Bellum South* (New York: Vintage Books 1956).

6 For a seminal discussion of the relationship between blackness, Canadianness, and modernity, see David Sealy, 'Canadianizing Blackness: Resisting the Political,' in Rinaldo Walcott, ed., *Rude: Contemporary Black Canadian Cultural Criticism* (Toronto: Insomniac Press 2000), 92–6.

7 Maureen G. Elgersman, *Unyielding Spirits: Black Women and Slavery in Early Canada and Jamaica* (New York: Garland Publishing 1999), 22.

8 Walker, *Racial Discrimination in Canada*, 8.

9 James W. St G. Walker, *The Black Loyalists: The Search for a Promised Land in Nova Scotia and Sierra Leone 1783–1870* (Toronto: University of Toronto Press 1992).

10 See Winks, *The Blacks in Canada*, chapter 5. See also Harvey Amani Whitfield, *Blacks on the Border: The Black Refugees in British North America 1815–1860* (Lebannon, N.H.: University of Vermont Press 2006).

11 Winks, *The Blacks in Canada*, 110.

12 Walker, *Racial Discrimination in Canada*, 10.

13 James W. St G. Walker, 'The Fall and Rise of Africville,' *Literary Review of Canada*, 2, no. 7 (1993): 5. Walker identities several different 'orientations' (rather than fully realized historiographical schools) which have characterized African Canadian historiography. The most salient characteristic of these orientations is the 'role assigned to Black people in the making of Black history.' The first is the 'Black Clients' orientation – that is, work that tends to focus on Whites in which Blacks are largely portrayed as the grateful and passive recipients of White beneficence. The second, the 'Black victimhood' orientation, focuses on Black abjection in the face of systemic discrimination. The third orientation stresses Black achievement in the face of insurmountable odds, and the fourth is comprised of studies that place the community at the centre of their analyses. Lastly, the most recent work tends to combine emphases on 'community' and the victim into what Walker calls the 'survivor' orientation.

14 See, for example, Fred Landon, 'The Anti-Slavery Society of Canada,' *Ontario History*, 48, no. 3 (1956): 125–31; and 'Canada's Part in Freeing the Slave,' *Ontario Historical Society Papers and Records*, 17 (1919): 74–5. For literature that points to the role of the law and the criminal courts in

maintaining this alleged haven, see Roman J. Zorn, 'Criminal Extradition Menaces the Canadian Haven for Fugitive Slaves,' *Canadian Historical Review*, 38 (1957): 284–7; and Alexander Murray, 'The Extradition of Fugitive Slaves from Canada,' *Canadian Historical Review*, 43, no. 4 (1962): 298–314. For later work that is more nuanced and sensitive but that nonetheless ultimately operates out of an overarching paradigm of Blacks being the beneficiaries of White benevolence, see Allan P. Stouffer, *The Light of Nature and the Law of God: Antislavery in Ontario 1833–1877* (Montreal and Kingston: McGill-Queen's University Press 1992).

15 Perhaps the most influential work to deal with this theme is Winks, *The Blacks in Canada*. See also William and Jane Pease, *Black Utopia* (Madison, Wis.: Madison Historical Society 1963); and William and Jane Pease, *They Who Would Be Free: Blacks' Search for Freedom, 1830–1861* (Champagne, Ill.: University of Illinois Press 1974); Jason Silverman, *Unwelcome Guests: Canada West's Response to American Fugitive Slaves* (New York: Associated Faculty Press 1985); and C. Peter Ripley, *The Black Abolitionist Papers Volume II: Canada, 1830–1865* (Chapel Hill: University of North Carolina Press 1986). For work that focuses on the emergence of all the Black settlements that were founded by Black and White abolitionists, see Howard Law, 'Self Reliance Is the True Road to Independence: Ideology and the Ex-Slaves in Buxton and Chatham,' in Franca Iacovetta et al., eds., *A Nation of Immigrants: Women, Workers and Communities in Canadian History: 1840s–1960s* (Toronto: University of Toronto Press 1998), 82–100; and Floyd J. Miller, *The Search for a Black Nationality: Black Emigration and Colonization 1878–1863* (Chicago: University of Illinois Press 1975).

16 See, for example, Ronald K. Burke, *Samuel Ringgold Ward: Christian Abolitionist* (New York: Routledge 1995); and Rosemary Sadlier, *Mary Ann Shadd: Publisher, Lawyer, Suffragette* (Toronto: Umbrella Press 1995).

17 Walker, *The Black Loyalists*.

18 Peggy Bristow et al., eds., *We're Rooted Here and They Can't Pull Us Up: Essays in African Canadian Women's History* (Toronto: University of Toronto Press 1994).

19 A recent work that speaks to this issue is Carol Tator and Frances Henry, *Racial Profiling in Canada: Challenging the Myth of a 'Few Bad Apples'* (Toronto: University of Toronto Press 2006).

20 See, for example, Paul Craven, 'The Law of Master and Servant in Mid-Nineteenth Century Ontario,' in David Flaherty, ed., *Essays in the History of Canadian Law, Volume I* (Toronto: Osgoode Society for Canadian Legal History / University of Toronto Press 1981), 175–211. For an example of an essay focusing on police court regulation of working-class behaviour, see

Paul Craven, 'Law and Ideology: The Toronto Police Court, 1850–1880,' in David Flaherty, ed., *Essays in the History of Canadian Law, Volume II* (Toronto: Osgoode Society for Canadian Legal History / University of Toronto Press 1983); Eric Tucker, '"That Indefinite Area of Toleration": Criminal Conspiracy and Trade Unions in Ontario, 1837–1877,' *Labour / Le Travail*, 27 (1991): 15–54, and 'The Faces of Coercion: The Legal Regulation of Labour Conflict in Ontario 1880–1889,' *Law and History Review*, 12 (1994): 277–340. On the emergence of the penitentiary, see Peter Oliver, *'Terror to Evil-doers': Prisons and Punishments in Nineteenth-Century Ontario* (Toronto: Osgoode Society for Canadian Legal History / University of Toronto Press 1998). For work on juveniles and the law, see Susan Houston, 'Victorian Origins of Juvenile Delinquency: A Canadian Experience,' *History of Education Quarterly*, 12, no. 3 (1972): 245–80; and Dorothy Chun, *From Punishment to Doing Good: Family Courts and Socialized Justice in Ontario, 1880–1940* (Toronto: University of Toronto Press 1992). For a post-Second World War study, see Franca Iacovetta, 'Gossip, Contest, and Power in the Making of Suburban Bad Girls: Toronto, 1954–1960,' *Canadian Historical Review*, 80, no. 4 (1999): 586–623.

21 Constance Backhouse, *Petticoats and Prejudice: Women and Law in Nineteenth-Century Canada* (Toronto: Osgoode Society for Canadian Legal History / Women's Press 1991).

22 Carolyn Strange, 'Patriarchy Modified: The Criminal Prosecution of Rape in York County Ontario, 1880–1930,' in Jim Phillips et al., eds., *Essays in the History of Canadian Law, Volume V: Crime and Criminal Justice* (Toronto: Osgoode Society for Canadian Legal History / University of Toronto Press 1994), 206–51, 209, 211.

23 Annalee Golz, '"If a Man's Wife Does Not Obey Him What Can He Do?" Marital Breakdown and Wife Abuse in Late Nineteenth Century Ontario,' in Susan W.S. Binnie and Louis Knafla, eds., *Law, Society and the State: Essays in Modern Legal History* (Toronto: University of Toronto Press 1995), 323–50, and 'Uncovering and Reconstructing Family Violence: Ontario Criminal Case Files,' in Franca Iacovetta and Wendy Mitchinson, eds., *On the Case: Explorations in Social History* (Toronto: University of Toronto Press 1998), 289–311; Judith Fingard, *The Dark Side of Life in Victorian Halifax* (Porters Lake, N.S.: Pottersfield Publishing 1989); Carolyn Strange, 'Wounded Womanhood and Dead Men: Chivalry and the Trials of Clara Ford and Carrie Davies,' in Franca Iacovetta and Mariana Valverde, eds., *Gender Conflicts: New Essays in Women's History* (Toronto: University of Toronto Press 1992), 289–311; Agnes Mclaren, 'Male Migrants and Murder in British Columbia, 1900–1923,' in Iacovetta and Mitchinson, eds., *On*

the Case, 159–180, and *The Trials of Masculinity: Policing Sexual Boundaries 1870–1930* (Chicago: University of Chicago Press 1997). Also see Steven Maynard, 'On the Case of On the Case: The Emergence of the Homosexual as a Case History in Early Twentieth-Century Ontario,' in Iacovetta and Mitchinson, eds., *On the Case*, 65–87, and 'Through a Hole in the Lavatory Wall: Homosexual Subcultures, Police Surveillance and the Dialectics of Discovery, Toronto 1890–1930,' in Joy Parr and Mark Rosenfeld, eds., *Gender and History* (Toronto: Copp Clarke 1996), 165–84.

24 Tina Loo, 'Savage Mercy: Native Culture and the Modification of Capital Punishment,' in Carolyn Strange, ed., *Qualities of Mercy: Justice, Punishment and Discretion* (Vancouver: UBC Press 1996), 108.

25 A few examples of works that explore Aboriginal history and the law are Sidney L. Harring, *White Man's Law: Native People in Nineteenth-Century Canadian Legal History* (Toronto: Osgoode Society for Canadian Legal History / University of Toronto Press 1998); Harmar Foster, '"The Queen's Law Is Better Than Yours": International Homicide in Early British Columbia,' in Phillips et al., eds., *Essays in the History of Canadian Law, Volume V*, 42–111; Tina Loo, 'The Road from Bute Inlet: Crime and Colonial Identity in British Columbia,' in Phillips et al., eds., *Essays in the History of Canadian Law, Volume V*, 113–42, and 'Tonto's Due: Law, Culture and Colonialization in British Columbia,' in Harmar Foster and John McLaren, eds., *Essays in the History of Canadian Law, Volume VI: British Columbia and the Yukon* (Toronto: Osgoode Society for Canadian Legal History / University of Toronto Press 1995), 128–70.

26 Clayton Mosher, *Discrimination and Denial: Systemic Racism in Ontario's Legal and Criminal Justice Systems 1892–1961* (Toronto: University of Toronto Press 1998), 28–30.

27 For more on the 'singled out' case method of historical analysis, a method pioneered by thinkers like Natalie Zemon Davis, see James W. St G. Walker, 'A Case for Morality: The Quong Wing Files,' in Iacovetta and Mitchinson, eds., *On the Case*, 217.

28 Constance Backhouse, *Colour-Coded: A Legal History of Racism in Canada, 1900–1950* (Toronto: Osgoode Society for Canadian Legal History / University of Toronto Press 1999), 15; Walker, *'Race,' Rights and the Law*, 303.

29 Walker, *'Race,' Rights and the Law*, 49.

30 Backhouse, *Colour-Coded*, 9, and 'The White Women's Labour Laws: Anti-Chinese Racism in Early Twentieth-Century Canada,' *Law and History Review*, 13, no. 2 (1996): 359.

31 Ann Laura Stoler, 'Racial Hierarchies and Their Regimes of Truth,' in

Philomena Essed and David Theo Goldberg, eds., *Race Critical Theories* (Malden. Mass.: Blackwell Publishing), 369–91.

32 Examples of work based on statistical data are C.H.S. Jaywardene, *The Penalty of Death: The Canadian Experiment* (New York: Lexington Books 1977); and David Chandler, *Capital Punishment in Canada: A Sociological Study of Repressive Law* (Montreal and Kingston: McGill-Queen's University Press 1976). See also Carolyn Strange, 'The Lottery of Death: Capital Punishment 1867–1976,' *Manitoba Law Journal*, 23, no. 3 (1996): 594–619.

33 In their examination of the trial and acquittal of a Black American circus performer tried for murder in Picton, Ontario, in 1903, Carolyn Strange and Tina Loo conclude that though the trial was atypical in its relative absence of class- and race-based arguments, the acquittal engendered self-congratulations as Pictonian jurists 'proved that even the lowest of the low benefited from His Majesty's justice ... [and] ... stood as an emblem of all that was best in Canada.' In the same vein, Strange's work on the trial of a 'mulatto' woman accused of the murder of a wealthy young White man in 1895 Toronto shows how chivalric paternalism and racialist notions of Black passion worked together for her acquittal. Karen Dubinsky and Franca Iacovetta use a similar approach in their study of an Italian immigrant woman convicted of murdering her husband. See Carolyn Strange and Tina Loo, 'Spectacular Justice: The Circus on Trial and the Trial as Circus: Picton, 1903,' *Canadian Historical Review*, 77, no. 2 (1996): 183–4; Carolyn Strange, 'Wounded Womanhood and Dead Men: Chivalry and the Trials of Clara Ford and Carrie Davis,' in Franca Iacovetta and Mariana Valverde, eds., *Gender Conflicts: New Essays in Women's History* (Toronto: University of Toronto Press 1993), 149–88; and Karen Dubinsky and Franca Iacovetta, 'Murder, Womanly Virtue and Motherhood: The Case of Angela Nepalitano, 1911–22,' *Canadian Historical Review*, 72, no. 4 (1991): 505–31. See also Mona Pon, 'The Case of the One Good Chinaman: Rex v. Charles Lee Hing, Stratford Ontario, 1909,' in Edgar Montigny and Lori Chambers, eds., *Ontario since Confederation: A Reader* (Toronto: University of Toronto Press 2000), 147–65. A fair bit of work that pushes these kinds of boundaries has been done in the U.S. context too. A few examples are: Walter Johnson, *Soul by Soul: Life inside the Antebellum Slave Market* (Cambridge, Mass.: Harvard University Press 1999); Diane Miller Sommerville, 'The Rape Myth of the Old South Reconsidered,' *Journal of Southern History*, 61 (August 1995): 481–518; Eugene Genovese, *Roll Jordon Roll: The World the Slaves Made* (New York: Vintage Press 1974); Martha Hodes, *White Women Black Men: Illicit Sex in the Nineteenth Century South* (New Haven, Conn.: Yale University Press 1997); and Lisa Linquist Dorr, 'Black

on White Rape and Retribution in Twentieth Century Virginia: Men, Even Negroes, Must Have Some Protection,' *Journal of Southern History*, 66 (November 2000): 711–48.

34 Carol A. Aylward, *Canadian Critical Race Theory: Racism and the Law* (Halifax: Fernwood Press 1999), 19–24. Critical Race Theory certainly fits this criteria. Its roots lie in Critical Legal Studies (CLS), an academic movement that emerged from left-leaning and mainly White male legal scholars in American legal institutions who were disgruntled with conventional liberal approaches to the study of law. They mounted a fierce battle in the temple of 'Legal Liberalism,' determined to topple the sacred pillars of rule of 'law, formalism, neutrality, abstraction, and individual rights.' Black legal scholars in the United States, as well as a much smaller cohort in Canada, were initially drawn to the CLS movement because it 'challenged the objectivity of laws that have oppressed people of colour.' It was not long, however, before scholars of colour began to see the limited utility of this particular brand of White academic radicalism. Aylward notes: 'While scholars of colour applauded the CLS movement's skepticism about the idea that law can produce determinate results free from reference to values, politics or historical conditions, they also believed that the Critical Legal Studies movement ignored the realities of people of colour.' The initial scepticism that developed among a cohort of Black and other non-White CLS scholars in the mid-1980s eventually developed into a full-blown critique. Minority legal scholars such as Richard Delgado raised concerns about CLS's 'disparagement of legal rules and rights,' its 'rejection of piecemeal change,' its 'idealism,' and, finally, its 'use of the concept of false consciousness.' Critical Legal Studies had an inherent inability to recognize that, for people of colour, a 'dual consciousness' was at work, simultaneously accommodating the idea of 'legal indeterminacy as well as the core belief in a liberating law that transcends indeterminacy.' Critical Race Scholars also expressed a marked discomfort with the CLS penchant for 'deconstructionist' approaches to the law that failed to move 'into the next vital stage of reconstruction.' Critical Race theorists argue that a world of repealed laws would not likely improve the lives of people of colour since they would still be subjected to the 'myriad insults, threats, indifference, and other micro aggressions' constantly directed towards non-Whites. They also argue that the 'utopian vision' free of rules and legal statutes so coveted by CLS scholars might very well lead to an increase in racist sentiment, thereby disempowering minorities. Simply put, 'jettison[ing] the rules and structures ... risk[s] losing the gains we have made in combating racism.'

35 Frantz Fanon, *The Wretched of the Earth* (New York: Grove Press 1963); Robert J.C. Young, *Postcolonialim: A Very Short Introduction* (New York: Oxford University Press 2003), 147.
36 See Sherene Razack, *Looking White People in the Eye: Gender, Race, and Culture in Courtrooms and Classrooms* (Toronto: University of Toronto Press 1998), Introduction.
37 Frantz Fanon, *Black Skins White Masks* (New York: Grove Press 1967), chapter 5, 'The Fact of Blackness.'
38 Edward Said, *Orientalism* (New York: Vintage 1994), 7–8.
39 Bhabha's work on the dynamic creation of the stereotype shows us that stereotypes do not merely consist of derogatory or harmful ideas that in turn establish a false image or a scapegoat which are then used to justify, reify, and institutionalize discriminatory practices. For Bhabha, the stereotype is a much more ambivalent and complex social and psychic phenomenon. Drawing on psychoanalytic theory and Foucauldian discourse analysis, Bhabha points to the existence of a realm of 'phantasmic' or fantasy beliefs which create in the colonizer a desire and longing for 'the Other' as well as a set of justifications for his continued subjugation. In the mind of the colonizer, the image of the colonized is invariably 'mixed and split,' for he is both a savage cannibal and an obedient servant, feeble-minded and a devious liar. For our purposes, Bhabha's work tells us two important things. First, the stereotype is neither a unified nor a coherent entity but mixed, messy, and contradictory. Second, both the colonizer and the colonized exist within the realm of colonial discourse. Homi Bhabha, 'The Other Question,' in Padmini Mongia, ed., *Contemporary Postcolonial Theory: A Reader* (New York: Arnold Publishing 1996).
40 Iacovetta and Mitchinson, eds., *On the Case*, Introduction.
41 Mariana Valverde et al., 'On the Case: Explorations in Canadian Social History: A Roundtable Discussion,' *Canadian Historical Review*, 81, no. 2 (2000): 281–7.
42 Margaret A. Banks, 'The Evolution of the Ontario Courts 1788–1981,' in Flaherty, ed., *Essays in the History of Canadian Law, Volume I*, 498.
43 Ibid., 514.
44 Ibid., 544.
45 Ibid., 511.
46 Ibid., 521.
47 Nancy Kay Parker, 'Reaching a Verdict: The Changing Structure of Decision-Making in the Canadian Criminal Courts, 1867–1905,' PhD thesis, York University, 1999.
48 Banks, 'The Evolution of the Ontario Courts,' 544.

49 Jim Phillips, '"Securing Obedience to Necessary Laws": The Criminal Law in Eighteenth-Century Nova-Scotia,' *Nova Scotia Historical Review*, 12, no. 2 (1992): 87–124; and Desmond H. Brown, *The Genesis of the Canadian Criminal Code of 1892* (Toronto: University of Toronto Press 1989), 43.

50 Brown, *The Genesis of the Canadian Criminal Code*, 56.

51 Carolyn Strange, *The Politics of Punishment: The Death Penalty in Canada, 1876–1976* (Winnipeg: Canadian History Project, Faculty of Law, University of Manitoba, 1992), 3.

52 Ibid.

53 Jonathan Swaiger, 'A Distant Edge of Authority: Capital Punishment and the Prerogative of Mercy in British Columbia, 1872–1880,' in Foster and McLaren, eds., *Essays in the History of Canadian Law, Volume VI*, 204–41.

54 Ibid.

55 Strange, *The Politics of Punishment*, 13.

56 Ibid.

57 Ibid.

58 Library and Archives Canada (LAC), RG 13, vol. 1407, *R. v. Curtley Bush.*

59 Chandler, *Capital Punishment in Canada*, 217, Appendix II.

60 See Benedict Anderson's foundational text *Imagined Communities: Reflections on the Origins and Spread of Nationalism* (New York: Verso 1991). For recent work on Canada as an 'imagined region,' see Gerald Friesen, '2005 Presidential Address: Space and Region in Canadian History,' *Journal of the Canadian Historical Association / Revue de la Société Historique du Canada* (New Series), vol. 16 (2005): 1–22.

61 See Strange, 'Introduction,' 8, and 'Discretionary Justice: Political Culture and the Death Penalty in New South Wales and Ontario, 1890–1920,' 139, in Strange, ed., *Qualities of Mercy*.

62 'Overdetermination' is a term that was coined by Freud to characterize 'the representation of a number of dream-thoughts in images privileged by their condensation in a number of thoughts in a single image, or by the transference of psychic energy from a particularly potent thought to apparently trivial images.' It was later employed by structural Marxists Louis Althusser and Etienne Balibar. Their conception of the term replaced images and dreams with social formations and practices (economic, political, and ideological). Althusser employed the term to describe how contradictions within these practices affected the social formation as a whole and how this in turn affected each individual social formation. Post-Althusserian uses of the term, particularly in post-colonial theory, tend to act as a bridge between the psychoanalytic and structuralist analyses, employing it to explain social and cultural structures under colonialism.

Homi Bhabha, for example, uses the term 'functional overdetermination' to explain how race and sex work in conjuction under the auspices of colonialism, and how they are mobilized to create stereotypes: within the apparatus of colonial power, the discourses of sexuality and race relate in a process of functional overdetermination, 'because each effect ... enters into resonance or contradiction with the others and thereby calls for a readjustment or a re-working of the heterogeneous elements that surface at various points.' See Louis Althusser and Etienne Balibar, *Reading Capital*, 5th ed. (New York: Verso 1990), 315; Bhabha, 'The Other Question,' 44.

1 Blackness and the Law in Slavery and Freedom

1 Elgersman, *Unyielding Spirits: Black Women and Slavery in Early Canada and Jamaica* (New York: Garland Publishing 1999), 31; quote from the *Upper Canada Gazette*, July 1795.
2 Samuel Ringgold Ward, editorial, *Voice of the Fugitive*, 4 November 1852, as cited in C. Peter Ripley, ed., *The Black Abolitionist Papers, Volume II, Canada, 1830–1865* (Chapel Hill: University of North Carolina Press 1986), 224–44.
3 James St G. Walker, *The Black Loyalists: The Search for a Promised Land in Nova Scotia and Sierra Leone, 1783–1870* (Toronto: University of Toronto Press 1992), 28, as cited in Barry Cahill, 'Slavery and the Judges of Loyalist Nova Scotia,' *UNB Law Journal*, 43, no. 31 (1994): 73–135.
4 Afua Cooper, *The Hanging of Angelique: The Untold Story of Canadian Slavery and the Burning of Old Montreal* (Toronto: HarperCollins 2006), 68.
5 Elgersman, *Unyielding Spirits*, 5; Robin Winks, *The Blacks in Canada*, 2nd ed. (Montreal and Kingston: McGill-Queen's University Press 1997), 1.
6 Elgersman, *Unyielding Spirits*, 4; Winks, *The Blacks in Canada*, 1–2.
7 Winks, *The Blacks in Canada*, 9; Marcel Trudel, *L'esclavage au Canada Français: Histoire et Conditions de l'Esclavage* (Quebec: Laval University Press 1960), 317.
8 Elgersman, *Unyielding Spirits*, 4.
9 Winks, *The Blacks in Canada*, 9–10.
10 Kenneth Donovan, 'Slaves and Their Owners in Île Royale, 1713–1760,' *Acadiensis*, 25, no. 1 (1995): 3–32.
11 Ibid., 4.
12 Winks, *The Blacks in Canada*, 3.
13 Ibid., 6.
14 Ibid., 10; Donovan, 'Slaves and Their Owners in Île Royale,' 5; Elgersman, *Unyielding Spirits*, 14.
15 Elgersman, *Unyielding Spirits*, 15.

16 Winks argues that 'the protection that was extended to slaves in the Antilles by the *Code Noir* was applied in New France even if the code was not law.'
17 Winks, *The Blacks in Canada*, 23.
18 Elgersman, *Unyielding Spirits*, 23; Winks, *The Blacks in Canada*, 24–5.
19 Elgersman, *Unyielding Spirits*, 23.
20 Ibid., 23.
21 Winks, *The Blacks in Canada*, 25.
22 Lord Mansfield, who presided over this famous case in 1772, ruled that slavery could not exist in England without a law to enforce it positively. The view that the Somerset case freed all slaves in Britain was widely held, but, according to legal scholar D.G. Bell, this was a misconception. Mansfield himself was willing to rule only that once a slave was in England he could not be exported. The importance of the Somerset case was that it called the legality of slavery into question, not that it abolished it. Winks, *The Blacks in Canada*, 25; D.G. Bell, 'Slavery and Judges of Loyalist New Brunswick,' *UNB Law Journal*, 31 (1982): 12–13.
23 Winks, *The Blacks in Canada*, 26.
24 Cooper, *The Hanging of Angelique*, 91.
25 Winks, *The Blacks in Canada*, 28.
26 Allen P. Stouffer, *The Light of Nature and the Law of God: Antislavery in Ontario, 1833–1877* (Montreal and Kingston: McGill-Queen's University Press), 11.
27 Winks, *The Blacks in Canada*, 23.
28 Ibid.
29 Ibid., 98.
30 Stauffer, *The Light of Nature and the Law of God*, 14–15.
31 J.M. Bumsted, *A History of the Canadian Peoples*, 3rd ed. (Toronto: Oxford University Press 2007), 88; Winks, *The Blacks in Canada*, 27; Walker, *The Black Loyalists*, 40.
32 Walker, *The Black Loyalists*, 1, 8.
33 Ibid., 41.
34 Ibid., 40.
35 Cahill, 'Slavery and the Judges of Loyalist Nova Scotia,' 43.
36 Ibid.
37 Ibid.
38 Ibid., 82.
39 James St G. Walker, *Racial Discrimination in Canada: The Black Experience*, Canadian Historical Association, Booklet no. 41 (Ottawa: Canadian Historical Association 1985), 8.
40 Ibid., 9.

41 Ibid., 11.

42 The figure cited in the official census for the Black population in 1861 was 13,566. However, both Daniel Hill and Michael Wayne have found that the number was 11,223. With regard to the issue of the grossly exaggerated Black population in Canada West in the 1850s, Wayne notes that in 1854 Benjamin Drew, a Black abolitionist, 'accepted uncritically the claim by the Anti-Slavery Society that there were almost 30,000 Blacks in Canada by 1852.' See Winks, *The Blacks in Canada*, 487; Daniel Hill, 'Negroes in Toronto, 1793–1865,' *Ontario History*, 55, no. 2 (1963): 73–91; and Michael Wayne, 'The Black Population of Canada West on the Eve of the American Civil War: A Reassessment Based on the Manuscript Census of 1861,' in Franca Iacovetta et al., eds., *A Nation of Immigrants: Women, Workers and Communities in Canadian History, 1840s–1960s* (Toronto: University of Toronto Press 1998).

43 Wayne, 'The Black Population of Canada West,' 62.

44 Ibid.

45 Winks, *The Blacks in Canada*, 486.

46 Ibid.

47 Census of Canada, 1931, vol. 2, Table 32, 'Population and Local Subdivisions'; Census of Canada, 1941, vol. 2, Table 31, 'Population by Racial Origin and Sex for Countries and Census Divisions, Total and Rural, 1941'; and Census of Canada, 1951, vol. 1, Table 32, 'Population by Origin and Sex for Province and Territories.'

48 Winks, *The Blacks in Canada*, 496.

49 Fred Landon, 'The Upper Thames Valley,' in Jessie Edgar Middleton and Fred Landon, eds., *The Province of Ontario: A History, 1615–1927, Volume II* (Toronto: Dominion Publishing 1927), 1025–7.

50 Winks, *The Blacks in Canada*, 493.

51 The data to support this claim were compiled from the Census of Canada for the years 1861 and 1881 and Winks, *The Blacks in Canada*, 493. In the 1951 census, the Black populations of Essex and Kent were absurdly enumerated under the category of 'Other,' a designation that also included Chinese, Japanese, and 'Other Asians,' as well as Indians and Eskimos. It is unlikely that the Black population decreased in these counties during the era, given the fact that, as noted above, a marked increase in the province's Black population was reported during this period. See Census of Canada, 1931, vol. 2, 'Population, Local Subdivisions'; Census of Canada, 1941, 'Population by Racial Origin and Sex for Counties and Census Divisions, Total and Rural'; Census of Canada, 1951, vol. 1, 'Population and Characteristics.'

52 Winks, *The Blacks in Canada*, 169.

53 Ibid.

54 Ibid., 169; Adrienne Shadd, Afua Cooper, and Carolyn Smardz Frost, *The Underground Railroad: Next Stop, Toronto!* (Toronto: Umbrella Press 2002), 68.

55 David Murray, *Colonial Justice: Justice, Morality, and Crime in the Niagara District* (Toronto: Osgoode Society for Canadian Legal History / University of Toronto Press 2002), 99.

56 Ibid., 174.

57 Winks, *The Blacks in Canada*, 174. See also William Teatero, *John Anderson: Fugitive Slave* (Toronto: Brown and Martin 1986); and Patrick Brode, *The Odyssey of John Anderson* (Toronto: Osgoode Society for Canadian Legal History / University of Toronto Press 1989).

58 Narrative of Henry Atkinson in Benjamin Drew, *The Refugee or the Narratives of Fugitive Slaves in Canada Related by Themselves with an Account of the History and Condition of the Colored Population of Upper Canada* (Toronto: Prospero 2000), 175, 82.

59 For an extensive discussion of these issues, see, for example, Jason Silverman, *Unwelcome Guests: Canada West's Response to American Fugitive Slaves, 1800–1865* (Millwood, N.Y.: Associated Faculty Press 1985).

60 See Winks, *The Blacks in Canada*, chapters 6 and 7; Howard Law, '"Self-Reliance Is the True Road to Independence": Ideology and the Ex-Slaves in Buxton and Chatham,' in Iacovetta et al., eds., *A Nation of Immigrants*, 82–100.

61 Winks, *The Blacks in Canada*, 248–9.

62 Wayne, 'The Black Population of Canada West,' 71.

63 Donald G. Simpson, *Under the North Star: Black Communities in Upper Canada* (Toronto: Africa World Press 2005), 13–14.

64 Benjamin Drew, *The Narrative of the Fugitive Slaves* (Toronto: Prospero Books 2000), 147.

65 Ibid.

66 Winks, *The Blacks in Canada*, 368.

67 Ibid., 367.

68 Kristin McLaren, '"We Had No Desire to Be Set Apart": Forced Segregation of Black Students in Canada West and Myths of British Egalitarianism,' *Social History / Histoire sociale*, 37, no. 73 (2004): 35.

69 Ibid., 34.

70 Winks, *The Blacks in Canada*, 368.

71 McLaren, '"We Had No Desire to Be Set Apart,"' 38; Winks, *The Blacks in Canada*, 370.

72 Winks, *The Blacks in Canada*, 370.
73 Ibid., 369.
74 Ibid., 375.
75 Peggy Bristow, 'Black Women in Buxton and Chatham,' in Bristow et al., eds., *We're Rooted Here and They Can't Pull Us Up: Essays in African Canadian Women's History* (Toronto: University of Toronto Press 1999), 117.
76 Brantford *Expositor*, 8 October 1858.
77 Ibid.
78 AO, RG 22, 392–0–2626, *R. v. Edward Harrison*.
79 AO, RG 22, 392–0–2645, *R. v. Ephrine Rodine*.
80 AO, RG 22, 392–0–2633, *R. v. Phillip Morton*.
81 AO, RG 22, 392–0–2628, *R. v. Aceleous Hurst et al.*; Chatham *Tri-Weekly Planet*, 29 October 1859.
82 AO, RG 22, 0–2727, *R. v. Nathaniel Farris*.
83 See, for example, Greg Marquis, 'Doing Justice to "British Justice": Law, Ideology, and Canadian Historiography,' in W. Wesley Pue and Barry Wright, eds., *Canadian Perspectives on Law and Society: Issues in Legal History* (Ottawa: Carleton University Press 1988), 50–1. Two articles cited by Marquis that deal with the issue of working-class encounters with the law in early Ontario are John Weaver, 'Crime, Public Order and Repression: The Gore District in Upheaval, 1832–1851,' *Ontario History*, 78 (September 1986): 175–207; and Paul Romney, 'From the Types of Riot to the Rebellion: Elite Ideology, Anti-Legal Sentiment, Political Violence and the Rule of Law in Upper Canada,' *Ontario History*, 79 (June 1987): 133–44. See also Susan Lewthwaite, 'Violence, Law and Community in Rural Upper Canada,' in Jim Phillips et al., eds., *Essays in the History of Canadian Law, Volume V: Crime and Criminal Justice* (Toronto: Osgoode Society for Canadian Legal History / University of Toronto Press 1994), 354–86.
84 Josiah Henson's life is well documented, including in a 1949 manuscript titled *The Life of Josiah Henson, Formerly a Slave, Now an Inhabitant of Canada: As Narrated by Himself* (London: Charles Gilpin, Bishopsgate Without 1851). Harriet Beecher Stowe's *Uncle Tom's Cabin* was believed to have been based on Henson's life, but, as Robin Winks points out, at no time during the publication of his narrative did Stowe publicly associate herself with Henson. However, ghostwriters of Henson's various later memoirs stubbornly insisted that he was the original 'Uncle Tom.' The story of Uncle Tom also inspired many theatrical blackface representations – popularly known as 'Tom Shows' – on both sides of the border well into the nineteenth century in Canada. See Winks, *The Blacks in Canada*, 185–6; Eric Lott, *Love and Theft: Blackface Minstrelsy and the American Working Class*

(New York: Oxford University Press 1995), 211–33; Josiah Henson, *Uncle Tom's Story of His Life: An Autobiography of the Reverend Josiah Henson 1789–1867, with a Preface by Mrs Harriet Beecher Stowe* (London: Cass Library of African Studies, Slavery Series, no. 13, 1971).

85 Chatham *Tri-Weekly Planet*, 27 October 1859.

86 AO, RG 22, 392–0–2627, *R. v. Josiah Henson and William Stewart.*

87 Lewthwaite, 'Violence, Law and the Community in Rural Upper Canada.'

88 AO, RG 22, 392–0–1422, *R. v. Isaac Mulder.*

89 AO, RG 22, 392–0–2826, *R. v. Felix Shreeve.*

90 AO, RG 22, 392–0–1405. Neither the indictment file nor the Windsor jail records indicate the sentence that was meted out.

91 AO, RG 22, 392–0–273, *R. v. John Cutley.*

92 AO, RG 22, 392–0–1301, *R. v. John Jackson.*

93 AO, RG 22, 392–0–2682, *R. v. John Thompson*; RG 22, 382–0–392–1375, *R. v. George Nolan*; RG 22, 392–0–2708, *R. v. Charles Oxentine.*

94 Chatham *Weekly Planet*, 12 May 1881.

2 Nationhood, Mercy, and the Gallows

1 See Tina Loo, '"Savage Mercy": Native Culture and the Commodification of Capital Punishment in Nineteenth Century British Columbia,' and Carolyn Strange, 'Discretionary Justice: Political Culture and the Death Penalty in New South Wales and Ontario, 1840–1920,' in Carolyn Strange, ed., *Qualities of Mercy: Justice, Punishment and Discretion* (Vancouver: UBC Press 1996), 104–29, 130–65; Constance Backhouse, *Colour-Coded: A Legal History of Racism in Canada, 1900–1950* (Toronto: University of Toronto Press 1999).

2 See George Elliott Clarke, 'Raising Raced and Erased Executions in African-Canadian Literature, or Unearthing Angelique,' in Camille A. Nelson and Charmaine A. Nelson, eds., *Racism Eh?: A Critical Inter-Disciplinary Anthology of Race and Racism in Canada* (Toronto: Captus Press 2004), 73.

3 LAC, RG 12, vol. 1407, *R. v. G.W. Johnston*, memo from Justice Morrison to the secretary of state, 24 November 1867.

4 Ibid., Privy Council memo, 6 December 1867.

5 Ibid.

6 LAC, RG 13, vol. 1407; attached to the petition was a form sent from the Department of Justice to the warden of the Kingston Penitentiary requesting that the warden report upon 'the conduct and remission' of George Johnston. The report, which formed the basis of the petition, noted Johnston's 'good conduct, his trade in stonework, and the fact that he had earned 19 months remission.'

7 Carolyn Strange, 'Lottery of Death: Capital Punishment 1867–1967,' *Manitoba Law Journal*, 23, no. 3 (1996): 610.

8 Ibid., 611.

9 LAC, RG 13, vol. 1411, file 82A, testimony of Mary Smith.

10 Joseph Smith was also indicted for murder along with James Smith as an 'accessory after the fact.' However, the charge was dismissed shortly before the trial.

11 LAC, RG 13, vol. 1411, file 82A, testimony of Joseph Smith.

12 Ibid., testimony of Dr James Sampson and Dr Daniel Samuelson.

13 Ibid., testimony of Benjamin Howe and Archibald Hunter.

14 Ibid., testimony of Robert Brightman.

15 Ibid., trial summary, Justice John W. Gwynne to the secretary of state, 29 October 1874.

16 Ibid., petition to Governor General Fredrick Temple. The petition was signed by roughly eighty people.

17 Ibid., letter from the sheriff of Kent County acknowledging news of the commutation of James Smith's sentence.

18 AO, RG 22, 392–0, *R. v. Frank Smith*, report of the Chatham Police Department.

19 Chatham *Daily Planet*, 3 March 1914.

20 The 6 February 1914 edition of the Chatham *Daily Planet* ran the story of Charles Guton, 'a young Negro [who] was convicted of highway robbery although his only loot was a white girl's kiss.' The article noted further that 'deputations of white women visited the judge … to demand that action be taken to save Guton from such severe punishment. Telephone messages informed him petitions were being taken to procure a pardon from the governor. Judge Willis explained the Negro had been convicted of highway robbery. He had taken a dime from the white girl, although he gave it back after he kissed her, and he had subjected six other white women to similar treatment, besides criminally attacking two Negro girls.'

21 AO, RG 22, 392–0, *R. v. Frank Smith.*

22 Ibid.

23 Ibid.; emphasis added.

24 Ibid.

25 Ibid.

26 AO, RG 22, 392–2621, *R. v. Andrew David*. There was also mention in the Chatham *Daily Planet* of a Native man named Paymahgay who was tried in the same year. I could find no mention of Paymahgay's trial in the legal records, and the likelihood of two such trials in the same year is slim. It is

more likely, therefore, that Paymahgay and Andrew David are the same person. David was tried and found guilty of murder at the 1859 Chatham assizes when he struck another Native man with a hoe while harvesting corn. The Chatham jail records of that year again shed light on the issue of interlocking racial representations of Blacks and Natives. Having no category for 'Indian' in their records, the jailers marked Paymahgay in the column headed 'Black.' The complexities inherent in racial performativity can be found in another aspect of Paymahgay's case. The Chatham *Daily Planet* reported that a few older residents of Chatham recalled that Paymahgay's hangman was a 'Negro well known in those days as Negro Steve.' Negro Steve was suspected to have been a 'white man who disguised himself by painting himself black.'

27 Ibid.

28 Ibid. Smith's sentence was commuted by the Duke of Connaught, a government official.

29 LAC, RG 13, vol. 1439, *R. v. Levi Steward*, report to the minister of justice, 18 January 1900.

30 AO, RG 22–392–0–1486, *R. v. Levi Steward*.

31 LAC, RG 13, vol. 1439, *R. v. Levi Steward*, memorandum for the honourable minister of justice (trial summary).

32 Ibid., trial transcripts, 235.

33 Ibid., Dr James Sampson to David Mills, minister of justice, 18 January 1900.

34 Ibid., trial transcripts, 190–1.

35 Ibid., trial transcripts, 166–74. See, for example, the testimony of defence witnesses Arthur Price, John Price, and James Samuel Austin. Each testified about Sarah Carter's general reputation for veracity in her hometown of Elmstead. Hanna's real intention, however, was to portray Carter as an immoral woman. It was a 'particular act of immorality' that interested Hanna: Carter's co-habitation with another man named Shanklin, a prosecution witness. The defence wanted to show that Carter was a loose woman who had taken up with another man shortly after Steward's arrest. The judge objected to this tactic, warning Hanna that such evidence was collateral and that immorality did not necessarily indicate a lack of truthfulness. 'Women in particular,' the judge continued, 'may be of the most lewd and immoral character yet speak the truth.' The key to uncovering the truth, then, was relying on the rules of the law by 'reflecting upon the evidence.'

36 Ibid., 192–3.

37 Chatham *Daily Planet*, 26 January 1900.

38 Ibid., Inquisition and Judgement of Death on the Body of Levi Steward, 6 February 1900.

39 LAC, RG 13, vol. 1580, *R. v. Franklin Jackson*, reports from Justice Sedgewick to the secretary of state, 22 February 1933.

40 Ibid.

41 LAC, RG 13, vol. 1580, *R. v. Franklin Jackson*, trial transcripts, 31.

42 Ibid., trial transcripts, 71.

43 Ibid., 106–7.

44 Ibid., newspaper clippings.

45 *R. v. Jackson* [1933] O.R. 522 (Court of Appeal), 524.

46 So pervasive was the view that the second trial was identical to the first that Justice Armour wrote the minister of justice 'to ascertain ... whether the report that the Hon. Mr. Justice Sedgewick made after the first trial of the prisoner would not be sufficient for his purposes? On the second trial before me, the evidence was the same as given before Mr. Justice Sedgewick.' The Department of Justice tersely replied: 'We will want the Judge's charge at the second trial, and we should also have Judge Armour's report in the usual way.' Ibid., correspondence between Justice Armour and the minister of justice, 17 October 1933.

47 LAC, RG 13, vol. 1580, *R. v. Franklin Jackson*.

48 Ibid., 31 October 1933, George Gordon to Hugh Guthrie, minister of justice.

49 Ibid., Inquiry into the Cause of Death of Edward Franklin Jackson, 30 November 1933. The inquest was held at the chambers of the Police Court of the city of Peterborough where a jury of twelve was summoned upon the authority of a police constable. Each gave sworn testimony as witnesses to Jackson's hanging and burial.

50 Carolyn Strange and Tina Loo, 'Spectacular Justice: The Circus as Trial and the Trial as Circus, Picton 1903,' *Canadian Historical Review* 77, no. 2 (1996): 182.

51 Ibid., 183.

52 LAC, RG 13, vol. 1407, *R. v. Charles Medley*, testimony of Eliza Rose.

53 By the twentieth century, concerns about the sexual dangers posed by Black men had crystallized in the form of White opposition to African American migration to the Canadian west. See Winks, *The Blacks in Canada*, 2nd ed. (Montreal and Kingston: McGill-Queen's University Press 1997), 298 and 309; and R. Bruce Sheppard, *Deemed Unsuitable: Blacks from Oklahoma Move to the Canadian Prairies in Search of Equality in the Early 20th Century Only to Find Racism in Their New Home* (Toronto: Umbrella Press 1997), 78–9.

54 LAC, RG 13, vol. 1407. See, for example, the testimony of James Hawkins and Samuel Taylor, both of whom testified that Charles Medley was in the vicinity on the night of the crime and that he was the man who administered the fatal blows to Captain Minor.

55 Ibid., testimony of Eliza Rose.

56 Ibid., testimony of William Stephens and William Burnett.

57 Ibid.

58 Ibid., 9 December 1868. On the order of the governor general, the government granted Bush a new trial on the basis of 'the Report and notes of Evidence of His Honour C.R. Beecher Esquire ... and on the recommendation of the Minister of Justice.'

59 LAC, RG 13, vol. 1407, the Reverend Isaac J. Rice to the governor general, 15 December 1868.

60 The legal record is strangely silent on Bush's ultimate fate. One can only assume that his sentence was also commuted given that he was not charged with murder but with aiding and abetting.

61 Strange, 'Discretionary Justice,' 148–53.

62 LAC, RG 13, vol. 1447, *R. v. Slaughter*, memorandum for the minister of justice.

63 While Delos Rogest Davis is widely cited as the first Black lawyer to practise in Canada, that distinction, as Constance Backhouse has pointed out, rightly belongs to Robert Sutherland, who was admitted to the bar in 1885. Davis was the son of an escaped Maryland slave. After a rather circuitous route that saw him work at a variety of jobs (including a brief stint as a teacher), he began to study law in 1871 under the tutelage of sympathetic Whites – one a county judge, the other an attorney. Racist barriers in the profession meant that no White attorney was willing to allow Davis to pursue the crucial step of articling. Two petitions to the Ontario legislature in 1884 and 1886 resulted in two special acts which allowed Davis to practise law and be called to the bar providing he passed the 'requisite examination.' Though Davis served as counsel on 'six important murder cases,' his specialty was 'drainage litigation.' See Backhouse, *Colour-Coded*, 374–5; and Owen Thomas, 'Davis, Delos Rogest,' *Dictionary of Canadian Biography*, vol. 14 (Toronto: University of Toronto Press / Quebec: Les Presses de l'Université Laval 1998), 274–5.

64 Carolyn Strange, 'Political Culture and the Death Penalty in New South Wales and Ontario 1890–1920,' in Strange, ed., *Qualities of Mercy*, 130–65.

65 Ibid., 149–50.

66 LAC, RG 13, vol. 1447, *R. v. Slaughter*, trial transcripts.

67 Davis crafted three main arguments: first, that 'paralysis from the blow

had disappeared'; second, that the '[a]bsorbtion of the blood clot had commenced, shewing that he was relieving and healing the injury'; and third, that the operation 'successfully and completely removed the effects of the blow of the cause of death.' Ibid.

68 Ibid., Davis's application before the High Court of Justice, sent to Charles Fitzpatrick, minister of justice, 20 October 1904.

69 Ibid., Davis to Fitzpatrick, 21 October 1904.

70 Ibid., A.H. Clarke to Fitzpatrick.

71 Approximately one year earlier, the surgeon of the Kingston Penitentiary reported that Slaughter was 'physically in good health, his mental condition also being favourable.' Though at this time the surgeon noted that Slaughter was confined to the insane ward, he felt that this was 'not owing to any mental enfeeblement, but owing to his restless condition ... he appears to be quite rational, converses quite intelligently, and conducts himself in an exemplary manner, performing such work as may be assigned to him.'

72 See, for example, the discussion of *R. v. Fred Fountain* in chapter 5. This theme has also been explored by Canadian historians interested in the areas of immigration policy and deportation. See Barbara Roberts, *Whence They Came: Deportation from Canada, 1900–1935* (Ottawa: University of Ottawa Press 1998); and Franca Iacovetta, '"Dangerous Men" in Cold War Canada, 1950s–1960s,' *Social History / Histoire Sociale*, 66 (November 2000): 361–89.

73 LAC, RG 13, vol. 1447, Remission Register No./Ticket of Leave File 3368–14, 9 December 1914. Also see a memorandum from the superintendent of immigration to the deputy minister of justice confirming the order for Slaughter's deportation to the United States.

74 The term 'Bohemian' is a rather slippery one. While defined as a native inhabitant of Bohemia in the Czech Republic, it is also, of course, a term to describe a 'person living free of conventional practices.'

75 LAC, RG 13, vol. 1592, *R. v. Frederick Turner*, trial summary and memorandum for the minister of justice.

76 This 'strategy of whitening' deployed by European immigrants has been noted in the American context. The seminal work on this issue is undoubtedly W.E.B. DuBois, *Black Reconstruction in America* (Philadelphia, 1935; repr. New York and Toronto: Free Press 1998).

77 LAC, RG 13, vol. 1592, trial transcripts, 95–6.

78 Ibid. In a telling moment during the direct examination dealing with Brown's knowledge of the fistfight, Beardall's frustration was clear:

Q: As soon as the fight was over what did you do?
A: We shook hands and I went back to the C.P.R. [Hotel] to pay my bill.

Q: Was anything said by anyone at or around the time that the fight ended?

A: What do you mean?

Q: About how they felt over the fight?

A: No. They said everything was all right; we would be friends again, that is all.

Q: Did Secka say anything?

A: No, he didn't, not that I remember.

Q: Did Secka say anything before he got up off the ground?

A: He said something in his own language that I didn't understand.

Q: Did he say anything in English about you?

A: Not that I remember.

Mr. Smith: That is your witness, Mr. Beardall.

Mr. Beardall: I am painfully aware of it.

79 Ibid., 118–23.

80 Ibid., 20.

81 Ibid., 46.

82 Ibid., 6.

83 Ibid. In his report, Kingstone made his regrets clear and pointed out that the jury had no idea that the verdict compelled him by law to pass a death sentence. He felt that this was particularly important because of the jury's recommendation for mercy.

84 Q: By the way, my learned friend has been referring to you as a boxer or fighter. Are you a skilled boxer?

A: No sir.

Q: Are you accustomed to being in fights?

A: It was the first fight I had since I left school.

Q: What age did you leave school at?

A: About twelve years old. [116–17]

85 Ibid., 124.

86 Ibid., 148.

87 The court felt that it was important to note that 'the communication from the Minister of Justice is a unique procedure. It is the first case of the kind that has ever come before me, or I think that has ever been before this court. We are really asked to interfere in the exercise of clemency. This court has no jurisdiction to exercise clemency. If it was a case where we had the right to reduce the penalty, well and good, but under section 1018, this being a capital case we have no right to modify the sentence in any way. But we should not wish our dismissal of the appeal to be construed

by the Government as either an adjudication by us or an expression by us against the exercise of clemency.' Ibid.

88 B.J. Spencer Pitt's role in the 1930s Oakville KKK case is extensively documented in Constance Backhouse's *Colour-Coded*, chapter 6.

89 Ibid.

90 PC 2966.

91 Memorandum from the director of Remission Services to the solicitor general, 25 October 1945.

92 *Border Cities Star*, 23, 26 February 1930.

93 The *Star*, reporting on the mood of the town, noted that though some protested Cross's commutation, others felt that 'Cross should not have been selected to give up his life when the other members of the bandit gang were given heavy sentences in the Kingston Penitentiary.' Between 1,200 and 1,500 signatures were obtained in Chatham alone, in addition to hundreds of others in the rural sections of Kent County. *Border Cities Star*, 19 May 1930.

94 LAC, RG 13, vol. 1736, CC 795 Transcripts.

95 Ibid.

96 *Regina v. Simmons and Lotharp* [1955] O.R. 118 [Court of Appeal]; and 'Her Majesty the Queen, Elizabeth II, versus Jerry Simmons and Glen Lothorp (the Case of the Murderer Who Returned to the Scene of the Crime), http://www.norfolklawassociation.com/chapter10.php.

97 C.H.S. Jaywardene, *The Penalty of Death: The Canadian Experiment* (Lexington, Mass.: Lexington Books 1997), 69.

98 Greg Marquis, *Policing Canada's Century: A History of the Canadian Association of Chiefs of Police* (Toronto: University of Toronto Press 1993), 223, 266, 285–9.

99 I am using the pseudonym 'M' here as per my research agreement with the Archives of Ontario.

100 AO, RG 4–32, Office of the Attorney General of Ontario, correspondence.

101 The Webster-Ashburton Treaty, signed between Britain and the United States in 1842, covered a range of outstanding areas of contention between the two powers. It settled boundary questions on the Great Lakes and on the New Brunswick-Maine border; it addressed the continued involvement of the United States in the (now banned) transatlantic slave trade and pressed the U.S. government to police this activity; and, most relevant for the case of M, it addressed the thorny question of the extradition of fugitive slaves from the Canada to the United States. The basic principle behind these extradition agreements was that extraditable offences had to be indictable offences in both British North America and the

United States. Theft of a slave, then, would not suffice as an extraditable offence. As well, the motives for the commission of fugitive slaves' offences were to be taken under consideration by Canadian legal and government authorities (e.g., theft of horse was a justifiable act if the horse was used to escape). See Winks, *The Blacks in Canada*, 172–4; Alexander Murray, 'The Extradition of Fugitive Slaves from Canada,' *Canadian Historical Review*, 43 (1962): 289–314; and http://www.u-s history.com/pages/h357.html.

102 http://www.u-s history.com/pages/h357.html.

103 George McLean Rose, ed., *A Cyclopaedia of Canadian Biography* (Toronto: Rose Publishing 1888), 743.

104 Ibid.

105 This was a volatile time in Kingston's history. The crime took place on the fourth anniversary of a major riot at the penitentiary and during the period with the lowest commutation rate among death-penalty cases.

106 LAC, RG 13, vol. 1610, CC 470 Transcripts and newspaper clippings; and Ottawa *PM Journal*, 14 September 1937.

107 LAC, RG 13, vol. 1438, memorandum for the minister of justice, 6 May 1899.

108 Toronto *Globe*, 25 March 1899.

109 LAC, RG 13, vol. 1438, memorandum.

110 Toronto *Globe*, 28 March 1899.

111 LAC, RG 13, vol. 1438, memorandum.

112 Toronto *Globe*, 29 March 1899.

113 Ibid., 28 March 1899.

114 Ibid.

115 Ibid.

116 LAC, RG 13, vol. 1438, trial transcripts.

117 Ibid.

118 LAC, RG 13, vol. 1610, newspaper clippings.

119 In reality, Crosley's physicality was far less imposing, bringing to mind Homi Bhabha's notion of the 'phantasmic knowledges' which inform how the 'colonized is constituted under the gaze of the colonizer.' In a RCMP reported dated 29 September 1937, Crosley was described thusly: 'Height 5'6", Weight 135 lbs, Complexion dark, Hair Black, Eyes Black, scar on right part of body, and three toes missing.' Clearly, then, this 'giant Negro' was principally a product of the White imagination. LAC, RG 13, vol. 1610.

120 Michael D. Wittingham, *The Role of the Reformers and Volunteers in the Advance of Correctional Reform in Canada since Confederation: Section II, The*

Role of Governmental Commissions: Provincial/Federal Inquiries (Ottawa: Programs Branch, Ministry of the Solicitor General, 1984), 11–13. See also *Report of the Royal Commission to Investigate the Penal System of Canada* (Ottawa: King's Printer 1938) (hereinafter *Report*).

121 C.W.S. Jeffrey, *Who's Who in Canada, 1930–31: An Illustrated Biographical Record of Men and Women of the Time* (Toronto: International Press 1932), 722.

122 *Report*, 3.

123 Wittingham, *The Role of Reformers and Volunteers*, 9.

124 LAC, RG 13, vol. 1610, newspaper clippings.

125 During this examination, Dr Wylie also told the court that before the start of the first trial he had injected Crosley with the drug ephedrine; this was done at the behest of the defence counsel, W.M. Nickle. The racist and class-biased undertones of such an undertaking (class is important here because this was routinely done to White patients/prisoners as well) become clear when one considers that the doctor went on, frankly (and frighteningly), to characterize the procedure as an 'experiment' and 'declared that he intended to write a paper on it.' Perhaps even more disturbing is that Nickle proceeded to ask the presiding judge if he could reproduce the experiment in court. Ottawa *AM Journal*, 3 March 1937.

126 LAC, RG 13, vol. 1610, report of Justice Jeffrey.

127 Ottawa *AM Journal*, 6 March 1937.

128 Ibid., 9 March 1937.

129 In fact, the jury was dismissed at 11:50 a.m. and did not render its verdict until 2:30 p.m. of the same day. While this might not seem to be an especially long deliberation period, it is likely, as crown counsel noted in correspondence to the deputy minister of justice, that had the judge not called an adjournment, the verdict may have been in much sooner. See LAC, RG 13, vol. 1610, transcripts, C.L Snyder to the deputy minister of justice, 28 September 1937.

130 Ottawa *AM Journal*, 1 March 1937.

131 Ibid., 2 March 1937.

132 Ibid.

133 James St G. Walker, *'Race,' Rights and the Law in the Supreme Court of Canada* (Waterloo, Ont.: Wilfrid Laurier Press 1997), 202–3, 217–19. Mackay heard the *Drummond Wren* case in October 1945. The Workers Educational Association had purchased a parcel of land in the Toronto suburb of East York, only to discover that it had a covenant restricting its sale to 'Jews or persons of objectionable nationality.'

134 Montreal *Gazette*, 21 September 1937.

135 Today Collin's Bay Penitentiary is within Kingston's expanded city limits.

136 Ottawa *AM Journal*, 22 September 1937.

137 Montreal *Gazette*, 23 September 1937; emphasis added.

138 This is the opposite of the muted body/'shadow' of the Indian peasant woman in Spivak's work. See Gayatri Chakravorty Spivak, 'Can the Subaltern Speak?,' in Bill Ashcroft et al., eds., *The Post Colonial Studies Reader* (New York: Routledge 2006), 24–8.

139 LAC, RG 13, vol 1610, trial transcripts.

140 Ibid.

141 A concrete example of how the disjunction between the Canadian nation and blackness played out can be found in a standard form, part of Crosley's case file, that was sent to the sheriff of Frontenac County. The form required that the sheriff provide the following information to E.H. Coleman, under-secretary of state: age, nationality, place of birth, marital status, religion, the date of the crime, the court in which the case was tried, the date of the trial, and the date of the sentence. Entered next to 'Nationality' was the word 'Canadian.' A little farther down the page, the same entry is entered next to 'Origin.' However, next to it the word 'Negro' was entered by what appears to have been a charcoal pencil.

142 LAC, RG 13, vol. 1610, trial transcripts.

143 Ibid.

144 Of the two letters found in Crosley's file, the first, signed by G.H. Glass, pointed out that Crosley was a 'ward of the government at the time of the crime' and, moreover, had been 'examined and found to have the mentality of a child of eleven.' The second letter, penned by the Reverend Dr Lion Penhall Rees of the First Church of the Illuminate in Toronto, not only mentioned Crosley's childlike 'mental equipment' but also queried whether Crosley was 'bullied' and 'Brow Beaten' by the prison officials. 'Or,' Rees continued, 'is this another example of what is popularly stated "THE MAN WHO KILLS A POLICE WORKER MUST DIE"?' Ibid.

145 Ottawa *AM Journal*, 4 November 1937; Montreal *Gazette*, 29 November 1937.

146 LAC, RG 13, vol. 1438.

147 Ibid.

148 Ibid.

149 Ibid., Archdeacon Davis to the minister of justice.

150 Ibid.

151 Ibid.

3 Black Patriarchy

1 There is now an extensive body of literature on this subject which has made an important contribution to Canadian historiography. See, for example, Annalee Golz, 'If a Man's Wife Does Not Obey Him What Can He Do? Marital Breakdown and Wife Abuse in Late Nineteenth Century and Early Twentieth Century Ontario,' in Susan Binnie and Louis Knafla, eds., *Law, State, and Society: Essays in Modern Legal History* (Toronto: University of Toronto Press 1995), 325–50, and 'Uncovering and Reconstructing Family Violence in Ontario,' in Franca Iacovetta and Wendy Mitchinson, eds., *On the Case: Explorations in Social History* (Toronto: University of Toronto Press 1998), 298–311; Karen Dubinsky, *Improper Advances: Rape and Heterosexual Conflict in Ontario, 1880–1929* (Chicago: University of Chicago Press 1993); and Carolyn Strange, 'Historical Perspectives on Wife Assault,' in Mariana Valverde et al., eds., *Wife Assault and the Canadian Criminal Justice System* (Toronto: University of Toronto Centre of Criminology 1995), 293–304. For an excellent example of a singled-out case of female spousal murder, see Karen Dubinsky and Franca Iacovetta, 'Murder, Womanly Virtue and Motherhood: The Case of Angela Napolitino,' *Canadian Historical Review*, 72, no. 1 (1991): 505–31. See also Constance Backhouse, *Carnal Crimes: Sexual Assault Law in Canada, 1900–1975* (Toronto: Osgoode Society for Canadian Legal History / University of Toronto Press 2008).

2 I first introduced and explored this concept in a 1998 Canadian Historical Association conference paper titled 'Sexual Conflict, Black Patriarchy and the Law: Reading the Story of George and Eliza Ross in Ontario's Criminal Case Files, Essex County, Ontario, 1882.'

3 Shirley Yee, 'Gender Ideology and Black Women as Community Builders in Ontario, 1850–1870,' *Canadian Historical Review*, 75, no. 1 (1994): 53–73, 60.

4 See Michael Awkward, 'A Black Man's Place(s) in Black Feminist Criticism,' in Marcellus Blount and George P. Cunningham, eds., *Representing Black Men* (New York: Routledge 1996), 3–26 at 18, where he provides a discussion of Black feminist literary theorists. See also Deborah McDowell, 'Reading Family Matters,' in Cheryl Wall, ed., *Changing Our Own Words: Essays on Criticism, Theory and the Writing of Black Women* (New Brunswick, N.J.: Rutgers University Press 1989), 75–97.

5 AO, RG 22, 392–0–1394, *R. v. George Ross.*

6 Ibid., testimony of Eliza Ross.

7 Ibid.

8 Ibid.

9 Ibid.

10 Lori Chambers has shown that there was a gradual change in married women's property rights between the years of 1837 and 1900, and that the Ross case took place just two years short of watershed statutory changes in this area of the law. To address the disadvantages that such women faced in the common law, various measures were taken, beginning with the establishment in 1837 of the 'local court of Chancery or Equity,' where 'wives could gain access to alimony and could protect some property for themselves through the use of trusts.' An 1859 act 'granted wives the right to own, but not manage or alienate, the property that they brought to marriage or inherited during coveture.' In 1872 wives won the right to 'manage and dispose of personal property' including wages, and a year later the Married Women's Real Estate Act granted 'disparities powers over their land.' By 1884, the most significant act of all was passed, abolishing 'the role of the husband as the trustee over his wife's separate estate.' Lori Chambers, *Married Women and Property Law in Victorian Ontario* (Toronto: University of Toronto Press 1997), 9–10.

11 AO, RG 22, 392–0–1394, *R. v. George Ross.*

12 While this was never explicitly mentioned in Eliza's sworn statement, it certainly does not take a great leap of faith to imagine that sexual tension may have been an element of their relationship.

13 LAC, RG 13, vol. 1407, *R. v. Jonathan George*, testimony of Hannah Brown.

14 Ibid.

15 Ibid.

16 Ibid.

17 Ibid., testimony of Hannah Woodson.

18 Ibid., testimony of Charles Jackson.

19 Ibid., testimony of Mrs Thomas.

20 Ibid., testimony of Theodore Dunn.

21 Ibid., petition to the governor general, 7 December 1867.

22 Ibid.; emphasis added.

23 Windsor's sheriff, acting on the direction of the warden of the town of Windsor and the County Council, presented more petitions on behalf of Jonathan George to the minister of justice. These petitions were drafted by the attorney who represented George at his trial and witnessed by the warden of the Kingston Penitentiary.

24 LAC, RG 13, vol. 1407, *R. v. Jonathan George*, petition to the governor general, 31 January 1871.

25 Ibid.; emphasis added.

26 Ibid.; emphasis in original. The story of Joseph and Potiphar's wife can be found in Genesis, chapter 39. Joseph, one of the patriarchs of the 'twelve tribes,' and Potiphar's slave, was charged with the rape of Potiphar's wife. It is widely held, however, that the charge was spurious. Potiphar's wife levelled the charges only after her unwanted sexual advances were spurned. Joseph was thrown in prison for the offence. However, through divine intervention, not only were his fellow prisoners placed in Joseph's charge, but he was released and ultimately named the 'overseer of all Egypt' because of his ability to decode dreams and foresee the future.

27 LAC, RG 13, vol. 1407, *R. v. Jonathan George*. See Brown, *The Genesis of the Canadian Criminal Code of 1892* (Toronto: Osgoode Society for Canadian Legal History / University of Toronto Press 1989), 169.

28 AO, RG 22, 392–0–1515, *R. v. Allan Saunders*.

29 Ibid., testimony of Timothy Gray.

30 Ibid.

31 Ibid., testimony of Mary Gray.

32 Ibid.

33 Ibid.

34 Ibid.

35 Ibid., testimony of Timothy Gray.

36 Ibid.

37 Clayton Mosher has noted: 'The magistrate hearing the case declared that such crimes [rape] were altogether too prevalent throughout the country. He understood the parties in the case were colored, but this made no difference as they were entitled to the same protection as other individuals.' Clayton Mosher, *Discrimination and Denial: Systemic Racism in Ontario's Legal and Criminal Justice Systems, 1892–1961* (Toronto: University of Toronto Press 1999), 192.

38 RG 22, 392–0–1501, *R. v. Jonathan George*, testimony of Sergeant Abraham Nash.

39 Ibid., testimony of Edith Vincent.

40 In the case file, however, there exists a small piece of paper – what appears to be a rent receipt for $10.50 dated 1 April 1904.

41 The shelf upon which these preserves were kept was lined with newspaper. Upon inspection, officer Nash surmised that the jars had been recently removed since there was no dust upon the newspaper rings.

42 RG 22, 392–0–1501, *R. v. Jonathan George*, testimony of Abraham Nash.

43 *Evening Record*, 7 October 1904.

44 Ibid.

45 Ibid.

46 Aside from a passing reference in Mosher's *Discrimination and Denial*, I was able to uncover only one account of the Anderson Veney trial: Patrick Brode, 'Veney, Anderson,' *Dictionary of Canadian Biography*, vol. 13 (Toronto: University of Toronto Press; Quebec: Les Presses de l'Université Laval 1990), 1073–4.

47 LAC, RG 13, vol. 1414, *R. v. Henry White*, testimony of George Farr.

48 Ibid.

49 Ibid., newspaper clippings.

50 LAC, RG 13, vol. 1414, *R. v. Henry White*.

51 Ibid.

52 Ibid.; emphasis added.

53 Ibid., Thomas L. Davidson to the minister of justice, 7 December 1875.

54 Ibid., Thomas James to Ontario Premier Oliver Mowat (forwarded to the federal minister of justice), 3 December 1875.

55 LAC, RG 13, vol. 1414, *R. v. Henry White*. A petition to the secretary of state dated 22 November 1875 reads: 'The undersigned recommends that communication be had by the Secretary of State with the Attorney General of Ontario, to the effect that it has been brought under the notice of the Governor General that Henry White, a colored man, now lying in the jail at Guelph under the sentence of death for the murder of his wife and to be executed on the 23rd day of December ... has made a confession of his guilt and requesting that the attorney general will be good enough, if such the case, to have the same furnished for the consideration of His Excellency.' Edward Blake, minister of justice, responded in a memo dated 27 November 1875: 'With reference to the case of Henry White convicted at Guelph of the murder of his wife Susannah White, the undersigned has the honour to report that the evidence leaves no room to doubt that the Convict willingly and deliberately murdered his wife, nor does the case present any extenuating circumstances. It therefore, becomes the duty of the undersigned to suggest that the law must be allowed to take its course.'

56 Toronto *Daily Mail*, 23 September 1892.

57 LAC, RG 13, vol. 1428, *R. v. Anderson Veney*, testimony of Hattie Primeaux.

58 Ibid., testimony of Weadon Johnson.

59 Eerily, during this conversation, Weadon Johnson extended his encouragement and support to Anderson Veney for having found religious faith. Johnson testified that he congratulated Veney, telling him, 'I am glad to understand that you have found Christ.' To this Veney responded: 'It is a good thing to try and live a Christian [life].' Ibid.

60 Ibid., trial transcripts.

61 Ibid., testimony of Weadon Johnson, 16–17.

62 Toronto *Telegram*, 23 September 1892.

63 Ibid.

64 AO, RG 22, 392–0–2793, Inquest on the Body of Martha Veney, testimony of Constable Lewis Lemay.

65 London *Free Press*, 14 September 1892.

66 AO, RG 22, 392–0–2793, Inquest on the Body of Martha Veney, testimony of Dr James T. Park.

67 Ibid., testimony of Forest T. Bell.

68 A newspaper headline read: 'AT THE SPRING ASSIZES TRIAL OF TWO MURDER CASES CROWDS THE COURT: RICHARDSON THE DRESDEN FIEND WHO DELIBERATELY KICKED HIS WIFE TO THE DEATH ON THE STREET.' See Chatham *Daily Planet*, 11 April 1894.

69 AO, RG 22, 487–1–12, box 1, bench books of Justice William Purvis Street, testimony of Mary Richardson.

70 Ibid.

71 Inquest on the Body of Martha Veney, testimony of Daphne Warren.

72 AO, RG 22, 487–1–12, box 1, bench books of Justice Street, testimony of Mary Richardson. This graphic testimony was corroborated by a man named William Fritz who also witnessed the murder. His testimony, represented as a moment of grotesque levity (Chatham *Daily Planet*, 11 April 1894), only serves to amplify the horror of the violence committed upon Hannah Richardson's body:

> Cross Examined: 'How near were you to them?'
> 'About 15 feet.'
> 'And you stood there and saw him beat his wife and never interfered? Is that the man you are?'
> 'Well sir, if you'd been there, you would have done the same thing.' (Laughter)

73 Ibid., testimony of Mary Richardson.

74 Ibid., testimony of Daniel Gailbraith.

75 A person of African descent with approximately one-quarter 'African Blood.' This way of categorizing Black bodies was most typically found in the New World slavery societies of Canada and the United States. According to the 'one drop rule' that was predominant in these societies, one drop of Black blood made a person racially 'Black.' Racial categories were more fluid in places like Brazil and the Caribbean. See Carl M. Degler, *Neither Black Nor White: Slavery and Race Relations in Brazil and the United States* (Madison, Wis.: University of Wisconsin Press 1971).

76 AO, RG 22, 392–2793, *R. v. Hiram Richardson*, testimony of Dr Irvine Wiley.

77 I have chosen not to explicitly pursue this method in this chapter, but for an excellent discussion of dramaturgy as an historical methodology which gives us 'insights that may be gained from reviewing the interaction of past people as though the episodes considered were displayed in a theatre,' see Rhys Isaac, *The Transformation of Virginia, 1740–1790* (New York: Norton 1982).

78 LAC, RG 13, vol. 1428, *R. v. Anderson Veney*, testimony of Hattie Primeaux.

79 Ibid.

80 Ibid.

81 See ibid., testimony of Lewis Lemay and James Lushington. Lemay, who was Amherstburg's chief of police, recalled that Veney remarked that he had killed [Martha Veney] in a fit of passion and moreover that 'if I had not minded the outside talk and letters [I] would be a free man today.' Similarly, Lushington, who after Veney's arrest accompanied him to see Dr Proudfoot, told the court of Veney's admission of his crime as well as the motives behind it. Veney told Lushington that his wife's unfaithfulness led him to commit the crime. When Veney was asked whether he had secured legal representation, he responded, according to Lemay: 'No, I have not, it is not necessary that I should have to do so … I committed the deed, and … there is no use of spending all the money I have got and the little piece of property I have; I would be doing it and deprive my children of it … I am satisfied that I will get the rope.'

82 Ibid., testimony of Lewis Lemay. Emphasis added. 'I cannot put a straw in either one of their roads' was a colloquial way of saying that someone was a person of good character.

83 For an extended discussion of this theme, see Kimberley White-Mair, *Negotiating Responsibility: Law, Murder and States of Mind* (Vancouver: UBC Press 2008); and Alison Kirk-Montgomery, 'Courting Madness: Insanity and Testimony in the Criminal Justice System of Ontario,' PhD thesis, University of Toronto 2001.

84 The duties of a steward on the lake included 'buy[ing] stores, look[ing] after [one's] boat and kneel[ing] everything in proper order.' See LAC, RG 13, vol. 1428, *R. v. Anderson Veney*, testimony of Roman Smith.

85 Ibid.

86 Ibid.

87 Ibid., testimony of Annie Foster.

88 Ibid., testimony of Mrs John Leslie.

89 Ibid., testimony of William H. Brown.

90 Ibid., testimony of Dr Thomas Hobley.
91 Ibid., testimony of Dr James Sampson.
92 Ibid.
93 Ibid., testimony of Dr Rémi Cosgrain.
94 AO, RG 22, 487–1–12, box 1, bench books of Justice William Purvis Street, testimony of Mary Richardson.
95 Chatham *Daily Planet,* 11 April 1894.
96 AO, RG 22, 487–1–12, box 1, bench books of Justice William Purvis Street, testimony of James Richardson.
97 Ibid., testiomony of Richard Lucas, Richard Morton, James Langstaff, and Joseph Jones. Brief synopses of witness testimony also appear in the Chatham *Daily Planet,* 11 April 1894.
98 AO, RG 22, 487–1–12, box 1, bench books of Justice William Purvis Street, testimony of Dr McKeough and Dr J.H. Bray.
99 AO, RG 22, 342–0–2793, *R. v. Hiram Richardson*, testimony of Hiram Richardson.
100 Chatham *Daily Planet,* 11 April 1894.
101 The following statement, which was likely made to the court during sentencing, appears in Justice Street's bench books: 'The crime was the most brutal and the woman was killed by repeated kicks to the head by her husband the prisoner – the provocation if any was very slight. A verdict of murder would have been well justified by the evidence.'
102 *R. v. Anderson Veney*, trial transcripts, Justice Malcolm Street's charge to the jury. Street's trial report to the secretary of state in Ottawa, which was composed the same day as the trial, was a little more nuanced. The trial now over, Street could step outside the strict confines of rather narrowly proscribed legal sentencing procedure. His report alluded to the fact that 'while the evidence left no doubt open as to the fact the prisoner killed his wife, and knew at the time he did so that he was committing a murder, there was some evidence which may have led the jury to believe that at the present time at all events, [he] was not perfectly sound in mind.'
103 Ibid., petitions to the governor general of Canada.
104 Ibid. See also Brode, 'Veney, Anderson.'

4 Tales of a 'Peculiarly Horrible Description': Archetypal Race Narratives

1 Cited in Constance Backhouse, *Petticoats and Prejudice: Women and Law in Nineteenth-Century Canada* (Toronto: Osgoode Society for Canadian Legal History / Women's Press 1991), 98; LAC, MG 26A, Macdonald Papers,

Letterbook 11–845, John A. Macdonald to Chief Justice William Johnson Richie of Nova Scotia, 8 June 1868.

2 In 1901 David Hawes, a fifty-year-old African Canadian sleeping-car porter, was sentenced to ten years in prison. Amidst much self-congratulation, the presiding judge lauded those involved in the case 'for having tried rather than lynched the man.' Hawes received a ten-year sentence; however, a sentence of this length for a man of his years was a de facto death sentence. Carolyn Strange, 'Patriarchy Modified: The Criminal Prosecution of Rape in York County, 1880–1930,' in Jim Phillips, Tino Loo, and Susan Lewthwaite, eds., *Essays in the History of Canadian Law: Volume 5 – Crime and Criminal Justice* (Toronto: Osgoode Society for Canadian Legal History / University of Toronto Press 1994), 233.

3 Backhouse, *Petticoats and Prejudice*, 98.

4 AO, RG 22, 3920-2617, *R. v. Daniel Oxentine*. What is not clear is how Mary Ann Lawrence might have found out about the alleged encounter between Oxentine and Steinhoff.

5 Chatham *Weekly Planet*, 22 October 1858.

6 AO, RG 22, 392–0–2625, *R. v. Levi Harris*.

7 Ibid.; emphasis added.

8 Ibid.; emphasis added.

9 Chatham *Planet*, 20 September 1859.

10 See my discussion of Josiah Henson in chapter 2.

11 AO, RG 22–392–0–2625, *R. v. Harris*.

12 Chatham *Tri-Weekly Planet*, 29 September 1859.

13 Ibid.; emphasis mine.

14 London *Advertiser*, 9 April 1888.

15 AO, RG 22, 441–1–11, bench books of Sir Mathiew Crooks Cameron, Ontario High Court of Justice, April 1884–April 1885.

16 See, for example, Strange, 'Patriarchy Modified'; and Backhouse, *Petticoats and Prejudice*.

17 Many doctors and jurists, believing that working-class women in particular routinely engaged in consensual rough sex, were sceptical of the medical evidence often submitted to substantiate charges of rape. See Constance Backhouse, *Carnal Crimes: Sexual Assault Law in Canada, 1900–1975* (Toronto: Osgoode Society for Canadian Legal History / Irwin Law 2008), 40.

18 No record exists of the sentence meted out to his alleged accomplice. Indeed, nowhere in the record is this other man even mentioned by name.

19 Stratford *Daily Herald*, 5 May 1909. The account of the arraignment hearing also showed how difficult a road Roughmond had ahead of him. The

newspaper account repeatedly referred to Roughmond as 'the Negro' and made it clear that he had no lawyer until the presiding judge assigned him one during his preliminary trial.

20 The account of the case is from LAC, RG 13, vol. 1455, memorandum for the acting minister of justice, 10 June 1909.

21 Karen Dubinsky, *Improper Advances: Rape and Heterosexual Conflict in Ontario, 1880–1929* (Chicago: University of Chicago Press 1993), 98–104.

22 The above quotations are from LAC, RG 13, vol. 1455, transcripts, 79–80, 83–4, 89–90.

23 Riddell even contributed historical articles to the 1920s and 1930s Black newspaper *The Dawn of Tomorrow*. See Constance Backhouse, *Colour-Coded: A Legal History of Racism in Canada, 1900–1950* (Toronto: Osgoode Society for Canadian Legal History / University of Toronto Press 1999), 123; and Robin Winks, *The Blacks in Canada*, 2nd ed. (Montreal and Kingston: McGill-Queen's University Press 1997), 298.

24 The Stratford *Daily Herald* also reported Roughmond's plea of innocence to Justice Riddell. However, the account that appeared in the paper perhaps reveals the inherent bias in how the trial was reported and even the newspaper's desire to embellish the details for its readers. The *Herald* reported that Roughmond claimed that Peake's true murderer 'was the son.' No such statement attributable to Roughmond can be found in the transcripts.

25 LAC, RG 13, vol. 1455, transcripts, 102.

26 Martha Hodes, *White Women, Black Men: Illicit Sex in the Nineteenth Century South* (New York: Yale University Press 1997), 4–5. Lisa Linquest Dorr, 'Black-on-White Rape and Retribution in Twentieth-Century Virginia: "Men, Even Negroes Must Have Some Protection,"' *Journal of Southern History*, 66, no. 4 (2000): 714.

27 See R. Bruce Sheppard, *Deemed Unsuitable: Blacks from Oklahoma Move to the Canadian Prairies in Search of Equality in the Early 20th Century Only to Find Racism in Their New Home* (Toronto: Umbrella Press 1997), chapters 3 and 7.

28 LAC, RG 13, vol. 1455, CC. 1609, letters from Dr C.K. Clarke and Dr R.W. Bruce Smith to Justice W.R. Riddell, 7 and 26 May 1909.

29 Ibid.; emphasis added.

30 AO, RG 4–32, *R. v. William McCathern*, transcripts, 10, 51, 53.

31 St Catharine's *Standard*, 29 October 1926.

32 *R. v. De Young, R. v. Liddiard, R. v. Darling* [1927] O.R. 155 (Appellate Division) at 156.

33 AO, RG 4–32, *R. v. William McCathern*, transcripts; emphasis added.

34 Ibid.; emphasis added.

35 Ibid., transcripts, 56.

36 Grace E. Hale, *Making Whiteness: The Culture of Segregation in the South, 1890–1940* (New York: Pantheon Books 1998).

37 I maintain that the frequency with which Canadian newspapers ran 'lynching stories' (and the rate at which they were consumed by various readers) might at worst have been a way for White Canadians to live vicariously through their cousins to the south, but more it was another manifestation of a general tendency towards a voyeuristic obsession with 'spicy stories,' in this instance the pornographic displays of lynched Black male bodies in the U.S. South.

38 AO, RG 4–32, *R. v. William McCathern*, transcripts; see also http://www.amnesty.ca/death penalty/canada.php.

39 In McCathern's file there is an interesting police report on McCathern's family, giving some indication of how delicate (and risky) a matter it was to bring forth family members as family witnesses. The report, penned by Chatham's chief constable, revealed that he had known McCathern 'for the last five years ... he was known around town as a general jobber ... his associates were of the lowest Element and usually he would be found around the slums of the city.' The chief continued: 'As far as known to me, there are eight children in the family[,] seven boys and one girl ... They have been in a lot of trouble around this city[,] one of them at present serving a term in the Guelph Reformatory for burglary. The girl, now married to a Belgian, is of a very loe [*sic*] moral type and was known to the police before her marriage as a common prostitute.' Nevertheless, the chief further opined that 'his parents are considered to be law abiding citizens, although they appear to be in poor circumstances, the father works steady, and it is said that they own the home they live in and about an acre of ground surrounding the home near the City Limits, and near to the home of Mrs. Alice McCall.' LAC, RG 13, vol. 1534.

40 AO, RG 4–32, *R. v. William McCathern*, affidavit of Ophelia Ann McCathern.

41 Ibid., affidavits of George Yott and Dr James Walter Coulter.

42 Ibid., testimony of Dr James Walter Coulter.

43 Ibid., affidavit of William McCathern, Sr. The cases referred to in this affidavit took place in St Catharines on 26, 27, and 28 October 1926. They are cited in the legal records as 'the cases of the King versus Frank De Young, Richard Darling, Walter Liddard and John Robert Gough.'

44 AO, RG 4–32, *R. v. William McCathern*. See also *R. v. McCathern* [1927] O.R. 334 (Appellate Division), at 335–6.

45 Ibid.

46 Ibid., memo from Deputy Attorney General E. Bayly to Attorney General H.D. Smith. Indeed, the importance of paternalistic constructions of blackness in this case is contained in the crown attorney case file. In this brief, the crown attorney argued that McCathern's sentence should not be overturned, on the grounds that the death penalty was 'still the law and whipping since 1922' and also that 'none of the matters that were urged [in the appeal] were urged at trial and no defence was offered.' What also appears, however, is the crown attorney's plan to 'refer to the fact that [McCathern] is a Negro which is unfortunate.' This point was crossed out in the brief, indicating, perhaps, that this strategy was abandoned.

5 Rape, Sex, and the Power of Dominant Rape Narratives

1 James Walker, *'Race,' Rights and the Law in the Supreme Court of Canada* (Waterloo, Ont.: Wilfrid Laurier University Press 1997), 127, 306; R. Bruce Shepard, *Deemed Unsuitable: Blacks from Oklahoma Move to the Canadian Prairies in Search of Equality in Early 20th Century Canada Only to Find Racism in Their New Home* (Toronto: Umbrella Press, 1997), 78–80.
2 Homi Bhabha, 'The Other Question,' in Padmini Mongia, ed., *Contemporary Postcolonial Theory: A Reader* (New York: Arnold 2003), 44.
3 AO, RG 22, 392–0–1373, *R. v. Peter Hines and William Beatty*.
4 Ibid., testimony of Margaret Murton.
5 Ibid.
6 Ibid., testimony of Constable Ronald Craig.
7 Ibid., testimony of Constable Donald Graves.
8 Aside from a few references in chapter 10 of Robin Winks's seminal work *The Blacks in Canada*, 2nd ed. (Montreal and Kingston: McGill-Queen's University Press 1997), I do not know of any scholarly treatments of blackface minstrelsy in Canada. The U.S. literature, by contrast, is rather extensive. My favourite more recent example of this kind of work is Eric Lott, *Love and Theft: Blackface Minstrelsy and the American Working Class* (New York: Oxford University Press 1995). For examples of the how the blackening of the lower stratum of the White working class blurred racial boundaries, see David Roediger, 'White Looks, Hairy Apes, True Stories and Limbaugh's Laughs,' in Mike Hill, eds., *Whiteness: A Critical Reader* (New York: New York University Press 1997), 37–9.
9 London *Daily Advertiser*, 9 March 1880.
10 Awad El Karim M. Ibrahim, '"Hey, Aain't I Black Too?": The Politics of Becoming Black,' in Rinaldo Walcott, ed., *Rude: Contemporary Black Canadian Cultural Criticism* (Toronto: Insomniac Press 2000), 113–14; Judith

Butler, *Gender Trouble: Feminism and the Subversion of Identity* (London and New York: Routledge 1990).

11 Chatham *Daily Planet*, 8 October 1883.

12 This was the site of the Brescina murder discussed in chapter 3.

13 Winks, *The Blacks in Canada*, 209.

14 Howard Law, '"Self Reliance Is the True Road to Independence": Ideology and the Ex-Slaves in Buxton and Chatham,' in Franca Iacovetta et al., eds., *A Nation of Immigrants: Women, Workers and Communities in Canadian History, 1840s–1960s* (Toronto: University of Toronto Press 1998), 84.

15 Winks, *The Blacks in Canada*, 213.

16 Chatham *Daily Planet*, 8 October 1893.

17 Karen Dubinsky, *Improper Advances: Rape and Heterosexual Conflict in Ontario, 1880–1929* (Chicago: University of Chicago Press 1993), 66–8.

18 Ibid., 69.

19 See Ann Laura Stoler, 'Sexual Affronts and Racial Frontiers: European Identities and the Cultural Politics of Exclusion in Colonial Southeast Asia,' in Nathaniel Gates, *Critical Race Theory Volume III: Racial Classification and History* (New York: Garland 1997), 208–45.

20 Chatham *Daily Planet*, 8 October 1893.

21 Ibid. The strong desire to punish George Freeman and the reality of an underfunded constabulary made this step necessary.

22 A summary of the findings of the coroner's report was provided by three doctors – J.P. Rutherford, D.G. Flemming, and R.V. Bray – on 23 January 1893. Their post-mortem exam revealed that the constable had suffered six different wounds on his scalp and brain trauma; both were caused by a 'great deal of force' through the use of a blunt instrument. AO, RG 22, 392–0–3793, *R. v. George Freeman et al.*

23 Chatham *Daily Planet*, 8 October 1893.

24 A 'rod' is equal to 5 1/2 yards or 16 1/2 feet.

25 Chatham *Daily Planet*, 8 October 1893.

26 Though the crime occurred in Kent County, the prosecution successfully asked for a change of venue to neighbouring Middlesex County. See Chatham *Daily Planet*, 8 October 1893; and Winks, *The Blacks in Canada*, 327.

27 Patrick Brode, 'Osler, Britton Bath,' *Dictionary of Canadian Biography*, vol. 13 (Toronto: University of Toronto Press; Quebec: Les Presses de l'Université Laval 1994), 795–6; 'B.B. Osler,' *Law Society of Upper Canada Gazette*, 2, no. 4 (1968): 27–35.

28 Chatham *Daily Planet*, 8 October 1893.

29 See Constance Backhouse, *Colour-Coded: A Legal History of Racism in Canada, 1900–1950* (Toronto: Osgoode Society for Canadian Legal History /

University of Toronto Press 1999), 196, particularly the discussion of anti-miscegenation sentiment in the Canadian Ku Klux Klan (KKK).

30 Constance Backhouse hints at this in her treatment of the 1930s trial (*R. v. Phillips*) of a member of the KKK for his attempt (along with other Klan members) to prevent the marriage of an interracial couple. What raised the concern of prominent local observers, says Backhouse, was not the Klan's racial attitudes but their 'un-Canadian' mob-like march through the streets. See Backhouse, *Colour-Coded*, 280–1.

31 Chatham *Daily Planet*, 9 October 1893.

32 AO, RG 22, 392–0–3797, *R. v. George Freeman et al.*, January 1893 inquiry into the death of Constable Rankin, deposition of Ida Jane Lizzart.

33 Ibid.

34 It is also possible, of course, that Ida Jane was lying to protect her lover. Perhaps, but there was no mention of carnal knowledge by the time the Freemans went to trial. It is also true that, since murder (unlike rape) carried the death penalty in Canada until 1976, this charge would have served the ends of George's accusers just fine, rendering the charge of carnal knowledge superfluous.

35 AO, RG 22, 392–0–3793, *R. v. George Freeman et al.*, deposition of George Freeman to the Chatham chief of police, January 1893. George's testimony at the assize trial mirrored this statement.

36 Ibid., testimony of Elizabeth Freeman.

37 Ibid., testimony of Jessie Freeman.

38 Ibid., testimony of George Freeman.

39 Chatham *Daily Planet*, 9 October 1893. Osler, citing a rather complex legal technicality, moved to have George Freeman's statement thrown out under sections 70 and 71 of the Criminal Code. Essentially, Osler argued that, because the police waited a day after laying the charge to take Freeman's statement, the statement could not be used.

40 Chatham *Daily Planet*, 9 October 1893. Pegley represented George Freeman at the police court hearings and at the inquest in the death of Constable Rankin.

41 Ibid.; emphasis added.

42 For an interesting, albeit cursory, account of the Freeman murder case, see Winks, *The Blacks in Canada*, 327.

43 See Clayton Mosher, *Discrimination and Denial: Systemic Racism in Ontario's Legal and Criminal Justice Systems, 1892–1961* (Toronto: University of Toronto Press 1999), 195–6, for similar kinds of cases.

44 AO, RG 22, 392–0–2886, *R. v. Frank Turner*, transcripts, 62–3.

45 LAC, RG 22, 392–0–2886, *R. v. Frank Turner*, transcripts, 69.

46 Ibid., transcripts, 74.
47 *Border Cities Star*, 15 February 1928.
48 Ibid. Emphasis added.
49 Ibid.
50 Ibid. Emphasis added.
51 Chatham *Weekly Planet*, 17 April 1884.
52 AO, RG 22, 392–0–2745, *R. v. James R. Charleston*.
53 Ibid.
54 Ibid.
55 Ibid.
56 The Chatham *Weekly Planet* reported that the judge pointed out a number of contradictions in Arabella's testimony, ensuring that her testimony carried even less weight that it otherwise might have.
57 Glencoe *Transcript*, 19 April 1900.
58 Ibid.
59 Ibid.
60 Ibid., 3 May 1900.
61 Chatham *Weekly Planet*, 30 April 1900.
62 Glencoe *Transcript*, 3 May 1900.
63 Chatham *Weekly Planet*, 30 April 1900.
64 For a history of the Mercer Reformatory, see Peter Oliver, *'Terror to Evil-doers': Prisons and Punishments in Nineteenth Century Ontario* (Toronto: University of Toronto Press 1998); and Kelley Hannah-Moffat, *Punishment in Disguise: Penal Governance and Federal Imprisonment of Women in Canada* (Toronto: University of Toronto Press 2001), 56–66.
65 Nathan Fillmore, the young stable boy, was not confined to the gaol (likely because of his age and the fact that he turned queen's evidence). Archie McCallum evidently managed to secure enough bail money to grant his release on bail while waiting for the fall assizes.
66 London *Free Press*, 27 September 1900.
67 Ibid.
68 Works that deal with this theme in the U.S. context are Grace Elizabeth Hale, *Making Whiteness: The Culture of Segregation in the South, 1890–1940* (New York: Pantheon Books 1998), 201; and Darlene Clark Hine, 'Rape and the Inner Lives of Southern Black Women: Thoughts on the Culture of Dissemblance,' in Virginia Bernhard, ed., *Southern Women: Histories and Identities* (Columbia: University of Missouri Press 1992), 177–90.
69 A good example is Martha Hodes, *White Women Black Men: Illicit Sex in the Nineteenth Century South* (New York: Yale University Press 1997), chapter 7.

70 See LAC, RG 13, vol. 653, *R. v. George Jones*, transcripts, 95.

71 See Sarah Carter, *The Importance of Being Monogamous: Marriage and Nation Building in Western Canada to 1919* (Edmonton: University of Alberta Press 2008); and Peggy Pascoe, *What Comes Naturally: Miscegenation Law and the Making of Race in America* (New York: Oxford University Press 2009).

72 LAC, RG 13, vol. 1505, *R. v. Fred Fountain*, transcripts, 2nd trial, 29.

73 Ibid., 17 October 1919 memorandum from Justice Logie to the secretary of state, Ottawa. Emphasis in original.

74 AO, RG 4–32, *R. v. Fred Fountain*, attorney general case file concerning the examination of the accused to determine his sanity. Memorandum from the minister of justice to the Ontario attorney general.

75 The deputy attorney general of Ontario argued that the provisions of section 19 of the Criminal Code were 'very clear,' and, while 'the experts' opinion as to his sanity or otherwise would be valuable in coming to a conclusion on the application of executive clemency, I cannot understand why that should be made the occasion for a new trial.' The minister expressed the view that, 'while of course the provisions of section 19 of the Criminal Code are in the opinion of many Alienists inadequate and unscientific[,] yet they are the law which binds the courts and my correspondence … with your Department led me to believe that the legal end of the case was not being seriously considered.' Thus, the minister continued, 'the Order for a new trial came as somewhat as a surprise and in view of the wording of the Criminal Code section 1022 before a new trial is directed it appears that the Minister of Justice must entertain a doubt whether such a person ought to be convicted. I shall be glad … to learn upon what provision [of] the Criminal Code [the decision] … was founded.' AO, RG 4–32, *R. v. Fountain*, Ontario deputy attorney general to the minister of justice.

76 See Kimberly White-Mair, 'Negotiating Responsibility: Representations of Criminality and Mind-State in Canadian Law, Medicine and Society, 1920–1950,' PhD thesis, University of Toronto 2001.

77 LAC, RG 13, vol. 1505, *R. v. Fred Fountain*, 2nd trial, transcripts, 60–1.

78 AO, RG 4–32, *R. v. Fred Fountain*, T.D. Cowper to E. Bailey, solicitor to the attorney general.

79 LAC, RG 13, vol. 1501, *R. v. Fred Fountain*, transcripts, 66.

80 Ibid., 68.

81 Ibid.

82 Ibid.

83 Ibid.; emphasis added. The deputy minister of justice concurred, referring to Fountain as an 'unfortunate man.'

84 Ibid.

85 Ibid., F.C. Blair, secretary, Department of Immigration and Colonization, to J.D. Clarke, chief of Remission Branch, Department of Justice, Ottawa, 23 June 1920.

86 Ibid.; emphasis added. J.D. Clarke to F.C. Blair, 26 June 1920.

87 Ibid., memorandum from the superintendent of penitentiaries for the deputy minister of justice, 27 January 1923.

88 Ibid.

89 Ibid., inspector of prisons and public charities of the province of Ontario to the minister of justice, 12 March 1924.

90 Ibid., commissioner, Department of Immigration and Colonization, to J.D. Clarke, chief of Remission Branch, Department of Justice, 6 June 1924.

91 Ibid., under-secretary of state, Governor General's Office, to the Department of Immigration, 26 January 1926.

92 Ibid., memorandum from the minister of justice for the chief of Remission Branch, 6 February 1926.

93 See, for example, Barbara Roberts, *Whence They Came: Deportation from Canada, 1900–1935* (Ottawa: University of Ottawa Press 1998); Franca Iacovetta, 'The Sexual Politics of Moral Citizenship: Containing "Dangerous Men" in Cold War Canada, 1950s–1960s,' *Histoire Sociale / Social History*, 33, no. 66 (2000); and Donald Avery, *Dangerous Foreigners: European Immigrant Workers and Labour Radicalism in Canada, 1896–1932* (Toronto: McClelland and Stewart 1979).

94 For a similar case in the 1920s, see LAC, vol. 1711, *R. v. George Jones*.

95 LAC, RG 13, vol. 1711, *R. v. Harry Lee*, memorandum for the chief inspector, Ontario Provincial Police, 4.

96 Lee's testimony was referred to as 'utterly fantastic' and full of contradictions and inconsistencies. Dr Arthur Doyle, a physician who examined Lee, concluded that he was suffering from a mental disorder but yet refused to be considered mentally ill, stating that he would rather hang. LAC, RG 13, vol. 1711, *R. v. Harry Lee*, report to the minister of justice.

97 For an extensive discussion of anti-Semitism in Canada, see Gerald Tulchinsky, *Branching Out: The Transformation of the Canadian Jewish Community* (Toronto: Stoddart 1998); Irving Abella and Harold Troper, *None Is Too Many: Canada and the Jews of Europe* (Toronto: Lester and Open Dennys 1982); and James Walker, *'Race,' Rights and the Law*, chapter 4.

98 See, for example, chapter 7 of Martha Hodes, *White Women Black Men*; and Jacqueline Dowd Hall, *Revolt against Chivalry: Jessie Ames and the Campaign against Lynching* (New York: Columbia Press 1979), 154–5.

99 LAC, RG 13, vol. 1711, *R. v. Harry Lee*. Emphasis added.

100 Under the heading 'Reputation,' the report said: 'Good.' Apparently she took part-time employment as a waitress to supplement the family income. Her husband testified that they had been married twenty years and that they were a happy family and his wife was proud of her home and children. In an Ontario Provincial Police memorandum, she was similarly described as a 'woman who loved her home, her husband and her children ... No one was found who even suspected she was keeping company with another man.'

101 This conclusion was reached even though shortly after Harry Lee's arrest he was found with greeting cards in his possession which were proven to have been signed by Rosenblatt and a watch which Harry had allegedly given to her. Both were summarily explained away by the police as insignificant.

102 Hamilton *Spectator*, 6 October 1952.

103 LAC, RG 13, vol. 1711, *R. v. Harry Lee.*

104 Much of the evidence for this assessment is an analysis of Lee's handwriting. Lee was simultaneously described as 'keenly comprehensive,' 'shrewd,' 'mechanically minded yet not skilled mechanically,' 'cunning' yet 'deceptive,' and 'yielding to desires coldly and selfishly.' Clearly, the contradictory images that characterized the place that Blacks occupied in the White mind are evident in Lee's diagnosis. LAC, RG 13, vol. 1711, *R. v. Harry Lee.*

105 Ibid., transcripts, 142–3.

106 For similar examples, see Mona Pon, 'Like a Chinese Puzzle: The Construction of Chinese Masculinity in Jack Canuck,' in Joy Parr and Mark Rosenfeld, eds., *Gender and History in Canada* (Toronto: Copp Clark 1996), 88–100; Karen Dubinsky and Adam Givertz, '"It Was Only a Matter of Passion": Masculinity and Sexual Danger,' in Kathryn McPherson et al., eds., *Gendered Pasts: Historical Essays in Femininity and Masculinity in Canada* (Toronto: Oxford University Press 1999), 65–79; and Franca Iacovetta, 'Defending Honour, Demanding Respect: Manly Discourse and Gendered Practice in Two Construction Sites, Toronto 1960–61,' in Kathryn McPherson, Celia Morgan, and Nancy M. Forestall, eds., *Gendered Pasts: Historical Essays in Femininity and Masculinity in Canada* (Toronto: Oxford University Press 1999), 199–222.

107 LAC, RG 13, vol. 1711, *R. v. Harry Lee*, transcripts, 144–5.

108 James R. Barret and David Roediger, 'Inbetween Peoples: Race, Nationality and the "New Immigrant" Working Class,' *Journal of American Ethnic History*, 16 (spring 1997): 3–44.

109 LAC, RG 13, vol. 1711, *R. v. Harry Lee*, transcripts, 42. Emphasis added.

110 See Eric Lott, 'The Whiteness of Film Noir,' in Hill, ed., *Whiteness*, 81–9.

111 LAC, RG 13, vol. 1711, *R. v. Harry Lee*, transcripts, 130.

112 Ibid., Dr Arthur M. Doyle to Argo and Kennedy and Argo and Kennedy to Stuart Carlson, minister of justice.

113 Ibid.; parentheses in the original.

114 LAC, RG 13, vol. 1711, *R. v. Harry Lee*, letter to the minister of justice, 14 February 1953. Emphasis in original.

115 For other examples of expressive leniency campaigns in high-profile capital-case files, see Carolyn Strange, 'Stories of Their Lives: The Historian and the Capital Case File,' in Franca Iacovetta and Wendy Mitchinson, eds., *On the Case: Explorations in Social History* (Toronto: University of Toronto Press 1998); and Karen Dubinsky and Franca Iacovetta, 'Murder, Womanly Virtue and Motherhood: The Case of Angela Napolitano, 1911–22,' *Canadian Historical Review*, 72, no. 4 (1991): 505–31.

116 The minister's attempt to convince the government to reopen the case fell upon deaf ears.

117 On 26 January 1953 the Ottawa *Evening Journal* reported that 'some 350 persons from Hamilton, Galt, Camfield, and Vineland joined in prayer for a last hour reprieve for Lee. Reverends Kerr and Blair, both in attendance, no doubt also had a hand in organizing this special service.'

118 LAC, RG 13, vol. 1711, *R. v. Harry Lee*, H.H. Blair, pastor, Central Gospel Tabernacle, to the minister of justice.

119 Ibid., pamphlet titled 'What God Did for Harry Lee: An Amazing Story of the Grace of God toward the Man Who Was Hanged in Barton Street Jail,' Hamilton, 3 February 1953.

Bibliography

Primary Sources

Archives of Ontario

Case Files:
RG 22–392, Criminal Assize Indictment Files, Essex and Kent Counties, 1858–1930

Jail Registers:
RG 20–65–1, Chatham Jail Registers, 1858–1930
RG 20–103–1, Windsor Jail Registers, 1858–1930

Judges' Bench Books:
Crooks, Matthew, RG 22–441
Falconbridge, William, RG 22–443
Kelley, Hugh J., RG 22–495
Street, William Purvis, RG 22–487

Minute Books:
RG 22–2669–0–1, County Judge's Criminal Court Minute Book, Kent County, 1907–1918
RG 22–2669–0–2, County Judge's Criminal Court Minute Book, Kent County, 1918–1929

RG 22–2669–0–3, County Judge's Criminal Court Minute Book, Kent County, 1929–1966

Library and Archives Canada

RG 13, Capital-Case Files:
Robert Berry
Marion Brown
Curtley Bush
Charles Cross
Chester Crossley
Fred Fountain
Jonathan George
Frank Jackson
George Johnston
George Jones
Delbert Knight
Harry Lee
Glen Lotharp
William McCathern
Frank Roughmond
Jerry Simmons
J.E. Slaughter
James Smith
Levi Steward
Frank Turner
Anderson Veney
Henry White

Newspapers:
Border Cities Star
Brantford *Expositor*
Chatham *Daily Planet*
Chatham *Planet*
Chatham *Tri-Weekly Planet*
Chatham *Weekly Planet*
Glencoe *Transcript*
Hamilton *Spectator*
London *Free Press*
Montreal *Gazette*
Ottawa *Citizen*
Ottawa *AM Journal*

Ottawa *PM Journal*
St Catharines *Standard*
Toronto *Globe*

Published Primary Sources

Canada. Bureau of Agriculture and Statistics. *Census of the Canadas, 1860–61.* Quebec: S.B. Foot 1863–4.

Canada. Bureau of Statistics. *Census of Canada, 1931.* Ottawa: J.O. Patenaude, King's Printer 1933–4.

Canada. Bureau of Statistics. *Census of Canada, 1941.* Ottawa: E. Cloutier, Printer to the King 1944–50.

Canada. Department of Agriculture. *Census of Canada, 1870–71.* Ottawa: I.B. Taylor 1873–8.

Canada. Dominion Bureau of Statistics. *Census of Canada, 1951.* Ottawa: Queen's Printer 1953–5.

Henson, Josiah. *The Life of Josiah Henson. Formerly a Slave. Now an Inhabitant of Canada: As Narrated by Himself.* London: Charles Gilpin, Bishopsgate Without 1851.

– *Uncle Tom's Story of His Life: An Autobiography of the Reverend Josiah Henson, 1789–1867. With a Preface by Mrs Harriet Beecher Stowe.* London: Cass Library of African Studies. Slavery Series, no. 13, 1971.

Jeffrey, C.W.S. *Who's Who in Canada, 1930–1931: An Illustrated Biographical Record of Men and Women of the Time.* Toronto: International Press 1932.

Johnson, J.K., ed. *The Canadian Directory of Parliament 1867–1967.* Ottawa: Queen's Printer 1968.

Law Society of Upper Canada Gazette, 2, no. 4 (1968).

Middleton, Edgar, and Fred Landon. *The Province of Ontario: A History: 1615–1927, Volume II.* Toronto: Dominion Publishing 1927.

Ontario Law Reports.

Report of the Royal Commission to Investigate the Penal System of Canada. Ottawa: King's Printer 1938.

Rose, Maclean George, ed. *A Cyclopaedia of Canadian Biography.* Toronto: Rose Publishing 1888.

Secondary Sources

Abella, Irving, and Harold Troper. *None Is Too Many: Canada and the Jews of Europe, 1933–1948.* Toronto: Lester and Orpen Dennys 1983.

Anderson, Benedict. *Imagined Communities: Reflections on the Origins and Spread of Nationalism.* New York: Verso 1991.

Althusser, Louis, and Étienne Balibar. *Reading Capital.* 5th ed. New York: Verso 1990.

Ashcroft, Bill, et al., eds. *The Post-Colonial Studies Reader.* London and New York: Routledge 1995.

Avery, Donald. *Dangerous Foreigners: European Immigrant Workers and Labour Radicalism in Canada, 1896–1932.* Toronto: McClelland and Stewart 1979.

Awkward, Michael. 'A Black Man's Place(s) in Feminist Criticism.' In Marcellus Blount and George P. Cunningham, eds., *Representing Black Men.* New York: Routledge 1996. 3–26.

Aylward, Carol A. *Canadian Critical Race Theory: Racism and the Law.* Halifax: Fernwood Publishing 1999.

Backhouse, Constance. *Carnal Crimes: Sexual Assault Law in Canada, 1900–1975.* Toronto: Osgoode Society for Canadian Legal History / Irwin Law 2008.

– *Colour-Coded: A Legal History of Racism in Canada, 1900–1950.* Toronto: Osgoode Society for Canadian Legal History / University of Toronto Press 1999.

– 'Nineteenth-Century Canadian Rape Law, 1800–82.' In David H. Flaherty, ed., *Essays in the History of Canadian Law, Volume II.* Toronto: Osgoode Society for Canadian Legal History / University of Toronto Press 1983. 200–37.

– *Petticoats and Prejudice: Women and Law in Nineteenth-Century Canada.* Toronto: Osgoode Society for Canadian Legal History / Women's Press 1991.

– 'The White Women's Labour Laws: Anti-Chinese Racism in Early Twentieth Century Canada.' *Law and Historical Review,* 14, no. 2 (1996): 315–68.

Banks, Margaret A. 'The Evolution of Ontario Courts, 1788–1981.' In David H. Flaherty, ed., *Essays in the History of Canadian Law, Volume II.* Toronto: Osgoode Society for Canadian Legal History / University of Toronto Press 1983. 492–572.

Barret, James R., and David Roediger. 'Inbetween Peoples: Race, Nationality and the "New Immigrant" Working Class.' *Journal of American Ethnic History,* 16 (spring 1997): 3–44.

Beaton, Elizabeth. 'An African Canadian Community in Cape Breton, 1901–1904.' *Acadiensis,* 24, no. 2 (1995): 65–97.

Bell, D.G. 'Slavery and the Judges of Loyalist New Brunswick.' *UNB Law Journal,* 31 (1982): 9–42.

Binnie, Susan, and Louis Knafla, eds. *Law, State and Society: Essays in Modern Legal History.* Toronto: University of Toronto Press 1995.

Brand, Dionne. *No Burden to Carry.* Toronto: Women's Press 1991.

Bristow, Peggy, et al., eds. *We're Rooted Here and They Can't Pull Us Up: Essays in African Canadian Women's History*. Toronto: University of Toronto Press 1999.

Brode, Patrick. *The Odyssey of John Anderson*. Toronto: University of Toronto Press 1999.

– 'Osler, Britton Bath.' *Dictionary of Canadian Biography*, vol. 13. Toronto: University of Toronto Press; Quebec: Les Presses de l'Université Laval 1994. 795–6.

Brown, Desmond H. *The Genesis of the Canadian Criminal Code of 1892*. Toronto: Osgoode Society for Canadian Legal History / University of Toronto Press 1989.

Burke, Ronald K. *Samuel Ringgold Ward: Christian Abolitionist*. New York. Garland Publishing 1995.

Butler, Judith. *Gender Trouble: Feminism and the Subversion of Identity*. London and New York: Routledge 1990.

Cahill, Barry. 'Slavery and the Judges of Loyalist Nova Scotia.' *UNB Law Journal*, 43 (1994): 73–135.

Calliste, Agnes. 'Canada's Immigration Policy: The Second Domestic Scheme.' In Jesse Vorst, ed., *Race, Class and Gender: Bonds and Barriers*. Toronto: Garamond Press / Society for Socialist Studies 1991. 136–68.

– 'Race, Gender and Immigration Policy: Blacks from the Caribbean, 1900–1932.' *Journal of Canadian Studies*, 28, no. 4 (1993–4): 131–48.

– 'Women of Exceptional Merit: Immigration of Caribbean Nurses to Canada.' *Canadian Journal of Women and the Law*, 6 (1993): 85–102.

Carter, Sarah. *The Importance of Being Monogamous: Marriage and Nation Building in Western Canada to 1915*. Edmonton: University of Alberta Press 2008.

Chambers, Lori. *Married Women and Property Law in Victorian Ontario*. Toronto: Osgoode Society for Canadian Legal History / University of Toronto Press 1997.

Chan, Wendy, and Kiran Mirchandi, eds. *Crimes of Colour: Racialization and the Criminal Justice System in Canada*. Peterborough, Ont.: Broadview Press 2002.

Chandler, David. *Capital Punishment in Canada: A Sociological Study of Repressive Law*. Toronto: McClelland and Stewart 1976.

Chun, Dorothy. *From Punishment to Doing Good: Family Courts and Socialized Justice in Ontario, 1880–1940*. Toronto: University of Toronto Press 1992.

Clairmont, D.H.J. *Africville: The Life and Death of a Canadian Black Community*. Toronto: Canadian Scholars Press 1999.

Clarke, George Elliott. *Odysseys Home: Mapping African-Canadian Literature*. Toronto: University of Toronto Press 2002.

Cooper, Afua. 'The Fluid Frontier: Blacks and the Detroit River Region: A Focus on Henry Bibb.' *Canadian Review of American Studies*, 2 (2000): 127–48.

– *The Hanging of Angelique: The Untold Story of Canadian Slavery and the Burning of Old Montreal.* Toronto: HarperCollins 2006.

Craven, Paul. 'Law and Ideology: The Toronto Police Court.' In David H. Flaherty, ed., *Essays in the History of Canadian Law, Volume II.* Toronto: Osgoode Society for Canadian Legal History / University of Toronto Press 1983.

– 'The Law of Master and Servant in Mid-Nineteenth Century Ontario.' In David H. Flaherty ed., *Essays in the History of Canadian Law, Volume I.* Toronto: Osgoode Society for Canadian Legal History / University of Toronto Press 1981. 175–211.

Curtis, Bruce. *The Politics of Population: State Formation and the Census of Canada.* Toronto: University of Toronto Press 2001.

Degler, Carl M. *Neither Black Nor White: Slavery and Race Relations in Brazil and the United States.* Madison: University of Wisconsin Press 1971.

Donovan, Kenneth. 'Slaves and Their Owners in Île Royale, 1713–1760.' *Acadiensis* 25, 1 (1995): 4–32.

Dorr, Lisa Linquist. 'Black on White Rape and Retribution in Twentieth Century Virginia: "Men, Even Negroes Must Have Some Protection."' *Journal of Southern History*, 66, no. 4 (2000): 711–48.

Drew, Benjamin. *The Refugee or the Narratives of Fugitive Slaves in Canada Related by Themselves with an Account of the History and Condition of the Colored Population of Upper Canada.* Toronto: Prospero 2000.

Dubinsky, Karen. *Improper Advances: Rape and Heterosexual Conflict in Ontario, 1880–1929.* Chicago: University of Chicago Press 1993.

Dubinsky, Karen, and Adam Givertz. '"It Was Only a Matter of Passion": Masculinity and Sexual Danger.' In Kathryn McPherson, Celia Morgan, and Nancy M. Forestall, eds., *Gendered Pasts: Historical Essays in Femininity and Masculinity in Canada.* Toronto: Oxford University Press 1999. 65–79.

Dubinsky, Karen, and Franca Iacovetta. 'Murder, Womanly Virtue and Motherhood: The Case of Angela Napolitano, 1911–22.' *Canadian Historical Review*, 72, no. 4 (1991): 505–31.

DuBois, W.E.B. *Black Reconstruction in America.* New York: The Free Press 1998.

Elgersman, Maureen. *Unyielding Spirits: Black Women and Slavery in Early Canada and Jamaica.* New York: Garland Publishing 1999.

Fanon, Franz. *Black Skins White Masks.* New York: Grove Press 1967.

– *The Wretched of the Earth.* New York: Palgrave 1963.

Fingard, Judith. *The Dark Side of Life in Victorian Halifax.* Potters Lake, N.S.: Pottersfield Press 1980.

– 'From Sea to Rail: Black Transportation Workers and Their Families in Halifax, c. 1870–1916.' *Acadiensis*, 24, no. 2 (1995): 49–64.

Foster, Cecil. *A Place Called Heaven: The Meaning of Being Black in Canada.* Toronto: HarperCollins 1996.

Foster, Hamar. 'The Queen's Law Is Better Than Yours: International Homicide in Early British Columbia.' In Jim Phillips and Tina Loo, eds., *Essays in the History of Canadian Law, Volume V: Crime and Criminal Justice.* Toronto: Osgoode Society for Canadian Legal History / University of Toronto Press 1994. 42–111.

Friesen, Gerald. '2005 Presidential Address: Space and Region in Canadian History.' *Journal of the Canadian Historical Association / Revue de la Société Historique du Canada* (New Series), vol. 16 (2005): 1–22.

Gates, Nathaniel, ed. *Critical Race Theory Volume I: The Concept of 'Race' in Natural and Social Science.* New York: Garland Publishing 1997.

– *Critical Race Theory Volume II: The Cultural and Literary Critiques of the Concept of 'Race.'* New York: Garland 1997.

– *Critical Race Theory Volume III: Racial Classification and History.* New York: Garland 1997.

– *Critical Race Theory Volume IV: The Judicial Isolation of the 'Racially' Oppressed.* New York: Garland 1997.

Genovese, Eugene. *Roll Jordon Roll: The World the Slaves Made.* New York: Pantheon Books 1974.

Gilroy, Paul. *The Black Atlantic: Modernity and Double Consciousness.* Verso: London 1993.

Goldberg, David Theo. *The Racial State.* Oxford: Blackwell Publishers 2002.

Golz, Analee. '"If a Man's Wife Does Not Obey Him What Can He Do?" Marital Breakdown and Wife Abuse in Late Nineteenth and Early Twentieth Century Ontario.' In Susan Binnie and Louis Knafla, eds., *Law, State and Society: Essays in Modern Legal History.* Toronto: University of Toronto Press 1995. 323–50.

– 'Uncovering Family and Restructuring Family Violence in Ontario.' In Franca Iacovetta and Wendy Mitchinson, eds., *On the Case: Explorations in Social History.* Toronto: University of Toronto Press 1998. 289–311.

Greenwood, Murray F., and Beverley Boissery. *Uncertain Justice: Canadian Women and Capital Punishment.* Toronto: Dundurn Press 2000.

Hale, Grace Elizabeth. *Making Whiteness: The Culture of Segregation in the South, 1890–1940.* New York: Pantheon Books 1998.

Hall, Jacqueline Dowd. *Revolt against Chivalry: Jessie Ames and the Women's Campaign against Lynching.* New York: Columbia University Press 1979.

Hannah-Moffat, Kelly. *Punishment in Disguise: Penal Governance and Federal Imprisonment.* Toronto: University of Toronto Press 2001.

Harring, Sydney L. *White Man's Law: Native Peoples in Nineteenth-Century*

Canadian Legal History. Toronto: Osgoode Society for Canadian Legal History / University of Toronto Press 1998.

Harris, Cole. *Making Native Space: Colonialism, Resistance, and Reserves in British Columbia*. Vancouver: UBC Press 2002.

Hill, Mike, ed. *Whiteness: A Critical Reader*. New York: NYU Press 1997.

Hine, Darlene Clark. 'Rape and the Inner Lives of Southern Black Women: Thoughts on the Culture of Dissemblance.' In Virgina Bernhard et al., eds., *Southern Women: Histories and Identities*. Columbia: University of Missouri Press 1992.

Hodes, Martha. *White Women Black Men: Illicit Sex in the Nineteenth Century South*. New York: Yale University Press 1997.

Houston, Susan. 'Victorian Origins of Canadian Delinquency: A Canadian Experience.' *History of Education Quarterly*, 12, no. 3 (1972): 245–80.

Iacovetta, Franca. 'Gossip, Contest, and Power in the Making of Suburban Bad Girls: Toronto: 1945–1960.' *Canadian Historical Review*, 80, no. 4 (1999): 585–623.

– 'The Sexual Politics of Moral Citizenship: Containing "Dangerous Men" in Cold War Canada, 1950s–1960s.' *Histoire Sociale / Social History*, 33, no. 66 (2000): 361–89.

Iacovetta, Franca, et al., eds. *A Nation of Immigrants: Women, Workers and Communities in Canadian History, 1840s–1960s*. Toronto: University of Toronto Press 1998.

Iacovetta, Franca, and Mariana Valverde, eds. *Gender Conflicts*. Toronto: University of Toronto Press 1995.

Iacovetta, Franca, and Wendy Mitchinson, eds. *On the Case: Explorations in Social History*. Toronto: University of Toronto Press 1998.

Jaywardene, C.H.S. *The Penalty of Death: The Canadian Experiment*. Lexington, Mass.: Lexington Books 1997.

Johnson, Walter. *Soul by Soul: Life inside the Antebellum Slavery Market*. Cambridge, Mass.: Harvard University Press 1999.

Kirk-Montgomery, Alison. 'Courting Madness: Insanity and Testimony in the Criminal Justice System of Ontario.' PhD thesis, University of Toronto 2001.

Landon, Fred. 'The Anti-Slavery Society of Canada.' *Ontario History*, 48, no. 3 (1956): 125–31.

– 'Canada's Part in Freeing the Slave.' *Ontario Historical Society Papers and Records*, 17 (1919): 74–84.

Law, Howard. 'Self Reliance Is the True Road to Independence: Ideology and the Ex-Slaves of Buxton and Chatham.' In Franca Iacovetta et al., eds., *A*

Nation of Immigrants: Women, Workers and Communities in Canadian History, 1840s–1960s. Toronto: University of Toronto Press 1998. 82–100.

Lewthwaite, Susan. 'Violence, Law, and Community in Upper Canada.' In Jim Phillips and Tina Loo, eds., *Essays in the History of Canadian Law, Volume V: Crime and Criminal Justice.* Toronto: Osgoode Society for Canadian Legal History / University of Toronto Press 1994. 113–42.

Loo, Tina. 'The Road from Bute Inlet: Crime and Colonial Identity in British Columbia.' In Jim Phillips and Tina Loo, eds., *Essays in the History of Canadian Law, Volume V: Crime and Criminal Justice.* Toronto: Osgoode Society for Canadian Legal History / University of Toronto Press 1994. 128–170.

– 'Savage Mercy: Native Culture and the Modification of Capital Punishment.' In Carolyn Strange, ed., *Qualities of Mercy: Justice, Punishment and Discretion.* Vancouver: UBC Press 1996. 104–29.

– 'Tonto's Due: Law, Culture and Colonization in British Columbia.' In Hamar Foster and John McLaren, eds., *Essays in the History of Canadian Law, Volume VI: British Columbia and the Yukon.* Toronto: Osgoode Society for Canadian Legal History / University of Toronto Press 1995. 128–170.

Loo, Tina, and Carolyn Strange. *Making Good: Law and Moral Regulation in Canada 1867–1939.* Toronto: University of Toronto Press 1997.

– 'Spectacular Justice: The Circus of Trial and the Trial as Circus, Picton 1903.' *Canadian Historical Review,* 77, no. 2 (1996): 159–84.

Lott, Eric. *Love and Theft: Blackface Minstrelsy and the American Working Class.* New York: Oxford University Press 1995.

Marquis, Greg. *Policing Canada's Century: A History of the Canadian Association of the Chiefs of Police.* Toronto: Osgoode Society for Canadian Legal History / University of Toronto Press 1993.

Maynard, Steven. 'On the Case of On the Case: The Emergence of the Homosexual as a Case History in Early Twentieth-Century Ontario.' In Franca Iacovettta and Wendy Mitchinson, eds., *On the Case: Explorations in Social History.* Toronto: University of Toronto Press 1998. 65–87.

– 'Through a Hole in the Lavatory Wall: Homosexual Subcultures, Police Surveillance and the Dialectics of Discovery, Toronto, 1890–1930.' In Joy Par and Mark Rosenfeld, eds., *Gender and History in Canada.* Toronto: Copp Clark 1996. 165–84.

McClintock, Anne. *Imperial Leather: Race, Gender and Sexuality in the Colonial Contest.* New York: Routledge 1995.

McLaren, Angus. 'Males, Migrants and Murder in British Columbia, 1900–1923.' In Franca Iacovetta and Wendy Mitchinson, eds., *On the Case: Explorations in Social History.* Toronto: University of Toronto Press 1998. 159–80.

– *The Trials of Masculinity: Policing Sexual Boundaries 1870–1930*. Chicago: University of Chicago Press 1999.

McLaren, Kristin. '"We Had No Desire to Be Set Apart": Forced Segregation of Black Students in Canada West and Myths of British Egalitarianism.' *Social History / Histoire sociale*, 37, no. 73 (2004): 27–50.

Mensah, Joseph. *Black Canadians: History, Experiences, Social Conditions*. Halifax: Fernwood Publishing 2002.

Miller, Floyd J. *The Search for a Black Nationality: Black Emigration and Colonization, 1863–1878*. Urbana: University of Illinois Press 1975.

Mongia, Padmini, ed. *Contemporary Postcolonial Theory: A Reader*. New York: Arnold 2003.

Mosher, Clayton. *Discrimination and Denial: Systemic Racism in Ontario's Legal and Criminal Justice Systems, 1892–1961*. Toronto: University of Toronto Press 1999.

Murray, Alexander. 'The Extradition of Fugitive Slaves from Canada.' *Canadian Historical Review*, 43, no. 4 (1962): 298–314.

Murray, David. *Colonial Justice: Justice, Morality, and Crime in the Niagara District 1791–1849*. Toronto: Osgoode Society for Canadian History / University of Toronto Press 2002.

Oliver, Peter. *'Terror to Evildoers': Prisons and Punishments in Nineteenth Century Ontario*. Toronto: University of Toronto Press 1999.

Parker, Nancy Kay. 'Reaching a Verdict: The Changing Structure of Decision-Making in the Canadian Criminal Courts, 1867–1905.' PhD thesis, York University, 1999.

Pascoe, Peggy. *What Comes Naturally: Miscegenation Law and the Making of Race in America*. New York: Oxford University Press 2009.

Pease, Jane, and William Pease. *Black Utopia*. Madison: State Historical Society of Wisconsin 1963.

– *They Who Would Be Free: Blacks' Search for Freedom, 1830–1861*. New York: Atheneum 1974.

Phillips, Jim. 'Recent Publications in Canadian Legal History.' *Canadian Historical Review*, 78, no. 2 (1997): 236–57.

– '"Securing Obedience to Necessary Laws": The Criminal Law in Eighteenth-Century Nova Scotia.' *Nova Scotia Historical Review*, 12 (December 1992): 87–124.

Pon, Mona. 'The Case of the One Good Chinaman: Rex v. Charles Ling, Stratford Ontario, 1909.' In Edgar Montigny and Lori Chambers, eds., *Ontario since Confederation: A Reader*. Toronto: University of Toronto Press 2000. 147–65.

– 'Like a Chinese Puzzle: The Construction of Chinese Masculinity in Jack

Canuck.' In Joy Par and Mark Rosenfeld, eds., *Gender and History in Canada*. Toronto: Copp Clark 1996. 88–100.

Pue, Wesley, and Barry Wright, eds. *Canadian Perspectives on Law and Society: Issues in Legal History*. Ottawa: Carleton University Press 1988.

Razack, Sherene. *Looking White People in the Eye: Gender, Race and Culture in Courtrooms and Classrooms*. Toronto: University of Toronto Press 1998.

Rhodes, Jane. *Mary Ann Shadd Cary: The Black Press and Protest in the Nineteenth Century*. Bloomington: Indiana University Press 1988.

Rhys, Isaac. *The Transformation of Virginia, 1740–1790*. New York: Norton 1982.

Ripley, Peter, ed. *The Black Abolitionist Papers Volume II: Canada, 1830–1865*. Chapel Hill: University of North Carolina Press 1986.

Roberts, Barbara. *Whence They Came: Deportation from Canada, 1900–1935*. Ottawa: University of Ottawa Press 1998.

Roberts, Dorothy. *Killing the Black Body: Race, Reproduction and the Meaning of Liberty*. New York: Random House 1999.

Romney, Paul. 'From the Types Riot to the Rebellion: Elite Ideology and Anti-Legal Sentiment, Political Violence and the Rule of Law in Upper Canada.' *Ontario History*, 79 (June 1987): 133–44.

Sadlier, Rosemary. *Mary Ann Shadd: Publisher, Teacher, Suffragette*. Toronto: Umbrella Press 1995.

Said, Edward. *Orientalism*. New York: Vintage 1994.

Sealy, David. 'Canadianizing Blackness: Resisting the Political.' In Rinaldo Walcott, ed., *Rude: Contemporary Black Canadian Cultural Criticism* (Toronto: Insomniac Press 2000). 92–6.

Sheppard, R. Bruce. *Deemed Unsuitable: Blacks from Oklahoma Move to the Canadian Prairies in Search of Equality in Early 20th Century Canada Only to Find Racism in Their New Home*. Toronto: Umbrella Press 1997.

Silverman, Jason. *Unwelcome Guests: Canada West's Response to the Fugitive Slaves, 1880–1865*. Millwood, N.Y.: Associated Faculty Press 1985.

Simpson, Donald G. *Under the North Star: Black Communities in Upper Canada*. Toronto: Africa World Press 2005.

Smith, Donald, and Edward S. Rogers. *Aboriginal Ontario: Historical Perspectives on the First Nations*. Toronto: Dundurn Press 1994.

Snell, James G. *In the Shadow of the Law: Divorce in Canada 1900–1939*. Toronto: University of Toronto Press 1991.

Sommerville, Dianne Miller. 'The Rape Myth in the Old South Reconsidered.' *Journal of Southern History*, 61 (August 1995): 481–518.

Spivak, Gayatri Chakravorty. 'Can the Subaltern Speak?' In Bill Ashcroft et al., eds., *The Post Colonial Studies Reader*. New York: Routledge 2006. 28–37.

Stamp, Kenneth. *The Peculiar Institution: Slavery in the Ante-Bellum South.* New York: Vintage Books 1956.

Stoler, Ann Laura. 'Racial Hierarchies and Their Regimes of Truth.' In Philomena Essed and David Theo Goldberg, eds., *Race Critical Theories.* Oxford: Blackwell Publishers 2002. 369–91.

– 'Sexual Affronts and Racial Frontiers: European Identities and the Cultural Politics of Racial Exclusion in Colonial Southeast Asia.' In Nathaniel Gates, *Critical Race Theory Volume III : Racial Classification and History.* New York: Garland Publishing 1997. 208–45.

Stouffer, Allan P. *In the Light of Nature and the Law of God: Antislavery in Ontario, 1833–1877.* Montreal and Kingston: McGill-Queen's University Press 1992.

Strange, Carolyn. 'The Criminal and the Fallen of Their Sex: The Establishment of Canada's First Women's Prison, 1874–1901.' *Canadian Journal of Women and the Law,* 1 (1985): 79–92.

– 'Historical Perspectives on Wife Assault.' In Mariana Valverde, ed., *Wife Assault and the Criminal Justice System.* Toronto: Centre of Criminology 1995. 293–304.

– 'Lottery of Death: Capital Punishment 1867–1967.' *Manitoba Law Journal,* 23, no. 3 (1996): 594–619.

– 'Patriarchy Modified: The Criminal Prosecution of Rape in York County, Ontario, 1880–1930.' In Jim Phillips et al., eds., *Essays in the History of Canadian Law, Volume V: Crime and Criminal Justice.* Toronto. Osgoode Society for Canadian Legal History / University of Toronto Press 1994. 206–51.

– *The Politics of Punishment: The Death Penalty in Canada, 1876–1976.* Winnipeg: Canadian History Project, Faculty of Law, University of Manitoba, 1992.

– 'Wounded Womanhood and Dead Men: Chivalry and the Trials of Clara Ford and Carrie Davis.' In Franca Iacovetta and Mariana Valverde, eds., *Gender Conflicts: New Essays in Women's History.* Toronto: University of Toronto Press 1993. 149–88.

Strange, Carolyn, ed. *Qualities of Mercy: Justice, Punishment, and Discretion.* Vancouver: UBC Press 1996.

Swaiger, Jonathan. 'A Distant Edge of Authority: Capital Punishment and the Prerogative of Mercy in British Columbia, 1872–1880.' In Hamar Foster and John McLaren, eds., *Essays in the History of Canadian Law, Volume VI: British Columbia and the Yukon.* Toronto: Osgoode Society for Canadian Legal History / University of Toronto Press 1995. 204–41.

Tator, Carol, and Frances Henry. *Racial Profiling in Canada: Challenging the Myth of 'A Few Bad Apples.'* Toronto: University of Toronto Press 2006.

Teatero, William. *John Anderson: Fugitive Slave.* Toronto: Brown and Martin 1986.

Thomas, Owen. 'Davis, Rogest Delos.' *Dictionary of Canadian Biography*, vol. 14. Toronto: University of Toronto Press; Quebec: Les Presses de l'Université Laval 1998. 274–5.

Trudel, Marcel. *L'esclavage au Canada Français*. Quebec: Les Presses de l'Université Laval 1960.

Tucker, Eric. 'The Faces of Coercion: The Legal Regulation of Labour Conflict in Ontario, 1880–1889.' *Law and History Review*, 12, no. 2 (1994): 277–339.

Tulchinksy, Gerald. *Branching Out: The Transformation of the Canadian Jewish Community*. Toronto: Stoddart 1998.

– *Taking Root: The Origins of the Canadian Jewish Community*. Toronto: Lester Publishing 1992.

Valverde, Mariana, et al. 'On the Case: Explorations in Canadian Social History: A Roundtable Discussion.' *Canadian Historical Review*, 81, no. 2 (2000): 281–7.

Walcott, Rinaldo. *Rude: Contemporary Black Canadian Cultural Criticism*. Toronto: Insomniac Press 2000.

Walker, Barrington. 'Finding Jim Crow in Canada.' In Janet Miron, ed., *A History of Human Rights in Canada*. Toronto: Canadian Scholars Press 2009. 81–98.

– 'The Tale of Ida Jane and George: Murder, Miscegenation and Bastardy in 1893 Raleigh, Ontario.' *Canadian Review of American Studies*, 30, no. 2 (2000): 211–27.

Walker, James W. St G. *The Black Loyalists: The Search for a Promised Land in Nova Scotia and Sierra Leone, 1783–1870*. Toronto: University of Toronto Press 1992.

– 'A Case for Morality: The Quong Wing Files.' In Franca Iacovetta and Wendy Mitchinson, eds., *On the Case: Explorations in Social History*. Toronto: University of Toronto Press 1998. 204–23.

– *'Race,' Rights, and the Law in the Supreme Court of Canada*. Waterloo, Ont.: Wilfrid Laurier University Press 1997.

– *Racial Discrimination in Canada: The Black Experience*. Canadian Historical Association, Booklet no. 41. Ottawa: Canadian Historical Association 1985.

– 'The Rise and Fall of Africville.' *Literary Review of Canada*, 2, no. 7 (1993): 3–5.

Wall, Cheryl, ed. *Changing Our Own Words: Essays on Literary Criticism: Theory and the Writing of Black Women*. New Brunswick, N.J.: Rutgers University Press 1989.

Wallenstein, Peter. *Tell the Court I Love My Wife: Race, Marriage, and the Law – An American History*. New York: Pallgrave Macmillan 2002.

Weaver, John. 'Crime, Public Order and Repression: The Gore District Upheaval, 1832–1851.' *Ontario History*, 78, no. 3 (1986): 175–207.

White Mair, Kimberly. 'Negotiating Responsibility: Representations of Criminality and Mind-State in Canadian Law, Medicine and Society, 1920–1950.' PhD thesis, University of Toronto, 2003.

Whitfield, Harvey Amani. *Blacks on the Border: The Black Refugees in British North America 1815–1860*. Lebannon, N.H.: University of Vermont Press 2006.

Winks, Robin. *The Blacks in Canada*. 2nd ed. Montreal and Kingston: McGill-Queen's University Press 1997.

Wittingham, Michael D. *The Role of Reformers and Volunteers in the Advance of Correctional Reform in Canada since Confederation: Section II: The Role of Governmental Commissions: Provincial/Federal Inquiries*. Ottawa: Programs Branch, Minister of the Solicitor General, 1984.

Yee, Shirley. 'Gender Ideology and Black Women as Community Builders in Ontario, 1850–1870.' *Canadian Historical Review*, 75, no. 1 (1994): 53–73.

Young, Robert J.C. *Postcolonialim: A Very Short Introduction*. New York: Oxford University Press 2003.

Zorn, Roman J. 'Criminal Extradition Menaces the Canadian Haven for Fugitive Slaves.' *Canadian Historical Review*, 38 (December 1957): 284–7.

Index

PUBLICATIONS OF THE OSGOODE SOCIETY FOR CANADIAN LEGAL HISTORY

2010 Judy Fudge and Eric Tucker, eds., *Work on Trial: Canadian Labour Law Struggles*
Christopher Moore, *The British Columbia Court of Appeal: The First Hundred Years*
Frederick Vaughan, *Viscount Haldane: 'The Wicked Step-father of the Canadian Constitution'*
Barrington Walker, *Race on Trial: Black Defendants in Ontario's Criminal Courts, 1858–1958*

2009 William Kaplan, *Canadian Maverick: The Life and Times of Ivan C. Rand*
R. Blake Brown, *A Trying Question: The Jury in Nineteenth-Century Canada*
Barry Wright and Susan Binnie, eds., *Canadian State Trials, Volume III: Political Trials and Security Measures, 1840–1914*
Robert J. Sharpe, *The Last Day, the Last Hour: The Currie Libel Trial* (paperback edition with a new preface)

2008 Constance Backhouse, *Carnal Crimes: Sexual Assault Law in Canada, 1900–1975*
Jim Phillips, R. Roy McMurtry, and John T. Saywell, eds., *Essays in the History of Canadian Law, Volume X: A Tribute to Peter N. Oliver*
Greg Taylor, *The Law of the Land: The Advent of the Torrens System in Canada*
Hamar Foster, Benjamin Berger, and A.R. Buck, eds., *The Grand Experiment: Law and Legal Culture in British Settler Societies*

2007 Robert Sharpe and Patricia McMahon, *The Persons Case: The Origins and Legacy of the Fight for Legal Personhood*
Lori Chambers, *Misconceptions: Unmarried Motherhood and the Ontario Children of Unmarried Parents Act, 1921–1969*
Jonathan Swainger, ed., *A History of the Supreme Court of Alberta*
Martin Friedland, *My Life in Crime and Other Academic Adventures*

2006 Donald Fyson, *Magistrates, Police, and People: Everyday Criminal Justice in Quebec and Lower Canada, 1764–1837*
Dale Brawn, *The Court of Queen's Bench of Manitoba, 1870–1950: A Biographical History*
R.C.B. Risk, *A History of Canadian Legal Thought: Collected Essays*, edited and introduced by G. Blaine Baker and Jim Phillips

2005 Philip Girard, *Bora Laskin: Bringing Law to Life*
Christopher English, ed., *Essays in the History of Canadian Law: Volume IX – Two Islands: Newfoundland and Prince Edward Island*

Fred Kaufman, *Searching for Justice: An Autobiography*

2004 Philip Girard, Jim Phillips, and Barry Cahill, eds., *The Supreme Court of Nova Scotia, 1754–2004: From Imperial Bastion to Provincial Oracle*

Frederick Vaughan, *Aggressive in Pursuit: The Life of Justice Emmett Hall*

John D. Honsberger, *Osgoode Hall: An Illustrated History*

Constance Backhouse and Nancy Backhouse, *The Heiress versus the Establishment: Mrs Campbell's Campaign for Legal Justice*

2003 Robert Sharpe and Kent Roach, *Brian Dickson: A Judge's Journey*

Jerry Bannister, *The Rule of the Admirals: Law, Custom, and Naval Government in Newfoundland, 1699–1832*

George Finlayson, *John J. Robinette, Peerless Mentor: An Appreciation*

Peter Oliver, *The Conventional Man: The Diaries of Ontario Chief Justice Robert A. Harrison, 1856–1878*

2002 John T. Saywell, *The Lawmakers: Judicial Power and the Shaping of Canadian Federalism*

Patrick Brode, *Courted and Abandoned: Seduction in Canadian Law*

David Murray, *Colonial Justice: Justice, Morality, and Crime in the Niagara District, 1791–1849*

F. Murray Greenwood and Barry Wright, eds., *Canadian State Trials, Volume II: Rebellion and Invasion in the Canadas, 1837–1839*

2001 Ellen Anderson, *Judging Bertha Wilson: Law as Large as Life*

Judy Fudge and Eric Tucker, *Labour before the Law: The Regulation of Workers' Collective Action in Canada, 1900–1948*

Laurel Sefton MacDowell, *Renegade Lawyer: The Life of J.L. Cohen*

2000 Barry Cahill, *'The Thousandth Man': A Biography of James McGregor Stewart*

A.B. McKillop, *The Spinster and the Prophet: Florence Deeks, H.G. Wells, and the Mystery of the Purloined Past*

Beverley Boissery and F. Murray Greenwood, *Uncertain Justice: Canadian Women and Capital Punishment*

Bruce Ziff, *Unforeseen Legacies: Reuben Wells Leonard and the Leonard Foundation Trust*

1999 Constance Backhouse, *Colour-Coded: A Legal History of Racism in Canada, 1900–1950*

G. Blaine Baker and Jim Phillips, eds., *Essays in the History of Canadian Law: Volume VIII – In Honour of R.C.B. Risk*

Richard W. Pound, *Chief Justice W.R. Jackett: By the Law of the Land*

David Vanek, *Fulfilment: Memoirs of a Criminal Court Judge*

1998 Sidney Harring, *White Man's Law: Native People in Nineteenth-Century Canadian Jurisprudence*

Peter Oliver, *'Terror to Evil-Doers': Prisons and Punishments in Nineteenth-Century Ontario*

1997 James W.St.G. Walker, *'Race,' Rights and the Law in the Supreme Court of Canada: Historical Case Studies*

Lori Chambers, *Married Women and Property Law in Victorian Ontario*

Patrick Brode, *Casual Slaughters and Accidental Judgments: Canadian War Crimes and Prosecutions, 1944–1948*

Ian Bushnell, *The Federal Court of Canada: A History, 1875–1992*

1996 Carol Wilton, ed., *Essays in the History of Canadian Law: Volume VII – Inside the Law: Canadian Law Firms in Historical Perspective*

William Kaplan, *Bad Judgment: The Case of Mr Justice Leo A. Landreville*

Murray Greenwood and Barry Wright, eds., *Canadian State Trials: Volume I – Law, Politics, and Security Measures, 1608–1837*

1995 David Williams, *Just Lawyers: Seven Portraits*

Hamar Foster and John McLaren, eds., *Essays in the History of Canadian Law: Volume VI – British Columbia and the Yukon*

W.H. Morrow, ed., *Northern Justice: The Memoirs of Mr Justice William G. Morrow*

Beverley Boissery, *A Deep Sense of Wrong: The Treason, Trials, and Transportation to New South Wales of Lower Canadian Rebels after the 1838 Rebellion*

1994 Patrick Boyer, *A Passion for Justice: The Legacy of James Chalmers McRuer*

Charles Pullen, *The Life and Times of Arthur Maloney: The Last of the Tribunes*

Jim Phillips, Tina Loo, and Susan Lewthwaite, eds., *Essays in the History of Canadian Law: Volume V – Crime and Criminal Justice*

Brian Young, *The Politics of Codification: The Lower Canadian Civil Code of 1866*

1993 Greg Marquis, *Policing Canada's Century: A History of the Canadian Association of Chiefs of Police*

Murray Greenwood, *Legacies of Fear: Law and Politics in Quebec in the Era of the French Revolution*

1992 Brendan O'Brien, *Speedy Justice: The Tragic Last Voyage of His Majesty's Vessel Speedy*

Robert Fraser, ed., *Provincial Justice: Upper Canadian Legal Portraits from the Dictionary of Canadian Biography*

1991 Constance Backhouse, *Petticoats and Prejudice: Women and Law in Nineteenth-Century Canada*

1990 Philip Girard and Jim Phillips, eds., *Essays in the History of Canadian Law: Volume III – Nova Scotia*

Carol Wilton, ed., *Essays in the History of Canadian Law: Volume IV – Beyond the Law: Lawyers and Business in Canada, 1830–1930*

1989 Desmond Brown, *The Genesis of the Canadian Criminal Code of 1892*
Patrick Brode, *The Odyssey of John Anderson*

1988 Robert Sharpe, *The Last Day, the Last Hour: The Currie Libel Trial*
John D. Arnup, *Middleton: The Beloved Judge*

1987 C. Ian Kyer and Jerome Bickenbach, *The Fiercest Debate: Cecil A. Wright, the Benchers, and Legal Education in Ontario, 1923–1957*

1986 Paul Romney, *Mr Attorney: The Attorney General for Ontario in Court, Cabinet, and Legislature, 1791–1899*
Martin Friedland, *The Case of Valentine Shortis: A True Story of Crime and Politics in Canada*

1985 James Snell and Frederick Vaughan, *The Supreme Court of Canada: History of the Institution*

1984 Patrick Brode, *Sir John Beverley Robinson: Bone and Sinew of the Compact*
David Williams, *Duff: A Life in the Law*

1983 David H. Flaherty, ed., *Essays in the History of Canadian Law: Volume II*

1982 Marion MacRae and Anthony Adamson, *Cornerstones of Order: Courthouses and Town Halls of Ontario, 1784–1914*

1981 David H. Flaherty, ed., *Essays in the History of Canadian Law: Volume I*

THE CANADIAN SOCIAL HISTORY SERIES

Terry Copp,
The Anatomy of Poverty: The Condition of the Working Class in Montreal, 1897–1929, 1974.
ISBN 0-7710-2252-2

Alison Prentice,
The School Promoters: Education and Social Class in Mid-Nineteenth Century Upper Canada, 1977.
ISBN 0-8020-8692-6

John Herd Thompson,
The Harvests of War: The Prairie West, 1914–1918, 1978.
ISBN 0-7710-8560-5

Joy Parr, Editor,
Childhood and Family in Canadian History, 1982.
ISBN 0-7710-6938-3

Alison Prentice and Susan Mann Trofimenkoff, Editors,
The Neglected Majority: Essays in Canadian Women's History, Volume 2, 1985.
ISBN 0-7710-8583-4

Ruth Roach Pierson,
'They're Still Women After All': The Second World War and Canadian Womanhood, 1986.
ISBN 0-7710-6958-8

Bryan D. Palmer,
The Character of Class Struggle: Essays in Canadian Working Class History, 1850–1985, 1986.
ISBN 0-7710-6946-4

Alan Metcalfe,
Canada Learns to Play: The Emergence of Organized Sport, 1807–1914, 1987.
ISBN 0-7710-5870-5

Marta Danylewycz,
Taking the Veil: An Alternative to Marriage, Motherhood, and Spinsterhood in Quebec, 1840–1920, 1987.
ISBN 0-7710-2550-5

Craig Heron,
Working in Steel: The Early Years in Canada, 1883–1935, 1988.
ISBN 978-1-4426-0984-6

Wendy Mitchinson and Janice Dickin McGinnis, Editors,
Essays in the History of Canadian Medicine, 1988.
ISBN 0-7710-6063-7

Joan Sangster,
Dreams of Equality: Women on the Canadian Left, 1920–1950, 1989.
ISBN 0-7710-7946-X

Angus McLaren,
Our Own Master Race: Eugenics in Canada, 1885–1945, 1990.
ISBN 0-7710-5544-7

Bruno Ramirez,
On the Move: French-Canadian and Italian Migrants in the North Atlantic Economy, 1860–1914, 1991.
ISBN 0-7710-7283-X

Mariana Valverde,
'The Age of Light, Soap and Water': Moral Reform in English Canada, 1885–1925, 1991.
ISBN 978-0-8020-9595-4

Bettina Bradbury,
Working Families: Age, Gender, and Daily Survival in Industrializing Montreal, 1993.
ISBN 978-0-8020-8689-1

Andrée Lévesque,
Making and Breaking the Rules: Women in Quebec, 1919–1939, 1994.
ISBN 978-1-4426-1138-2

Cecilia Danysk,
Hired Hands: Labour and the Development of Prairie Agriculture, 1880–1930, 1995.
ISBN 0-7710-2552-1

Kathryn McPherson,
Bedside Matters: The Transformation of Canadian Nursing, 1900–1990, 1996.
ISBN 978-0-8020-8679-2

Edith Burley,
Servants of the Honourable Company: Work, Discipline, and Conflict in the Hudson's Bay Company, 1770–1870, 1997.
ISBN 0-19-541296-6

Mercedes Steedman,
Angels of the Workplace: Women and the Construction of Gender Relations in the Canadian Clothing Industry, 1890–1940, 1997.
ISBN 978-1-4426-0982-2

Angus McLaren and Arlene Tigar McLaren,
The Bedroom and the State: The Changing Practices and Politics of Contraception and Abortion in Canada, 1880–1997, 1997.
ISBN 0-19-541318-0

Kathryn McPherson, Cecilia Morgan, and Nancy M. Forestell, Editors,
Gendered Pasts: Historical Essays in Femininity and Masculinity in Canada, 1999.
ISBN 978-0-8020-8690-7

Gillian Creese,
Contracting Masculinity: Gender, Class, and Race in a White-Collar Union, 1944–1994, 1999.
ISBN 0-19-541454-3

Geoffrey Reaume,
Remembrance of Patients Past: Patient Life at the Toronto Hospital for the Insane, 1870–1940, 2000.
ISBN 978-1-4426-1075-0

Miriam Wright,
A Fishery for Modern Times: The State and the Industrialization of the Newfoundland Fishery, 1934–1968, 2001.
ISBN 0-19-541620-1

Judy Fudge and Eric Tucker,
Labour Before the Law: The Regulation of Workers' Collective Action in Canada, 1900–1948, 2001.
ISBN 978-0-8020-3793-0

Mark Moss,
Manliness and Militarism: Educating Young Boys in Ontario for War, 2001.
ISBN 0-19-541594-9

Joan Sangster,
Regulating Girls and Women: Sexuality, Family, and the Law in Ontario, 1920–1960, 2001.
ISBN 0-19-541663-5

Reinhold Kramer and Tom Mitchell,
Walk Towards the Gallows: The Tragedy of Hilda Blake, Hanged 1899, 2002.
ISBN 978-0-8020-9542-8

Mark Kristmanson,
Plateaus of Freedom: Nationality, Culture, and State Security in Canada, 1940–1960, 2002.
ISBN 0-19-541866-2 (cloth)
ISBN 0-19-541803-4 (paper)

Robin Jarvis Brownlie,
A Fatherly Eye: Indian Agents, Government Power, and Aboriginal Resistance in Ontario, 1918–1939, 2003.
ISBN 0-19-541891-3 (cloth)
ISBN 0-19-541784-4 (paper)

Steve Hewitt,
Riding to the Rescue: The Transformation of the RCMP in Alberta and Saskatchewan, 1914–1939, 2006.
ISBN 978-0-8020-9021-8 (cloth)
ISBN 978-0-8020-4895-0 (paper)

Robert K. Kristofferson,
Craft Capitalism: Craftworkers and Early Industrialization in Hamilton, Ontario, 1840–1871, 2007.
ISBN 978-0-8020-9127-7 (cloth)
ISBN 978-0-8020-9408-7 (paper)

Andrew Parnaby,
Citizen Docker: Making a New Deal on the Vancouver Waterfront, 1919–1939, 2008.
ISBN 978-0-8020-9056-0 (cloth)
ISBN 978-0-8020-9384-4 (paper)

J.I. Little,
Loyalties in Conflict: A Canadian Borderland in War and Rebellion, 1812–1840, 2008.
ISBN 978-0-8020-9773-6 (cloth)
ISBN 978-0-8020-9525-1 (paper)

Pauline Greenhill,
Make the Night Hideous: Four English Canadian Charivaris, 1881–1940, 2010.
ISBN 978-1-4426-4077-1 (cloth)
ISBN 978-1-4426-1015-6 (paper)

Rhonda L. Hinther and Jim Mochoruk,
New Directions in the History of Ukrainians in Canada, 2010.
ISBN 978-1-4426-4134-1 (cloth)
ISBN 978-1-4426-1062-0 (paper)

Reinhold Kramer and Tom Mitchell,
When the State Trembled: How A.J.

Andrews and the Citizens' Committee Broke the Winnipeg General Strike, 2010.
ISBN 978-1-4426-4219-5 (cloth)
ISBN 978-1-4426-1116-0 (paper)

Barrington Walker,
Race on Trial: Black Defendants in Ontario's Criminal Courts, 1858–1958, 2010.
ISBN 978-0-8020-9909-9 (cloth)